Action Research

Edited by Julian Edge

Case Studies in TESOL Practice Series

Jill Burton, Series Editor

Teachers of English to Speakers of Other Languages, Inc.

Typeset in Berkeley and Belwe
by Capitol Communication Systems, Inc., Crofton, Maryland USA
Printed by Kirby Lithographic Company, Inc., Arlington, Virginia USA
Indexed by Coughlin Indexing Services, Annapolis, Maryland USA

Teachers of English to Speakers of Other Languages, Inc.
700 South Washington Street, Suite 200
Alexandria, Virginia 22314 USA
Tel 703-836-0774 • Fax 703-836-6447 • E-mail tesol@tesol.org • http://www.tesol.org/

Director of Communications and Marketing: Helen Kornblum
Managing Editor: Marilyn Kupetz
Additional Reader: Ellen Garshick
Cover Design: Charles Akins and Ann Kammerer

ISBN 0-939791-92-7
Library of Congress Catalogue No. 00-136374

Dedication

As we approach the 50th anniversary of the death of

John Dewey (1859–1952)

it is to his memory, and to the continuing, daily struggle for democracy and education, that we dedicate these footnotes to his work.

Table of Contents

Acknowledgments

The editor and authors of this collection would like to express their sincere thanks to Series Editor Jill Burton for her speedy and sensitive feedback on earlier drafts of these chapters, and to Marilyn Kupetz and her team for their caring and careful work from our manuscripts to this book, which brings us all together in craftsmanship.

Series Editor's Preface

The Case Studies in TESOL Practice series offers innovative and effective examples of practice from the point of view of the practitioner. The series brings together from around the world communities of practitioners who have reflected and written on particular aspects of their teaching. Each volume in the series will cover one specialized teaching focus.

◈ CASE STUDIES

Why a TESOL series focusing on case studies of teaching practice?

Much has been written about case studies and where they fit in a mainstream research tradition (e.g., Nunan, 1992; Stake, 1995; Yin, 1994). Perhaps more importantly, case studies also constitute a public recognition of the value of teachers' reflection on their practice and constitute a new form of teacher research—or teacher valuing. Case studies support teachers in valuing the uniqueness of their classes, learning from them, and showing how their experience and knowledge can be made accessible to other practitioners in simple, but disciplined ways. They are particularly suited to practitioners who want to understand and solve teaching problems in their own contexts.

These case studies are written by practitioners who are able to portray real experience by providing detailed descriptions of teaching practice. These qualities invest the cases with teacher credibility, and make them convincing and professionally interesting. The cases also represent multiple views and offer immediate solutions, thus providing perspective on the issues and examples of useful approaches. Informative by nature, they can provide an initial database for further, sustained research. Accessible to wider audiences than many traditional research reports, however, case studies have democratic appeal.

◈ HOW THIS SERIES CAN BE USED

The case studies lend themselves to pre- and in-service teacher education. Because the context of each case is described in detail, it is easy for readers to compare the cases with and evaluate them against their own circumstances. To respond to the wide range of settings in which TESOL functions, cases have been selected from diverse EFL and ESL settings around the world.

The 12 or so case studies in each volume are easy to follow. Teacher writers describe their teaching context and analyze its distinctive features: the particular demands of their context, the issues they have encountered, how they have effectively addressed the issues, what they have learned. Each case study also offers readers practical suggestions—developed from teaching experience—to adapt and apply to their own teaching.

Already published or in preparation are volumes on

- assessment practices
- bilingual education
- community partnerships
- content-based language instruction
- distance learning
- English for specific purposes
- intensive English teaching
- interaction and language learning
- international teaching assistants
- journal writing
- mainstreaming
- teacher education
- teaching academic writing
- technology in the classroom
- teaching English as a foreign language in primary schools

◈ THIS VOLUME

Through reflective investigation, the authors in this volume discover how to implement changes or sustain practices that make their teaching more productive for learners. Action research is demonstrated as manageable intervention that educates as it sustains. Thus, it is potentially a means of continuing professional renewal. These teacher authors certainly demonstrate how successful teaching practice entails researching and learning as well as teaching, how effective as investigators teachers can be—and how rewarding language teaching can be.

Jill Burton
University of South Australia, Adelaide

CHAPTER 1

Attitude and Access: Building a New Teaching/Learning Community in TESOL

Julian Edge

◈ TEACHING WITH ATTITUDE

Action research is well described as *boundary work* (MacLure, 1996) in the sense that action researchers live and act between and across some very well-established social, philosophical, and educational demarcation lines. It can be enormously frustrating to be dismissed by both of the communities to which one sees oneself belonging—too theoretical for the teachers, too practical for the theorists—and yet, out along the borderline, communities are also built. And it is in the frontier nature of these endeavors, undoubtedly, that some of the attraction lies. Although I do want to consider the pressing rational arguments for action research, from teaching and research perspectives, I suspect that affective issues of character and personal preference also play their part in leading people toward this style of work. I would like to celebrate that first.

> People will tell you where they've gone,
> They'll tell you where to go,
> But till you get there yourself, you never really know.

(Mitchell, 1976)

Simple lines, but resonant for me, and evocative of the reasons action research means as much to some of us as it does. Mitchell goes on to write of "Icarus ascending, on beautiful, foolish arms," and I find a direct link to Wilson's (1999) search for *consilience*—for the basic interlocking answers to fundamental issues in all areas of human knowledge, and to his intriguing question as to whether we should best understand the Icarus myth as one of punished pride or rather as definitive of an important aspect of our humanity, as we seek (always and ever) to push back the envelope, to see how deep, how far, and how high we can go, "before the sun melts the wax in our wings" (p. 4).

Wilson draws on references to astrophysics, to Eddington and Chandrasekhar, but my thoughts take me directly back to a seat in a London theater, and hearing lines from Stoppard's (1993) *Arcadia,* which moved the hairs on the back of my neck: "It's wanting to know that makes us matter; otherwise, we are going out the same way we came in" (p. 75).

I begin here because I believe that this is the core of my response to the ideas of action research. One aspect of human maturation, more important to some people than to others, is to want to know—wanting not to go out the same way we came in.

To respond to this Icarus impulse does not so much involve dichotomizing between theory and practice as it involves making decisions about the level of conscious awareness at which one wishes to operate in the various aspects of one's life.

Any ESOL teachers who wish to see themselves in such a light, at the beginning of the third millennium of the common era, are standing at a nexus of some of the most pressing issues of our time:

1. What are the relationships between the great laws of the natural sciences and the individual experiences of contextualized human learning and teaching? Why has humanity made such progress in the former area, yet still stumbles so badly in understanding the latter?

2. What are the key processes of human learning, particularly the learning of that defining human trait, language? How can we affect these processes?

3. How can TESOL professionals adequately respond to the sociopolitical pressures that increase the use of English and simultaneously create resistance to its spread?

4. Are there ways to encourage authentic communication while respecting cultural diversity?

5. Where does language education find a footing in the apparently unstoppable flow of commercial globalization?

I am not so foolish as to suggest that definitive answers to these questions are about to be formulated by English language teachers, not even the ones represented in collections of action research papers. My point is that one way of being alive as a person-who-teaches-English is to recognize, rather than ignore, the larger issues in which one is involved, to celebrate the significance to these issues of the data of our quotidian lives, and to want, actively and reflectively, to go out other than the way we came in.

From this perspective, we are central actors in the above issues, whether we wish to acknowledge the fact or not. Together with such an acknowledgment comes a sense of increasing responsibility, and also the realization that our responsibility is not to debate abstractions or to propose universal procedural solutions (both of which have failed us in the past), but rather, difficult as it is, to act as well as we can, in collaboration with the other actors in our own complex environments, and then to communicate our experiences to colleagues around us and elsewhere.

From the perspective of the continuing development of the person-who-teaches, therefore, in all his or her intellectual, emotional, social, cultural, and professional richness, I find myself arriving at a way of life that is committed to something like action research, even if it is not named as such, and even if I have not yet attempted to formulate just exactly what I mean by the term. I am ready to go there now.

◈ HISTORY AND DEFINITION

As in other areas that he addressed, Dewey's (1916, 1933) work here is seminal. His statements on the fundamental issues of how experience, thought, and action need to relate to each other in the educational processes of a democracy are as compelling today as when they were written and can be poorly represented by brief citation or summary. But with specific reference to our theme of action research, we might note this comment on thinking: "Thinking includes all of these steps—the sense of a problem, the observation of conditions, the formation and rational elaboration of a suggested conclusion, and the active experimental testing" (Dewey, 1916, p. 151).

Moreover, Dewey's arguments, although broad in their sweep, consistently place changes of philosophical attitude toward experience, thought, and action in specific historical, social, and political settings. Of what he saw as the exaggerated and debilitating separation of theory and practice, he writes: "The antithesis of empiricism and rationalism loses the support of the human situation which once gave it meaning and relative justification" (Dewey, 1916, p. 273).

With regard to the specific formulation of the term *action research* in the social psychology of Lewin (e.g., 1946), and to mainstream educational projects based on these principles (e.g., Elliott & Adelmann, 1975; Stenhouse, 1975), I refer readers to Adelmann (1993). I am going to move on to more recent definitions from the educational literature in order to focus this introduction more toward our own purposes.

Elliott (1991) defines action research briefly as "the study of a social situation with a view to improving the quality of action in it" (p. 69).

As Altrichter, Posch, and Somekh (1993) point out, this definition highlights the characteristic purpose of action research, which is not simply to describe, interpret, analyze, and theorize—the stuff of traditional research—but to act in and on a situation in order to make things better than they were. The procedure generally associated with action research (see, e.g., Kemmis & McTaggart, 1988) is one of a continuing, not necessarily linear, spiral of increasingly aware experience, which is most simply represented as a succession of stages, beginning with

- *action* in the sense that one is in the middle of action

- *observation* of what is happening, leading to a more specific focus of interest

- *reflection* on the focus which has been identified, leading to

- *planning* that forms the basis for future

- *action* to improve the situation, supported by

- *observation* in order to evaluate the changes made

Some of the writers in this collection refer specifically to this procedure and, where they do not, it is implicit in their accounts. This is not to say that the procedure is itself constitutive of action research, but this schema does provide a powerful, useful, and explanatory way of describing what is going on in terms of the major elements involved.

We can also see in Elliott's definition an emphasis on the study of a social situation in its own right. Implicit is the contention that responses to issues in specific contexts will arise most usefully from those contexts; they can rarely, with success, be imported from outside and applied.

We can illuminate action research further by looking at another proposed definition. Carr and Kemmis (1986) see action research as: "self-reflective inquiry, undertaken by participants in social situations in order to improve the rationality and justice of their own practices, their understanding of these practices, and the situations in which these practices are carried out" (p. 220).

What arises here is the typical preference in action research that the research involve more than one person, that at least some of the researchers should be insiders to the situation, and that improvements to the quality of action available cannot be seen only in utilitarian, procedural terms, but must make reference to the broader fields of conceptual argument and social justice. Implicit here are issues of differing perspectives, multiple understandings, and questions of how such data is to be collected and evaluated.

Let me expand briefly on some of those points. The link with rational argument is important if action research is to make a serious contribution to the human sciences and to education as our particular interest. The action researcher works to understand the specifics of a situation and to make links with the established educational literature. The crucial point, to use Prawat's (1991) terminology, is that the trajectory has changed from *outside-in* to *inside-out*. Local understandings are primary, and it is in the articulation of these understandings that actual educational practice can be theorized (the contribution to theory) and improved (the contribution to practice).

If action research can establish the appropriate lines of communication, there is an unbroken link between improved practice and authentic theory—the kind of theory that accounts for data. There is a long way to go, but if one accepts that action is complex and that the point of theory is to make simple, this approach holds out at least the hope of a coherence to which a misplaced theory/application discourse cannot even aspire (Clarke, 1994; Guba & Lincoln, 1982).

Please notice how those five major issues I mentioned above are always there in the background. The argument about theory/application is key to the dispute about the nature not just of research but also of reality and truth. Is there one reality out there to be discovered, or are there many perceptions to be understood? Is truth single and indivisible, or are there many equally, or more-or-less, valid perspectives to be taken into account? Do we give the same answer to these questions when we think about chemical formulae as when we think about discipline issues with adolescents (Denzin & Lincoln, 1994; Edge & Richards, 1998a, 1998b)?

Moving on to the social justice aspect of action research, we also see a relationship between large-scale themes and personal action. The idea that action research should contribute to the empowerment of individual teachers is an important part of the whole. The whole of which it is a part is the vision of a more just society of fully empowered citizens living fulfilled lives according to their own freely embraced values. This underlying aim is clearly seen as the driving motivation in the work of Dewey and Lewin to which I have already referred.

That is not to say, however, that ESOL teachers who engage in action research are equally called upon to engage in direct struggle for worldwide liberation. One can sympathize with the weariness in Zeichner's (1993) comments on the failure of 25 years of teacher development to add up to breakthroughs in social justice, but the relationship cannot be so direct, and anyway the timescale must necessarily be much longer. No individual is going to see such change in a working lifetime—that kind of personal gratification is simply not available. The most basic ideas of empowerment, participation, stakeholding are still news to a lot of people. But every little shift made by a language teacher, for example, from the fragile security of given knowledge to the robust uncertainty of emergent awareness is of a piece with the underpinning values of a sense of social justice that is shared, if not always trumpeted. Or, to express this in interpersonal terms, our individual responsibility is not to attempt to impose large-scale change, but to act in our everyday exchanges with others in ways that instantiate the values that we value (Clark, 1997).

The outcomes that we seek can be identified in many ways—not just a certain number of ways, but in the multiple, overlapping ways in which thought and action do interact. As with the typical action research procedure (action, observation, reflection, planning) outlined above, one can represent the possibilities most clearly by separating them out. Under each heading that follows, I have asked examples of relevant TESOL questions. Allow me to emphasize that these are only examples, there to exemplify possibilities, not to define or limit them. The focus of contribution of a piece of action research, then, may be

- means oriented: We know that we are trying to teach people to write English on this course. How can we improve the ways in which we do so?

- ends oriented: We know that these students want to become librarians. How sure are we about the importance of teaching them to write in English?

- theory oriented: As we investigate our teaching of writing, how can we articulate our increased understanding of what is happening here? How can we connect with other written records in order to theorize our practice and, perhaps, contribute to the theory that informs us?

- institution oriented: To what extent is my writing course, through its goals, its topics, and my practice, contributing to an integrated educational program through which the institution mediates between its students and its social context?

- society oriented: To what extent is my writing course, through its goals, its topics, and my practice, promoting values that I believe in (e.g., contributing to a healthy dialogic relationship among students, teachers, institution, and society at large)?

- teacher oriented: Where is my own personal and professional development in this? What is the contribution to collegiality and, thereby, the kind of society I want to live in?

Let us take these TESOL examples as a bridge into a more specific consideration of action research in TESOL.

◈ ACTION RESEARCH IN TESOL

As we begin a new century, it is difficult not to sense that something, anyway, is afoot, even in the mainstream, and that this change has moved us in a direction that might be at least loosely characterized as action research. Let me show you what I see here, closer to home.

In terms of this mainstream change in TESOL, I would identify Nunan's (1991) textbook, *Language Teaching Methodology*, as pivotal. There were other important and paradigm-shaking books around that time, of course (Allwright & Bailey, 1991; Nunan, 1989; and Peck, 1988, among them), but Nunan (1991) provided a core methodology textbook for teachers' courses that was based to a serious extent in the transcribed data of classroom interaction. Moreover, the purpose of this basis-in-action was explicitly "not to provide instances of exemplary practice, that is, to show what should be done, but to demonstrate what actually is done in language classrooms" (p. xiv).

Perhaps the measure of the change in our field is the extent to which this statement of purpose now seems uncontroversial. But prior to this time, it went without saying that a methodology course would consist of a series of arguments for, and explanations of, what teachers ought to be doing, based on whatever set of linguistic, psycholinguistic, sociolinguistic (and later humanistic, callisthenic, neuro-mystic), principles were the order of the day. It no longer goes without saying.

I believe that the thinking heart of TESOL as a field has moved away from the proposition that the future directions of our teaching are to be established by theorists from related disciplines. I believe that we have reached a point at which we accept our responsibility to raise our awareness first of what our current practice is, and then, on the basis of that awareness, to set our directions and seek the information we require. The thinking teacher is no longer perceived as someone who applies theories, but as someone who theorizes practice. Good teaching is no longer by definition somewhere else; good teaching is right here, so long as we are working on developing it.

To the extent that the above claims are true, I see the TESOL field as committed to a mode of operation for which the umbrella title, action research, is appropriate. In order to substantiate this claim, I put up an umbrella broad enough to cover not only the more explicit titles of Auerbach (1994), Edge and Richards (1993), Field, Graham, Griffiths, and Head (1997), Head (1998), Wallace (1998), Burns (1999), and De Decker and Vanderheiden (1999) but also Bailey and Nunan (1996), Graves (1996), Nunan & Lamb (1996), Richards (1998b), Freeman (1998), Johnson (1999), and further back from that, Nunan (1992a) and Wallace (1991). Of course, perspectives and foci vary, but the broad sweep of the movement is undeniable.

I hope it is clear from all this that I am not interested in building an essentialist argument about what action research really is and what it is not. I hope to have evoked a backdrop against which the reader will want to take a deeper interest in the figures moving across the foreground. Let us now turn our attention to the chapters that have made this collection what it is.

◈ THE MAKING OF A COLLECTION OF CASE STUDIES IN ACTION RESEARCH

In the opening lines of the preface to his (for me, life-changing) *The Making of the English Working Class*, Thompson (1968) writes: "This book has a clumsy title, but it is one which meets its purpose. 'Making' because it is a study in an active process, which owes as much to agency as to conditioning. The working class did not arise like the sun at an appointed time. It was present at its own making" (p. 9).

Similarly, among the many other excellent papers that I received, the ones gathered here insisted on their place, not simply through their individual qualities, but because they jostled their way together to create the style and purpose of a collection that I had not foreseen.

If I am to be frank, I suppose I should have to admit that I started out with the not-quite-articulated vision of a collection that was drawn from all corners of the globe, would equally represent men and women, would contain only a few authors with English-sounding names, and would explicitly exemplify the various interactions between thought and action that I have referred to above. And there would have been nothing wrong with that. But it is not exactly what happened. And action research is something that happens. It would be as much of a disservice to action research to present it as an idealized construct for others to adopt and adapt, as it has been for all these years to represent good teaching as a model for others to copy, or a theory for others to apply. Just as we say that there is no such thing as good teaching in the abstract—only particular teachers and learners in interaction, just as Thompson (1968) writes in his discussion of class—"We cannot have love without lovers, nor deference without squires and labourers" (p. 9)—we cannot have action research without action researchers, and the emergent generation of action researchers is present in its own making.

The pressing issue of our time, it seems to me, is the facilitation of access to this way of being a person-who-teaches, and it is this sense of becoming that these writers have used to insist on the nature of the collection that they have built. The work is all participatory, in the sense that the writers are first-person investigators of their own practice in their own situations. As I have already said, I am not interested in trying to build a definition of action research as necessarily participatory in this way, but the more we focus on action research as a way of being, as an orientation, as an attitude, and the more we concern ourselves with questions of access, of becoming, the more we want to hear firsthand accounts of personal involvement and significant outcomes for the teller of the research.

In some cases, with the current writers, there is a tentativeness about the relationship between their work and a preexisting idea of what action research is or should be. Perkins's title (chapter 2) is actually taken from the note she wrote across the top of her draft paper and indicates her own doubts about her claim to be a teacher researcher. But I know of no more evocative description of classroom space than her "There is just enough room for me to pass round the backs of all the students if they have their chairs pulled in," and her theorization of that space is not only insightful in its own right but also has the strength to point up the weaknesses she sees in her investigative procedures.

Similar doubts are explicitly expressed in Cowie's title (chapter 3), but it would also be a mistake not to notice the sensitive sureness of touch in the long-term development of his approach to the teaching of writing, a process he calls "a struggle that I intend to be encouraging to others."

Becoming an action researcher is a theme that runs very clearly through the next four chapters. Santana-Williamson (chapter 4) gives us a portrait of a teacher going through a telephone directory and calling local schools in order to collect data to back up an intuition regarding the recency of their establishment and the qualifications of their teachers. This is a part of her response to a pedagogic project that she sees as necessarily embedded in a social situation. Furthermore, her work with her teacher learners aims to empower them in terms of their response to this environment, just as it feeds her own development as teacher researcher. I see here a direct embodiment of Prawat's (1991) observation: "Although education is situation dependent, development is context interactive, as external influences are incorporated into the teacher's own world, and the teaching context is made to fit individual teachers' conceptual model of how and what the teacher wants the classroom to be" (p. 728).

A certain irony pointed up by Cox and Assis-Peterson (1999) about Brazilian educationists finding inspiration in a literature in turn inspired by the work of Freire is present again here.

Like Santana-Williamson, Rogers (chapter 5) is working with teacher learners, looking to investigate and develop his own practice as a teacher educator while introducing his course participants to an exploratory, interactive mode of working with their students. Although teacher educators' investigations are sometimes referred to as "second-order" action research (Elliott, 1993, p. 177), there is an important distinction to be made in instances such as this.

If teacher educators are investigating other teachers' practice, then *second-order* is an appropriate term for their research. Dadds's (1995) excellent study of the importance of emotion in teacher research, for example, explores no emotions of her own. But where a teacher educator's own practice is under investigation, second-order is no longer appropriate. Not only are these teacher educators engaged in first-order action research in their own right, they are also establishing exactly the kind of reflexive relationship with their teacher learners that is most likely to lead these same teachers to see the power of action research and to adopt similar attitudes to their own practice and development. If theory/practice is the most pernicious dichotomy that teacher education has to deal with, then perhaps the most undermining one is the gulf sometimes perceived between what teacher educators do and what they say, between what they practice and what they preach (Gore, 1991). As well as drawing satisfaction from the evaluative data of his own situation, Rogers's final reflection is a challenge to any approach to educational innovation, or to educational research, that does not at least include action research components (cf. Somekh, 1993).

Maneekhao and Watson Todd (chapter 6) provide us with a multilayered account of becoming in the area of action research, in which Maneekhao's description of her early motivation reminds us that involvement in action research does not always derive from an innate desire for professional self-development. Fear and uncertainty are endemic in many educational situations, and external pressures are unremitting, but this is, as Fullan (1993) expresses it, simply a case of educational situations mirroring life itself, and where, at our best, "seeking assistance is a sign of strength, where simultaneous top-down bottom-up initiatives merge, where collegiality and individualism co-exist in a productive tension" (p. viii).

Maneekhao and Watson Todd's interactive storytelling lends itself less to the drawing of general conclusions than to reflection on the experiences that they recount. I take this to be the very point of collecting case studies, and these writers give us perhaps the clearest example here of the change in illocutionary force that we are enjoying in our enriched paradigm of educational research. The researcher is no longer called upon to draw general conclusions, but to communicate the perceived value of the experience-in-context. Responsibility has now shifted to us, the readers, to decide on the significance for ourselves of what we read. The value that we find in the telling (Edge, 1989) is no longer a direct evaluation of the value experienced by the researcher. In just the same way, a teaching technique that regularly brings you success in your teaching may be of no use to me, without devaluing its worth to you. We are learning differing forms of evaluation and more subtle styles of reader/writer pragmatic relationships as we learn to establish more meaningful ways to research and theorize our practice.

Hales and O'Donoghue (chapter 7) are also involved in the reflexive building of investigatory approaches through their work with teacher learners, and one of the features of this chapter that I treasure is their reminder that short-term experimentation is not what they are talking about: "For the purposes of this chapter, we will in fact be discussing a project that encompasses most of our career in teacher education."

Quirke's chapter (8) is similarly one of explicit cycles of exploration, and one of the highlights of this, for me, is his unembarrassed delight at the personal discovery of the importance of collegial collaboration, an outcome that he acknowledges "will probably have many readers nodding sagely that they were aware of this all along."

It is worth pausing to consider what is at stake here and why Quirke makes such a point of it. This is hardly an original discovery, after all. It is quite easy to read about the importance of collaboration in teacher research, even at book length (Burns, 1999; Edge, 1992; Heron, 1992), and anyone writing even an assigned essay about action research is likely to make the point. What makes the difference here is that Quirke is writing from an immediate experience of the power of cooperation, and this immediacy shines through. Do not just believe it. Experience it. What is the point of simply knowing it? Do it.

Related to this point is the extent to which action research wastes a lot of time and energy by having people all over the place reinvent the wheel, as the saying goes. The challenge lies exactly in the saying itself, and in the choice of metaphor. If mechanistic invention and dispersion were what we require, then educational aspirations would surely have been met a long time ago. It is exactly because this approach has proved so unsatisfactory that we see why action research, with its emphasis on direct, lived experience, is so necessary. We get more of a feel for this if we shift metaphorical reference away from wheels and invention and toward the sense of the traditional North American saying: If you want to know why a person is the way they are, you need to walk a week in their moccasins. We are currently gathering, interpreting, and theorizing the data of our varied contexts. From these understandings, the experience of teaching and learning will begin to have a more influential role in the building of future professional preparation.

I have already noted that action research can operate along the different dimensions of means, ends, and theory, oriented toward the individual, the institution, or society at large, and that questions asked in one dimension resonate in others. Let me try to evoke this effect by referring briefly to the remaining chapters in this collection. Although the authors continue to concern themselves with issues of pedagogic principle and procedure, they do so in ways that enrich our thinking across these interlocking dimensions, as well as in interaction with various literatures.

Nicol's turning to theories of speech acts and face (chapter 9) reminds us that a disinclination to view what we do any longer as an application of linguistics does not cut us off from an involvement with its literature. What also stands out for me here is Nicol's exploration of data-collection procedure and his clearly keen enjoyment of the re-creative engagement technique he develops.

Adams's (chapter 10) concern with the way in which her language learners regularly passed through their environment experiencing only superficial interaction with it leads her to develop a theorizing in the terms of an ecology of language learning.

Jackstädt & Müller-Hartmann (chapter 11) are concerned with issues of culture, specifically with the role of background culture in the attempts of learners to communicate internationally with each other in ways that lead to both effective language learning and more aware citizenship.

Hadley pursues his concern with the culturally differentiated construction of social reality by setting out to find a researcher (Evans) with the appropriate expertise, and together they theorize the classroom experience of Japanese learners in terms that illuminate Kelly with Confucius and Confucius with Kelly.

Melles (chapter 13) shares Jackstädt and Müller-Hartmann's concern with computer-mediated communication (CMC), as he and his colleagues work to establish more coherence between CMC provision-in-practice and espoused CMC policy in their institution.

Pierre (chapter 14) takes the data of her teaching context to the workbench of conversation analysis and crafts there not only a perceptive understanding but also the basis for further pedagogic intervention. I know of no better way of setting a collection of work such as this squarely in the world of social action than to face up to Pierre's closing lines: The race is truly not to the swift.

As I review the collection now, there are three connected comments I feel I need to make. First, I think that we have done well in terms of geographical coverage, pedagogic issues, and types of learner, less well in terms of gender share, and English-sounding names remain overrepresented. One could argue for a quota system, but I would not.

These reflections lead me to my second comment, which is that I persuaded the authors to give up most of the discussion that they had originally included of action research itself as a topic. They have stripped their work, therefore, of much of the overtly intellectual and ideological framework in which they had set it, and this has left them more in the role of reporters and storytellers than they had set out to be. I have taken it upon myself to provide a discussion and a set of sources to follow up, and I hope that I have not done the contributors to this volume a disservice in this. My thinking is that the collection now *acts* in the sense of action research; it is more *of* action research and less *about* it. And by editing out some discussion, I have, in the very simple sense of pages available, made space for another chapter. I have also hoped to increase the urgency of the invitation to the reader not only to find out more about action research but to get and stay involved in it.

Third, and arising in turn from the above, the collection is resolutely focused on pedagogy in a way that the current favoring of ideologically oriented discussion might wish to question. Readers seeking further contributions to a debate on critical perspectives in a postmodern era will be disappointed. There certainly are important, related issues to explore further, regarding, to take just a few examples, the language politics of asylum seekers and refugees (Perkins); the relationships between teachers and researchers as separate people (Hadley & Evans; Jackstädt & Müller-Hartmann); as well as those between academic and technical support staff (Melles); the native speaker/international language debate (Nicol; Hadley & Evans); and the ideology of communication within commercial globalization (Pierre), but these are not explicitly pursued here.

Not because the debate is not important, not because the authors here do not have ideological positions or are naïve about their significance, not because I have my own thoughts on the issues (Edge, 1996) and share Johnston's (1999) enthusiasm and reservations, or even because there is currently plenty to read in the area (Canagarajah, 1999; Pennycook, 1994, 1999; Phillipson, 1992b; Tollefson, 1995), but so very simply because that is not the focus that this collection of chapters established as it made itself.

We have all become familiar with the Chinese saying to the effect that if you give a person a fish, you feed them for a day, but if you teach a person how to fish, you feed them for life. And we have seen beyond it. We know that if we see some people teaching other people how to fish, we need to check who has old fishing equipment that they are seeking to off-load or a new fast-freezing technology that they wish to market, who controls the system of fishing permits, whether local waters are already overfished, to what extent dietary or religious customs will permit the eating of fish, and what the local levels of mercury poisoning are. All of this and more must be done, and those who do it deserve as much, but not more, honor as those who feel the weight of the wet rope in their hands. In the space allotted to us in this collection, I take responsibility for having steered a course away from the corridors of power and toward the smell of the sea. Some readers might find it bizarre that I feel a need to defend a focus on pedagogy in a collection offered to ESOL teachers, but these are our times as I understand them.

To conclude, then, the two main themes here are those of

1. attitude: exploratory, investigative, participatory, collegial, and empowering of self and others

2. access: here is some of the work that men and women around the world are doing; take this as an invitation.

> We do not have perfect theoretical and epistemological foundations; we do not have perfect methods for data collection; we do not have perfect or transparent modes of representation. We work in the knowledge of our limited resources. But we do not have to abandon the attempt to produce disciplined accounts of the world that are coherent, methodical, and sensible. (Atkinson, 1992, p. 51)

If you are already engaged in this kind of work, please do communicate your experiences to others. If you are not, we hope some day you'll join us. Imagine . . . .

◈ ACKNOWLEDGMENTS

My thanks to Jill Burton, Keith Richards, and my fellow contributors to this collection for their comments on an earlier draft of this article.

◈ CONTRIBUTOR

Julian Edge has been involved in TESOL and teacher education since 1969, working and living in Europe, the Middle East, and Southeast Asia. He now works at Aston University, England, teaching on their distance-learning MSc in TESOL, as well as supervising doctoral studies in the area of professional discourse and development. His next book, *Continuing Cooperative Development,* will appear with The University of Michigan Press in 2002.

CHAPTER 2

Here It Is, Rough Though It May Be: Basic Computer for ESL

Alison Perkins

◈ INTRODUCTION

I am a novice teacher. There are moments of uncertainty, hesitation, and rejoicing every single class. I have waited patiently for the feelings of trepidation to be replaced by confidence. It has not happened. What I have become cognizant of is that it is during these moments of uncertainty, uniqueness, and value conflict—situations that Schon (1987) refers to as the "indeterminate zone of practice" (p. 6)—I have experienced the greatest moments of professional development.

Am I a teacher yet? Is this a professional identity that I may now claim? The name tag "Teacher! Teacher!" was the easy part; the daily activities have come with time. I can put together a lesson plan and live through a 3-hour class now. Does that count? I have conquered the overhead projector and the photocopier, and I can put together cooperative and uncooperative groups of students. Yet an inner satisfaction that I was seeking with this career change has remained elusive during my first forays into the teaching world. I have not felt like a professional. Most times, I have felt like a technician.

Survival in the classroom during my first year was dependent upon mastery of what I have come to see as the doingness of teaching. But there was only minimal satisfaction in getting through a class. I had not yet cracked the code. I was not satisfied. I felt as if I was dabbling, and professionals do not dabble, do they? Professionals know what they are doing.

I have found teaching in the TESOL world to be incredibly complex. Faced with the multitude of decisions that all teachers are faced with, I began to realize that most are not dichotomous. Each classroom dilemma is a multifarious, bewildering mix of value clashes and theoretical options. As a new teacher, I am often stymied by the goings-on in my 10-ft by 10-ft square.

What I have needed is a model through which I can fight my private battles and uncover my personal values, theoretical assumptions, and gaps of knowledge. Action research is providing such a model.

My first career involved health care, and I am no stranger to scientific articles replete with statistics and research jargon. However, the research model that dominates the scientific world seems out of place with the multifaceted world of teaching. What has helped me more are the stories that are born in the classrooms and shared among peers.

When I listen to these anecdotes, I hear the voices of teachers knowing what to do (Freeman, 1996), and that is the kind of teacher I want to be, of course. I seek their advice because at many times I do not know what to do, and I do not have the repertoire of tricks up my sleeve that a more experienced teacher has ready.

My search for the next useful idea (which often I get from these exchanges) has provided an unexpected benefit. The process by which I decide whether to adopt, modify, or reject the helpful hints that I have been given so generously has opened the door to the discovery of my own personal paradigm. The thought, "I love that idea!", can quickly be followed by the question "Why do I love that idea?" Reflection interrogates theory and practice. Introspection: what a powerful tool!

My primary motives in undertaking this action research project were twofold: to improve the situation in my classroom and to foster my own professional development as a teacher. The guided process of inquiry and reflection provided me with unexpected insights and paths that I would have otherwise left unexplored. I would like to acknowledge that my focus on this initial project was on the personal inquiry process and not on current thinking in TESOL. A primary outcome of the project was a familiarity with a practical research model that leads to professional growth. The action research model as outlined by Altrichter, Posch, and Somekh (1993) gave me the courage to cross that border from technician to professional.

◈ SITUATION

The action research project occurred in the context of adult education in a class entitled "Introduction to Basic Computer for ESL." This is an adult education class taught in a 10-week block that meets twice a week for 2 hours in the evening. The ethnic backgrounds of the students include Bosnian, Somalian, Vietnamese, Chinese, and Albanian. All of the students are defined by the adult school system as at an intermediate level of English (having completed at least Level 3 of a possible five levels of basic English offered).

Inherent in adult education are attendance issues that revolve around the adults' lives outside the classroom. In this particular class, two of the students arrived late every class due to work conflicts, and one left early to pick up her husband from work. The average attendance each meeting was 70%. Classes were held in the school's computer lab, which consists of 10 computers in a square shape with the server in the middle. There was just enough room for me to pass around the backs of all the students if they have their chairs pulled in.

The broad goal of the class is for the students to understand how a personal computer works and what it can do. It is an introduction to keyboarding, word processing, spreadsheets, database, and basic computer terminology. None of the students had ever used a computer or a typewriter prior to this class. I had taught this course twice before.

◈ FOCUS

For the first 2 weeks of class, I kept a diary. There are many formats that could be adopted for a research diary. The one I chose is my own hybrid method. I divide the paper into three columns. The middle section is for immediate observations and interpretations that I write down every day. The two outside columns are for later entries that pertain to the writing in the middle column. The right-hand column I leave for later thoughts and insights that occur when I reread the diary, and the left-hand column I use for theoretical notes that have come from literature searches that were initiated by questions that came up in the diary (see Appendix).

The driving force behind action research is the desire for improvement in the classroom situation. Focusing the research can be one of the most challenging and time-consuming beginning steps. My initial attempts at beginning a research project were thwarted by a lack of focus. Where does one begin? I decided to let my frustration level be the indicator and began to search my diary for the most charged entries. The following two excerpts are the ones that seemed to capture the essence of my frustrations.

> Diary Entry 1: I want to change my name. I can't possibly meet the demands of four students yelling out "Teacher! Teacher!" at once.

> Diary Entry 2: As usual, I have spent hours planning a creative, interactive lesson plan which has quickly dissolved into a question and answer session between individual students and myself.

Following Altrichter et al. (1993), I decided to analyze the individual elements of what I thought might be going on in the classroom in an attempt to answer the following questions:

1. What is happening in this situation?
2. Which events, actions, and features of the situation are important?
3. Which people are involved and in what kind of activities?

I returned to the two diary entries to see if I could add detail that might provide a richer picture of the scene at those moments of peak frustration. The following is a compilation of observational notes.

- After I have demonstrated a skill on the computer, and the students are practicing, they are requesting one-on-one assistance.
- The students appear to get stuck during lessons. When they are stuck, they do not continue with the lesson until unstuck.
- Three of the students keep calling out repetitively until they receive assistance.
- Some of the students never ask for help.
- The pattern of communication in the classroom begins with teacher to class and then changes to predominately teacher to individual student.

Unanswered questions began to emerge.

- Is it the same students asking for help all the time?
- Are they really stuck when they ask for help?
- Is it the students who are coming late or leaving early who are asking for help?
- Are other students also stuck but afraid to ask for help?
- Is it disruptive for the other students when some are calling out?
- Do the students have resources other than me for help?

- Am I interpreting how they are asking for help as impolite?
- How do I respond when they are asking for help?
- What forms of help do I want the students to utilize?
- Is there anything specific to this subject matter that is fostering this behavior?
- Are the students afraid to make a mistake?
- Do the students know when they know something?

The monitoring of classroom behaviors and questioning of the situation brought me into a role through which I could be more of a participant-observer and also reflect on the experience. Theory and practice infiltrate, question, and test each other. Why was I making particular choices in the classroom? Which model was I following? Were unexplored alternatives available? I began to reach deep inside and attempt to bring to the surface underlying assumptions and values so that they could be better examined. I also prioritized the issues based on what I thought would make the most meaningful changes in the classroom experience.

First, I acknowledged that I was interpreting the students' requests for help as impolite demands. Acceptance of cultural diversity was a struggle for me with this particular class. We needed to discuss the concept of politeness in the classroom and agree upon acceptable modes of communication when asking for help.

Second, I thought about the role of adult education in my students' lives and felt I owed them a practical, meaningful educational experience that related to their adult lives outside the classroom. The role of teacher as the only source of knowledge would not serve as a useful model outside of the computer classroom. Whether at home or in the workplace, basic personal computer use is an individual task. The availability of one-on-one assistance would be highly unlikely.

Within these two focuses, I formulated the following hypotheses about the situation in the computer classroom.

1. If the students are unaware of what I consider to be polite communication for requesting help, they will not be able to fulfill my expectations.

2. If politeness is a value that the individual students bring to the classroom, then communicating to them about cultural norms should establish an acceptable (to me) level of politeness.

3. If the students are afraid of doing something wrong with the computer, then they will not experiment.

4. If the students are not confident that they know something, then they may ask questions as reassurance.

5. If there are no other recognized resources for help in the classroom, then the teacher will be the only legitimate source.

◈ RESPONSE

I created a series of action strategies to implement and evaluate during the remaining 6 weeks of the semester. Their implementation overlapped, so I present them here not in a particular chronological order.

Action Strategy 1: Speak With Individual Students and the Class as a Whole Regarding Expectations for Politeness

I first spoke with a couple of the students who were very quiet during the class and asked them if they had unanswered questions and if they felt they were getting enough attention. The general feedback from this group was that they felt that the other students were getting all of the help and that their questions went unanswered.

I then spoke with the students who were asking most of the questions, and we discussed ways to ask questions in class that would be acceptable for politeness. The students did try and ask for help more politely, but the calling out for help continued throughout the semester when help was needed. This remains a frustration for me and doubtless for the less vocal students.

Action Strategy 2: Develop a Worksheet to Accompany the Lesson That Would Allow the Student and Me to Acknowledge Independent Skills Versus Emerging Skills

I realized that I was not exactly sure which students were capable of what specific skills on the computer. I wanted to differentiate the amount of help a student needed to accomplish a particular skill. To this end, I implemented a worksheet asking the student to identify whether they had accomplished the task completely independently, with some assistance, or with complete assistance. My short-term goal was to identify where individual students were on their skill acquisition. A longer term goal was to create cooperative learning groups with students of various skill levels. An excerpt from a worksheet is shown in Figure 1.

The students all gave very positive feedback on the worksheets. They liked the sequential nature of the activities and reported a feeling of accomplishment as they looked back through past sheets and saw the emerging independence. I had not anticipated the value that they would have as an assessment tool. The sheets also highlighted for me that I was taking a bottom-up approach to teaching computer. I had been aiming for a project-based, top-down approach, so this was an eye-opener.

Action Strategy 3: Introduce the Students to Sources of Help Other Than the Instructor: For Example, the Help Function of the Software, the Computer Software Manual, and Their Peers

The Help key and computer software manual did not prove to be a viable resource for this particular class because of the level of difficulty in the language found in those two sources. Without an appropriate text, and with the software manual inaccessible, I started to realize that I was the only resource they readily saw. My next goal was to help them learn from each other. I was hoping that the worksheets would

		Can't do	Received help	Independent
1	Boot the computer			X
2	Open the file "lesson 5" on your floppy		X	
3	Print the file	X		

FIGURE 1. Sample Worksheet From Computer Class

give me a way to identify a skill differential and create classroom experts regarding various aspects of computer usage.

A colleague who is a kindergarten teacher proposed the concept of *classroom experts* to me. She saw a similarity between her classroom needs and mine despite the obvious demographic differences. There were many discrete tasks that students accomplished throughout the year at different rates that were essential to the smooth functioning of the kindergarten's daily routine. Whereas I was dealing with booting the computer and saving files, she dealt with tying shoes and managing zippers.

The teacher alone could not efficiently assist all the students with those tasks, so she choose to identify classroom experts—those students who were competent at specific skills—and encouraged them to help those who were still working on skill development. I believed that there was an analogy here worth exploring (cf. Lantolf & Appel, 1994).

As soon as I started working with the concept of classroom experts, I started to confront my own biases. Does the term *expert* have a generally positive or negative connotation? Did I want to segregate my classroom into those who knew something and those who did not? Who designates the person as an expert? Can the students identify themselves as such, or does the designation need to come from an outside source? In a class where everyone starts at ground zero, how can I find a differential in skill levels?

I kept track of the sheets, observed the students at different tasks, and started to plan my lessons with groupings of students based on a skill differential. These lesson plans took a tremendous amount of time. Inevitably, students would be absent or come late to the class, which would stymie the plan.

During the last 2 weeks of class, I had a brainstorm. Instead of planning the lesson so that it was dependent upon people being there to make it work, I would reverse the process and take advantage of who had not come to class to provide an opportunity for a learning differential. I envisioned a learning differential as a different learning opportunity for different groups of students. Those who had been absent or late had not been exposed to certain information due to their absence or tardiness.

Creating a learning differential as opposed to identifying a skill differential was more congruous with my goal of building self-confidence with computer use. I did not have to separate the students who were catching on more quickly from those who were not. They self-selected themselves into groups with differing amounts of information.

This last strategy showed the most potential in the limited time that I was able to implement it. I could look at the class attendance list and assign people to teach those who were not present as a way of reinforcing the lesson plan for those who were there and as a way of catching up those who had been absent. (I am aware that there exists in adult education a tolerance for absences that is not as common in other educational settings.)

❖ OUTCOMES

The most important overall outcome of this project was that it gave me a way to contribute professionally, not merely technically. The structure of carrying out an action research project gave me the opportunity to observe, to be reflective, to think hard, to theorize, and to try new things in the classroom. I believe these processes take teachers beyond the role of technicians into the realm of professionals.

◈ REFLECTIONS

This action research project was a first-time experience for me, and I would like to address some of the shortcomings that I have identified. One in particular is the absence of multiple perspectives. I have made steps forward in making sense of my environment and my particular experience in this classroom, but I did not seek other perspectives in anything other than via very informal, spontaneous conversation with individual students and a classroom volunteer. This is an area that I will improve in the next project. The data collection was entirely through a personal research diary. There were opportunities where interviews, tape recordings, or surveys would have been more appropriate.

However, as Covey (1989) states, "Private victory precedes public victory" (p. 51). This is my story so far.

◈ CONTRIBUTOR

Alison Perkins has owned and operated a physical therapy, orthotic, and prosthetic facility for 18 years. In the mid-1990s, she decided to explore a new professional path, and she received her MA TESOL in 1998. She currently teaches content-based vocational courses at Portland Adult Education, in Maine, in the United States.

◈ APPENDIX

A Diary Extract: Class Notes 5/26/99

Vygotskian Approaches p. 37–

Participants' motives shape and guide the particular activity

For Vygotsky— social interaction is a mechanism for individual development—the novice is drawn into the space of the expert's strategic processes for problem-solving

My 3.30 (early group) came to type but of course Mario wants to surf the net to check soccer scores.

10 students showed up today for 9 computers. Oh my. I came in one and a half hours early and still wasn't ready for them. Where does the time go? This sporadic attendance is driving me nuts!

We warmed up on the computer and then reviewed vocabulary for storage devices. We did a cooperative project requiring saving and finished. Lots of progress today, but who will be at the next class?

I am so frustrated by all the lesson planning time that goes to waste because a different group shows up than I planned for. I really like the theme running through the book on Vygotsky and want to try to match expert and novice.

??? Could I use the sporadic attendance as an asset rather than a frustration [the group that attended or showed up on time = expert?

CHAPTER 3

An "It's Not Action Research Yet, But I'm Getting There" Approach to Teaching Writing

Neil Cowie

⬦ INTRODUCTION

Action research writers often describe various models of action research as involving cycles or spirals, typically of issue identification, data collection and analysis, reflection, and action (see Burns, 1999). The process described is one of disciplined and planned teacher research to improve conditions, both in the classroom and beyond, backed up by rich descriptions of data collection and analysis. The case study described below is, unfortunately, not one in which I describe a disciplined and planned way to improve my teaching. It consists of rather less than expertly focused reflections on how I addressed a series of puzzles about teaching writing. It is an account of a novice teacher researcher's struggle to get going on the action research path, a struggle that I intend to be encouraging to others because of its familiarity.

For 3 years, I have thought about how best to teach writing, constantly trying new classroom approaches and ways in which to respond to student work. In the account that follows, I describe briefly some of the teaching issues that are important to me, in particular how I have structured my feedback to students. I have found that this is an extremely complex area in which it is difficult to make any firm conclusions, and I have really only begun to scratch the surface. As well as describing my rationale for written comments, I discuss the benefits of using audiotapes to motivate novice writers to revise their work. I finish by identifying areas for further research and follow-up with an emphasis on much greater collaboration with my students.

⬦ SITUATION

This report is about an undergraduate writing class in the liberal arts faculty of a Japanese public university. There are several reasons this class can be difficult to teach. For many of the students, it is the first time that they have had any kind of writing lessons, in Japanese or English. The weekly lesson is 90 minutes long, 25 times a year; some quick sums will indicate that this is not a very great amount of contact time. This is compounded by the often relatively large numbers of students (20–40), and lateness and absence are common. Ability levels also vary enormously and, because students come from a variety of specializations within liberal arts, they may be reluctant initially to work with new faces of a different age or major. One further possible negative factor is that the course only carries two credits, half that of other courses, so students may not feel it is worthwhile putting as much effort in as they might if more credits were at stake. On the positive side, the students, although novice writers, are often very keen and enthusiastic, especially as for many of them it is their first opportunity to study with a native-speaking teacher of English. My teaching environment is rather isolated in that there is little discussion with my colleagues concerning pedagogy and innovation, so to enlist my students as partner researchers is a practical and motivational way to further my development as a teacher.

After experimenting with several approaches, I now focus on one specific genre, the report, and students have the chance to write several versions of that report over a 3- or 4-week period. A report is a very nebulous concept, but in broad terms I want students to be familiar with some kind of expository writing in which they have to take a side or give an opinion, research an issue and argue logically about it. This kind of writing may be useful to them in their immediate academic careers or future employment, but I think above all it is a very good way to stimulate their thinking (i.e., writing as thinking).

During the course of an academic year, students should write seven or eight reports, and I hope they will produce several drafts for each report. One of my main goals is to encourage novice writers to write as much as possible and to get used to the idea of redrafting their work several times. My approach is largely based on process writing during which writers go through a cycle or spiral of stages including getting ideas, organizing them, drafting and crafting, editing and rewriting. The two main parts I emphasize are the initial generation of ideas and rewriting. I try to make students aware of strategies to overcome their initial fear of writing and to get on with writing and rewriting their texts as often as they can. Such strategies include the familiar range of brainstorming ideas: mind maps, questioning surveys, readings, discussions, quickwriting. Once the students have the germ of an idea, they work, often collaboratively, to improve and fashion it into an organized and clear text.

As well as emphasizing the writing process, I show students models of writing. I am very careful to limit this, as once they have seen a model text, they tend to feel that there is only one correct way to write—which they must copy. In addition, I give them practical strategies that will help them become more independent writers, for example, get them to ask questions of their texts, or show them useful organizational patterns to help them plan. I choose the broad area for each report (e.g., a problem) while the students choose their own topics (their own personal problem).

Typically during a 3- or 4-week class cycle, students work together in class to generate ideas, write initial drafts, and then revise them at home. Of course, students vary enormously in the amount of out-of-class work they do, so I usually have two or three groups within the class (those who have done all the work, some of the work, and none of the work). Once the students submit their reports, I check them, return them and hope that the students will revise the reports using my comments and corrections. This mention of feedback brings me to the focus of my investigation.

🔷 FOCUS

Cochran-Smith and Lyttle (1990) note that most teachers begin researching because of some external course requirement, and that was certainly a factor for me. My first report for a master's course was about feedback, and I subsequently published it in my university journal (Cowie, 1995).

Reading about feedback has been a constant source of ideas during my action research, and I found Ferris and Hedgcock (1998) particularly helpful. The summary below reflects how I feel looking back rather than how I felt during the process.

Does Feedback Help?

Feedback can be problematic and confusing because students may not understand what teachers write or how to deal with suggestions, but there does seem to be some consensus that feedback, especially on early drafts, does help.

How Do Teachers Give Feedback?

There has been a tradition for teachers to give students feedback at sentence level, focusing on mechanics (e.g., verb-subject agreements, spelling), which is sometimes called *form*. This is in contrast to more global concerns about content, ideas, and organization. Some writers (e.g., Zamel, 1985) have suggested giving global feedback on early drafts and feedback on form on later drafts, whereas other writers (e.g., Fathman & Whalley, 1990) suggest neither has much effect. Truscott (1996), in a controversial but persuasive article, argues strongly that grammatical error correction is not beneficial and may even be harmful. However, again there seems to be a measure of consensus that some feedback on both global concerns and form is needed throughout the writing process.

How Do Students Respond to Feedback?

Cohen (1987) found that many students did not even reread their corrected papers, never mind redraft them. Ferris (1997) drew two opposing conclusions: Students either pay a great deal of attention to feedback and revise their writing, or they ignore or avoid suggestions altogether. Again, the evidence is contradictory, but it would appear some students do revise their work as a result of getting feedback.

Ferris and Hedgcock (1998) conclude that in giving feedback teacher comments should

- be personalized
- give guidance and direction
- be text specific, although some comments can carry through to subsequent texts
- be encouraging and constructively critical

Ferris (1997), in an earlier paper, suggested that the two strategies of asking for information and providing a general summary of grammar points are the most likely ways that teachers will encourage student revision. In addition, teachers should clearly explain to students what their feedback strategies are, encourage reflection and questions on the feedback, and integrate feedback into the lesson cycle.

As a result of this previous investigation, I use four guiding principles, similar to Ferris and Hedgcock's advice, when giving my responses to student reports:

1. Respond to the ideas students have. By this I mean that it is very important to be a real reader: to agree or disagree with what they have said, to respond openly and honestly and involve them in a dialogue.

2. Be positive about the writing, and try very hard not to cut down the student, who may be extremely sensitive to criticism.

3. Respond, at least initially, in terms of the global organization of the text. For example, are the ideas set out clearly and logically? Are there enough details and examples? Is there a good plan?

4. Focus student attention on errors of form by underlining or pointing, and by giving an end comment on consistent problems.

The following is from a typical end comment given to a student comparing the roles of mothers in Japan and England. I think it illustrates Points 1–3, with comments on form interspersed through the text.

> This is a very good topic to examine and you came up with some good examples. If you wanted to rewrite again, it would be good to have some more examples, both of the English and Japanese mothers. I think you do have a point about different attitudes but it is too easy to generalise. You've only really compared two women so you need more evidence to make your case strong.

In sum, my general priorities reflect the needs of the students. Most of them are novice writers who need a lot of encouragement in planning and organizing their work and perhaps are unnecessarily preoccupied with sentence formation. They are in Grabe and Kaplan's (1996) terms *knowledge tellers* rather than *knowledge transformers* (after Bereiter & Scardamalia, 1987). I believe that activities focused mainly on global concerns may help them make the transition from unskilled to skilled writer, by moving from simple retelling strategies to the more "reflective, problem solving nature of expert writing" (Grabe & Kaplan, 1996, p. 122).

Part of this process is to revise their writing several times and to incorporate teacher feedback into a final draft. However, that is very difficult to do given the constraints of the course, especially when many students only write one draft or nothing at all. My research focus, then, at least initially, was to see how the way in which I gave feedback and the type of feedback I gave could motivate students to rewrite.

◈ RESPONSE

I would now like to examine how I have varied my writing feedback over a 3-year period. The process has gradually become more disciplined and systematic, but I am still very much a novice teacher researcher. In Year 1, I tried various approaches but have little evidence of their effect, other than instinct, that what I was doing was improving the situation. In Year 2, I collected more information, in particular from students, that shows I may have improved my practice. Subsequently, in Year 3, a different set of research questions emerged, which shows that such improvement may not be gained so easily. These questions will be the basis for the next cycle of research.

The main ways in which I give feedback to students have been through written comments and by making comments on audiotapes. These are not the only ways, though, as I also use peer feedback and reformulation. I try to structure classes so that most work is collaborative, and student giving and getting of feedback is no exception to this.

In a feedback lesson, I encourage students to look through their work together, give supportive, constructive comments to each other, and work together to understand and act on my comments. About half of the feedback lessons also involve reformulation, a technique described by Tribble (1996) in which students work on one rewritten paper trying to identify improvements from the original. It may be that peer feedback and reformulation have had just as much as an impact on students' revision strategies as teacher comments, but I chose to focus on comments as I spent much more time thinking about and making them.

Usually, teachers write brief comments inserted throughout a paper, finishing with some kind of end summary (see Ferris, 1997). Examples of variations from this format include those of Charles (1990), and Storch and Tapper (1996), who only responded to student-annotated questions about their papers. However, my written comments are perhaps typical in that I write brief error corrections or underlining (usually in red) on the text and give a 50- to 100-word summary at the end.

Year 1

In Year 1 (1997–1998), I used written comments without consciously involving the students in an explicit action research focus. Of course, I explained the four main principles behind the comments (I would respond to their ideas, try to be positive, give priority to global concerns, and provide a limited focus on form), but I did not really involve them in my plans, probably because my plans were so vague. I do, nevertheless, have three sources of information: postcourse evaluations, some of the reports, and administrative records of attendance and reports submitted. The latter show that of the 140 reports I checked, only 11 were rewritten after I had handed them back (the figures for the previous year were 163 and 4, so perhaps I was doing something better). Although my statistics are neither sophisticated nor robust, they do give a rough idea of the rate of revision, which did not appear to be very high. I wrote in my teaching diary at the end of the course:

> I was disappointed with my performance this year in the writing lessons. I didn't really build on what I had discovered previously—just did more of the same. It's very difficult to get students to do rewriting so I tried to give more time this year in class than previously.

So what could I do to improve things?

Year 2

In Year 2 (1998–1999), I started giving feedback through audiotaped comments. My motivation for this was threefold:

1.   decrease the amount of time I spent marking

2.   give students more comments and listening practice

3.   motivate students to rewrite more

The way in which I do this is similar to giving written comments. First, I read through the paper and write brief marginal comments throughout the paper and a brief end summary; then I talk into a tape expanding on the points alluded to in my written summary (still trying to use the same 4-point framework).

By the end of Year 2, I had checked 199 reports of which 28 were rewritten once and 2 were rewritten twice. Although a small core number of students accounted for most of the rewriting (4 students rewrote 15 of the papers), 14 different students did rewrite at least once during the year after they received the tapes from me. I felt that the tapes were having a positive effect, perhaps motivating some to rewrite their papers again, or at least getting some students to write a paper in the first place.

In addition to the administrative record, I kept copies of all the reports as well as some of the tapes I made (students kept them after the course finished, but I copied six). I also received written responses about the tapes twice during the year. I asked the students to talk about how they used the tapes and what impact they had on their rewriting strategies. I would like to quote from these to give some idea of how the students felt:

> I listened about four times. First only listening, second listen carefully, third with reading my, writing, fourth only listening. When I listened to the tape I mostly corrected my writing or rewrote the matter. (This student did not rewrite the whole draft but penciled in corrections.)

> The tape you gave me was very useful and helpful for me and my friend. I listened many times the tape, and I could understand what you want to say. I and my friend listened the tape again and again and I explained what she couldn't understand. (The friend referred to was not on the writing course.)

> The tape that you gave me made me astonished because your comment for my homework was very long and very polite. It was very helpful and taught me lack of homework and how to rewrite it.

> It (the tapes) is a good system for us because we can listen when we want to listen. After I think to rewrite. Your comments on the tape was "why" "what" "where" or "when". It was good for me. If your comments was grammatical I couldn't rewrite.

Overall, these comments are very positive about the tapes, and a commonsense judgment would be that the students are motivated by them, but whether that is enough to make them rewrite, I do not know. In this first year of using the tapes, I paid little attention to training the students in what to do with the tapes or to monitoring their behavior. On reflection, I just handed the tapes over and expected them to get on with listening to them. In Year 3, I felt that I needed to be more careful in helping students get the most from the tapes and to find out what they do with them. This became another focus for my Year 3 approach.

As well as motivating students, I wanted audiotapes to be a more efficient way of giving feedback. It is true that I can say comments in less time than I can write them. I transcribed some of my tapes and found that I can say between 120 and 150 words a minute, compared to about 70 words in 2 minutes of writing. My written end comments tended to be 50–100 words, but my audiotaped comments range from 200 to 500 words, so I tend to give much more information on the tapes in a shorter amount of time (Flick, 1990, reached similar conclusions about the efficiency of talking versus writing).

Other advantages that tapes have over written comments are that students get more listening practice, and it may benefit those who prefer aural to visual input. Also some students mention the flexibility tapes give (they can listen in the car or on the train), and there is the possibility that the more personal extended comments I can give on tape are very positive in creating a good relationship with the students. One drawback is that I find making the tapes very draining compared to writing and cannot concentrate for such a long time. Written comments can also be done almost anywhere, whereas tapes need to be made in a quiet environment.

After Year 2, I felt confident that I was on to something positive. My students had reacted well to the tapes, and the amount of rewriting appeared to be higher than in Year 1. During Year 2, I had joined a small group of teacher researchers interested in writing and feedback, and I made a short presentation on my findings at a conference. My action research career appeared to be starting.

Year 3

At the time of writing, I was halfway through Year 3 (1999–2000) and had gone through four more report cycles. I was much more explicit with this group of students, explaining early on that I was giving them the tapes because I wanted them to rewrite their work. I also gave the students much more guidance on how to use the tapes effectively. After the relative success of Year 2, I was expecting an even greater number of rewrites, but only 3 students (out of 40) rewrote any of their reports—a dismal rate. And to compound this, the 3 students who did rewrite are mature, auditing students who have more time than most other students. So what happened?

I think two things can explain this. First, when I look at the reports handed in, it seems students were actually doing several initial drafts before the draft that they submitted. (I ask students to hand in all their drafts, even their rough quickwriting). I may have been allowing more time in lessons for rewriting, in response to some of the evaluation comments from Years 1 and 2, and as a result, when students handed in their report, it may have been their second or third attempt anyway. Second, I asked students why they did not rewrite (after I gave my feedback) more often. They gave replies that confirmed how high rewriting was on their list of priorities.

I felt I don't have to rewrite. I suggest you decide a deadline so I'll rewrite.

Basically it's troublesome.

I think rewriting is very important but my five tests this week is more important for my graduation.

New things are coming to me every moment it's pretty hard for me go back to a previous essay.

I don't have better idea about the same topic.

There was also one comment that links to Ferris and Hedgcock's (1998) notion that some comments should look forward to the next paper: "I use the comments to plan ahead for the next report."

It became clear that students are not rewriting because

*   it takes too much time and trouble

*   they mainly write in pencil, so revision is very time-consuming

*   the class is not so important to them in the bigger picture of university (e.g., other classes, jobs)

*   the class structure itself means that when we have moved on to other reports, it may be difficult to go back to revise old ones

On the positive side, students do realize it is important to revise, and many do so before they hand in their final draft. It may be that my preoccupation with the impact of feedback on revision is misplaced: Perhaps I should be looking at how my feedback methods and principles can help students improve their future reports, and I need to look at the lessons from a much wider perspective. In particular I need to pay much more attention to how the students write and what I can do to best help them.

⬖ OUTCOMES

I started my investigations by looking at feedback, but more and more I have come round to the view that I need to see feedback as part of a wider teaching situation. Of course, students expect, perhaps demand, a teacher response to their work, and I think that feedback has three main benefits:

1. It validates student work and effort by showing that their teacher cares about and is interested in their writing.

2. It helps a few students rewrite their past work by giving text-specific advice.

3. It can motivate other students for their next piece of work.

It is this third point on which I wish to focus the next spiral of action research, by finding ways to structure the feedback so that it will help students write their future papers.

Ferris (1997) claimed that the two strategies of asking for information and giving grammar summaries would be most likely to result in student revision of their work. I examined my taped and written comments in Year 2 (I transcribed some of the tapes) to see if I used these strategies, and I also wanted to check whether I adhered to my own 4-point framework (be positive, respond to ideas, focus on global concerns, give some pointers to issues of form).

I found that I was certainly positive, making supportive statements about even the weakest work. I did respond to ideas, often at some length and very often by giving my own opinions about a topic. My most common response regarding global concerns was to ask students for more information and more details. Although I did indirectly focus on form by underlining or pointing out errors, I hardly gave any end summaries, so it may be that I did not give students enough useful information about form for subsequent papers.

I therefore need to reexamine how I can better give students information on form, always bearing in mind Truscott's (1996) conclusions that grammar correction can be unhelpful or even harm writers' development. I think I need to find ways to help students become more independent in finding their own errors rather than pointing out errors for them. Finally, I would like to further investigate student responses to the audiotapes, perhaps not requiring revision of reports, but using some kind of reflective activity that will focus students' attention on key issues.

◈ REFLECTIONS

Just as with any other kind of research, to be effective, action research needs to be done in a planned and disciplined way. It is very important to take some time to work out just what it is that you want to do and how you are going to go about doing it. In many ways I feel I have been doing research not for my current group of students but for ones to come. In the same sense that the feedback I gave on their work may have been too late for their current reports, the lessons I am learning are perhaps too late to benefit my current classes.

So I need to get better at anticipating possibilities, think my plans through, and start collecting information as soon as possible. Of course, I can resolve to do this by myself, but I think that there are two other ways in which I can ensure a better chance of this happening: through working with others and writing collaboratively about research.

It is very important to involve other people early on so that they know what you are doing and can help. The primary group of people are my student partners in education. I have involved them more and more, by explaining what I am doing and getting their opinions, but I feel it is still not enough. I have thought about why this is so: Maybe I have not been confident enough in what I am doing to trust them to help, or perhaps I have not really viewed them as participants in the research process, but as objects of it. As McNiff (1988/1997) says, action research is research *with* not *on* people (emphasis hers). This may be where the process of doing action research is so important, and different from less participative approaches: By involving students in it, desired changes may be more likely to happen. Goswami and Stillman (1987) identify a number of things that happen when teachers do action research, including the following very important observation:

> They (teachers) collaborate with their students to answer questions important to both, drawing on community resources in new and unexpected ways. The nature of classroom discourse changes when inquiry begins. Working with teachers to answer real questions provides students with intrinsic motivation for talking, reading, and writing and has the potential for helping them achieve mature language skills. (n.p.)

As well as working more with my students, I would like to improve my collaboration with teacher colleagues. In the past, I have used Edge's (1992) cooperative development techniques as a means of professional development: once in weekly meetings with a colleague from another faculty, and once over a 12-week period contacting a colleague from another university by e-mail (Cowie, 1997). Cooperative development is a superb way to become motivated and disciplined about research, but I found it draining physically and emotionally.

Less taxing has been to start two support groups: one with colleagues from the same university but different departments (looking at student motivation), and one with teachers from other universities (focusing on writing). Both groups serve as a way of giving discipline and a framework for inquiry, and as an important reality check on what I am doing. Both groups have been instrumental in generating ideas, reflecting on the research process, and encouraging the act of public reporting, both informally at group meetings and through more formal written reports and presentations.

The two groups are very different in character, but there are some common factors: Social relationships are very important in making a group work, and these take some time and patience to develop. Members need to truly listen to each other and find out exactly what the respective teaching situations are like. Once common ground has been reached, then group members can work together on a research issue. In the case of the writing group, teacher response to students emerged as a common issue, and it has been refreshing and stimulating to learn in great detail about how other teachers work. Our regular meetings have resulted in a joint presentation at a conference, and we are planning to move on to write a collaborative report of our work.

I have come to agree with Greenwood (1999), not least as a result of writing up this case study, that "writing is a major tool of action research," and that, "by putting off writing, practitioners fail to consolidate their own learning for themselves and other AR [action research] practitioners" (p. 92). I think that a weakness of my research is that I have not done enough writing throughout the process. Of course, there are various kinds of writing: field notes, reflective journals, chapters in books such as this one, and so on. At all levels I have not done enough regularly, and it is something I want to improve. I tell my students often enough that writing is thinking, but I still have not followed my own advice. Therefore, I think the external push to report collaboratively will be very helpful in motivating me to write more consistently.

One final lesson I have learned is that I do not know enough about research methods and statistics in particular. Action research may be characterized by qualitative approaches (Altrichter et al., 1993), but it is very useful to know when statistics may be useful as support, and even more useful to know when they are inappropriate. Throughout the history of action research in education, there has been a tension with researchers in the positivist tradition who often express the view that action research is somehow inferior because it is less valid or robust (Crookes, 1993). Even in the small-scale work I have done, I have come across such opposition, and it would be comforting to argue from a position of knowledge rather than ignorance.

In conclusion, then, I find that I have learned a lot about teaching writing. Feedback is an important part of the teaching process and should be embedded in it, and students should be made aware of the reasons for giving feedback and given time to reflect and respond to the feedback they are given. There is no one way to give feedback, but audiotaped responses are motivating and relatively efficient to produce. The type of feedback given will vary according to student level and motivation. Those relatively few students who will rewrite their final drafts need text-specific comments that ask students questions about their work. The majority probably need more general summaries that will guide their next report.

In this chapter, I have tried to describe how my approach to teaching writing has changed over a number of years. I am not claiming that it has changed through a disciplined and planned cycle of action research; rather it has emerged from a much less organized process of reading, reflection, data collection, and change. From that experience, I have come to realize that I need to make my research efforts more disciplined and, I hope, more fruitful.

How? Through better planning and reflection, I hope to anticipate issues and be more sensitive to potential data, for example, by using a research diary and field notes more consistently. Through more collaboration with students as partners in research (via more regular collection and review of student comments and interviews with selected students), as well as with colleagues as critical friends, I hope to be more open to alternative perspectives and priorities. Through more consistent writing, which will help refine and focus research issues, and through more study of research methods themselves, I hope to use the power of increased articulation and formalization both to take my ideas forward and to communicate them more effectively.

In the next phase of my research, I want to look more at student writing behavior, in particular how the majority can be encouraged to improve from report to report and what role feedback might have in this process. I would also like to look at my teaching in general and how my classroom behavior affects rewriting. This will probably involve observation, either from a critical friend or through some kind of video self-observation. It is not action research yet, but I am getting there.

◈ ACKNOWLEDGMENTS

Many thanks to Tim Ashwell, Andy Barfield, Julian Edge, Cheiron McMahill, Mike Nix, Ethel Ogane, and Anthony Robins for your kind and helpful comments.

◈ CONTRIBUTOR

Neil Cowie has taught in the Liberal Arts Department of Saitama University, in Japan, since 1994. Aside from action research, he is very interested in teacher development, especially in looking for ways to collaborate with others.

CHAPTER 4

Early Reflections: Journaling a Way Into Teaching

Eliana Santana-Williamson

◈ INTRODUCTION

This chapter is a description of the process I went through to help preservice course participants in northern Brazil write reflective journals as an aid to the development of critical thinking skills. The focus on critical thinking is particularly problematic in the region because official education has only recently turned their attention to the development of critical pedagogy (Cox & Assis-Peterson, 1999).

The first part of this chapter presents a sketch of the broad context of the field of TESOL in northern Brazil as well as my own institutional situation. This is followed by the results of library research that I did in order to raise my own awareness regarding the state of the art in TESOL teacher education in general. I then discuss my beliefs concerning what the basis of the new program needed to be, before going on to show how my specific aims were formulated and focused, how I pursued them, which data were collected, and how the results led to further reflection on teacher education in general.

◈ SITUATION

The Setting

In northern Brazil, the context for teaching English contains a circle of linked problems that is difficult to break into. First of all, there is a huge demand for TESOL by the community, which envisages the knowledge of English as a sign of status, a way to get a better job, and a means of communicating with others all around the world, especially through the Internet.

In response to this, many schools have opened, and an informal survey, which a colleague carried out by phoning every school listed in the Belém telephone directory, confirmed that they had all been founded within the past 20 years.

With so many English language schools being opened, a large demand for ESOL teachers has been created. Where are they to be found? Two universities, Universidade da Amazônia and Universidade Federal do Pará, offer degrees called *Licenciatura em Letras,* English being among the languages offered. These traditional undergraduate degrees contain courses in language and literature, as well as pedagogy. When I interviewed the heads of the departments in the two universities, both acknowledged the demand for more TESOL-specific courses, including a graduate program, but both also emphasized that they did not have enough accredited staff to teach such programs, and one added that the cost of bringing in lecturers from outside the region would be prohibitive. Their concern about the situation became all the more urgent with the passage of a law requiring all teachers to be properly accredited by the year 2006 (Gilda Chaves, personal communication).

When I contacted the language schools mentioned above, I asked them how many teachers they employed and what qualifications these teachers held. The figures showed that only 20% of the total number of teachers had the Licenciatura em Letras credential, with no one holding a higher degree. The fact that most of the teaching force is thus unqualified in official terms, along with the fact that the private language schools operate in a highly competitive market, inevitably keeps teachers' salaries low. The low salaries act as a disincentive to potential teachers.

Furthermore, the state of Pará does not host professional organizations, which could offer EFL teachers tools for professional growth. Whenever teachers want to participate in conferences, short-term programs, seminars, and graduate programs, they have to travel further south. Because Pará is located in the very north of Brazil, far away from these centers, teachers need to be able to afford travel and living expenses that may go beyond what most of them can pay for. All these difficulties restrict access to better education and preparation as language instructors. The problem thus comes full circle.

Against this background, I must state that I was in a fortunate situation. With an undergraduate degree in economics and some pedagogic training, I had had a teaching post for 7 years at the Centro Cultural Brasil-Estados Unidos-Belém (CCBEU), a nonprofit binational center established 45 years ago and geared to the idea of cultural exchange. I had then been abroad to study for my master's degree in TESOL, and when I returned, the CCBEU was going through changes, with innovative projects being developed by the new academic team. In August 1998, because they felt they needed to work on the development of a teacher education program, they invited me to join them as an academic coordinator.

One of my responsibilities was to rebuild the curriculum of the teacher training program, which is equivalent to a certificate in TESOL. This is a year-long program that has the objective of giving initial training to those in the community who want to become English language teachers. Classes meet twice a week for an hour and 40 minutes, which makes it a 122-hour program. It is the only certificate in TESOL offered in the state of Pará that is both recognized by the community and required by some English language schools as a prerequisite for a language teaching position.

With this in mind, I looked again at our own teaching operation and was struck by two characteristics that certainly affected my thinking. First, although the new academic team of CCBEU had undoubtedly created one of the most stringent teacher selection processes in the state, and only the best educated and most experienced teachers were hired, my observations and interviews still led me to conclude that few teachers

- reflected on their teaching
- valued theory or research
- considered having a qualification in language teaching important in order to become a competent professional

- saw their participation in conferences or workshops as important for their advancement

Second, although the foreign language teaching context in the north of Brazil is completely different from the second language teaching contexts in the United States and the United Kingdom, most of the books and models of language teaching and teacher education to be found here are imported from those two countries.

My aim as a teacher educator was to ground the certificate in TESOL program in the teaching variables of the city of Belém, and the social, educational, and political context in which it is embedded. It seemed to me more important to begin with the context in which course participants were teaching than to seek to apply the latest theories by copying models from abroad (see Gebhard & Duncan, 1991). With my own situation clear in my mind, I turned to the literature.

The State of the Art in TESOL Teacher Education

In order to build a program with high chances of success, I found it important to research the general history of language teacher education and to form my own idea of its development. The big picture I perceived made me think of language teacher education as having developed different emphases in different historical settings.

In some times and places, language teacher training syllabi have been made up essentially of linguistics and second language acquisition theories, with the focus of teacher preparation on the teacher as the knower of the language. This content/cognitive approach has also sometimes been extended so that "teacher preparation programs generally included generic courses in educational psychology, philosophy of education, and general methods" (Jarvis & Bernhardt 1987, p. 1). In other times and places, teacher preparation programs have used prescriptive methodological approaches, and language teaching has been seen as made up of microelements that can be observed and taught, with teacher preparation seen essentially as behavioral training (see Ur, 1996; Wallace, 1991).

Nowadays, however, teaching is seen more as a holistic activity in which teachers constantly try to discover things that work, discarding old practices and taking on board new ones through a process of decision making, reflection, analysis, and assessment. Thus, metacognition has become as important as cognition, and teachers can become "leaders and agents for change, responsible for their own continuing professional development and that of their colleagues. They should conduct action research, reflect on their teaching and on their students' learning, and use their knowledge and experience to make necessary changes in collaboration with others" (Guntermann, 1992, p. 1). With the change from a prescriptive to a reflective model in language teaching, approaches to teacher education now involve teachers in "developing theories of teaching, understanding the nature of teacher decision making, and strategies for critical self-awareness and self-evaluation" (Richards & Nunan, 1990, p. xi).

It was now necessary for me to formulate my own position, living and working in Belém.

My Own Beliefs

After getting acquainted with new trends in teacher education, I explored my own beliefs again. I believed that experiential as well as received knowledge (Wallace, 1991) should be explored together from the beginning of the learning-teaching process and that what bridged them was the thinking about what had been done and how that had worked or not, and the comparison of the experience to the information received. In other words, reflection was the basis for all this learning.

I also believed the teacher learners could start moving toward reflective practice from the beginning of their careers. Becoming reflective—that is, being able to think about what the teacher is going to do, is doing, or has done, as well as being able to spot difficulties and work on them—was therefore set as an important goal for the new certificate in TESOL.

It was equally clear to me on a broader scale that course participants needed to become aware of the social-political-educational situation of TESOL so they could change it. For that, they needed to have critical thinking skills. Having critical thinking skills also implies reflecting on what is done, read, or discussed. This way, once again, reflection appeared to be a tool to reach goals at the level of awareness. And awareness would be the tool to trigger changes in the status quo. The attitudinal key of the program was set: a reflective approach to learning teaching.

To put this explicitly, I saw the redesigning of the teacher training course as an opportunity to make a small contribution to my home context. I hoped to shatter the circle of linked problems by acting as a change agent, raising the awareness of course participants in the Brazilian sociopolitical-educational tradition of Freire (1982; cf. Cox & Assis-Peterson, 1999). I also wanted to respond to the internationalist call expressed by Nunan (1998) in a local interview, in which he suggested that all of us engaged in TESOL act on a broader educational agenda, "because it's hard to think of another subject that is more suitable to creating citizens for the twenty-first century" (p. 9).

◈ FOCUS

In this chapter, I shall concentrate on one of the tools I chose in order to work on course participants' reflective abilities: the use of dialogue journals. Doubting that I would be effective by simply asking my students to reflect, I decided first to get to know their experience with reflection. In order to collect this information, student teachers responded to a survey on their first day of class (see the Appendix). This survey provided me with some quantitative data, such as if they had taught before and for how long, if they had ever had any training as language teachers, what it was like, if that had included the writing of journals, and if so, if that had been difficult or easy, and why.

The data collected showed that out of the 18 course participants, 6 were already working as teachers, and 12 had never had any teaching experience. Out of those who had teaching experience, 1 had been teaching for 6 years, 2 had been teaching for 4 years, 2 had been teaching for 1 year, and 1 had just started. When asked if they had had any training as language teachers, 8 responded they had, and 10 stated they had never experienced any training. However, when they described their training, the survey showed that 2 teachers had had a 1-month training course in a certain school's method; 4 had had a 1-day experience; and 2 had attended other teachers' classes for a period of 2 months. Concerning the writing of journals, the survey showed that 7 of the course participants had had some experience in writing journals as students, and 11 had not ever written journals. When those who had written journals before were asked how difficult that experience had been, 2 stated that it had been easy, 4 found it not easy, and 1 found it difficult.

These data showed widespread inexperience of writing journals, but that did not mean that course participants would not be able to write reflective journals or that the participants who had had experience writing journals as students would be able to write truly reflective journals. I decided, therefore, to collect some qualitative data. For that I used two approaches.

First, at the end of the first day of class, and after talking about the program, its goals, as well as the writing of journals, I asked participants to ask me any questions they wanted about what I had just said. While they asked me their questions, I wrote them down in order to examine them later and see if any pattern would emerge. The questions asked were the following:

- What is a journal?
- So, we have to write about our days, what we did and how we felt?
- What do you mean by reflection?
- But, what is all this for?
- Do we have to write it every day?
- How lengthy does it need to be?
- How are you going to grade it?
- If I have many mistakes, what grade am I going to have?
- But isn't what authors and the teacher say what we have to learn?
- Shouldn't a teacher know everything?

The questions confirmed what the quantitative data suggested: that the course participants did not know much about journals in teacher education; they did not know what content journals had or what to write in them; they did not see any purpose in doing journal writing; and they were worried about how they would be graded. They also worried about form and accuracy instead of ideas and thoughts, and they had the misunderstanding that they were in the program in order to receive knowledge from the trainer and their readings and then apply it in their classrooms. They were not aware of the importance of reflection and how that could help them learn to teach, or even how to begin to reflect.

The second qualitative tool I used was their first two journal entries. Without guiding them, I asked them to write journals at the end of the first 2 days of class. I read the journals and identified what student teachers were doing that was not reflection. As I found a problem for the first time, I would name it and write it on a sheet. As I found it again, I would put a mark beside that same problem so I could keep track of the problems found and their frequency. After reading all the journals, I had a big picture of the most common problems found. One extract from each of the four most common categories identified is shown below:

1. a tendency to praise the teacher: "The first moment that I saw you, I felt you were going to be a nice teacher. And I am glad I still think like that. I have to confess that I am a little bit dizzy, because of the first class. I have no more words to say, I don't know what to say, do you know what I mean?"

2. an unquestioning attitude: "Actually, when we are at school we are used to accepting passively what the teachers and authors say. They don't teach us to think, but to absorb information, since they are considered to be the owners of knowledge."

3. ungrounded assertions: "The process used in class was important. Reading the text about the grammar translation method at home and discussing it was really essential."

4. listing events without reflection: "Yesterday, you asked us to be in pairs and read a text and answer the questions following it. Then, you asked us to say what we had learned by doing it. Afterwards, you asked us to be in groups, each group read a part of the text. Then, each student went to a different group and talked about the part of the text he/she had read."

With the quantitative and qualitative data in my hands, I realized that course participants were not ready to write real reflective journals and that, therefore, they needed to learn how to do so, or the success of the whole program would be in jeopardy.

◈ RESPONSE

Rather than deal directly with the more abstract issues of a reflective and critical attitude, I decided to approach reflection as something that could be taught. I saw this more-or-less skills-based approach as one that would better suit the previous learning experiences of my course participants, while also helping them develop the necessary underlying critical attitudes. So, based on the four most common categories of lack of reflectivity identified above, as well as the questions asked on the first day of class, I came up with five objectives for us to work toward. Course participants would learn to

1. be more aware of what is actually happening in class

2. differentiate generally useful processes from specific content

3. present their own ideas and not see the trainer as the owner of all relevant knowledge

4. ground what they say on concrete evidence

5. focus on the learning potential of their journals, rather than on their linguistic form

Toward these goals, I developed a number of techniques, of which the following are a sample. Although there are no simple, one-to-one correspondences between goals and techniques, I invite the reader to make the connections.

1. At the end of a class, I put participants in groups and asked them to come up with what they remembered we had done the class before. That was a memory game, and they had to give me a step-by-step description of it. After their lists were ready, I would elicit the steps from them and write them on the board. Afterwards, the students and I would connect another topic to a certain number of steps. Then they could see that the topic was the content to be explored whereas the steps were the process they went through in order to get to know that content.

2. In their journals, teacher learners had to give me suggestions for our classes and for the program in general. These suggestions were discussed and voted on in the classroom. Many of them were adopted as part of the program.

3. I showed journal extracts that I had created myself (I did not know to what extent using their own journals would make them defensive and self-conscious), and asked them to identify when there was grounding and when there was not. For example,

> I learned a lot about the grammar translation method, but I didn't like the discussion.

> When you asked us to discuss the grammar translation method, I got kind of lost. I did not know what to talk about. Maybe, if you had given us questions to discuss, that would have helped because we would have a focus.

4. Right after the activity above, I asked them to take a look at their own journals and identify examples of ideas and feelings that were grounded and those that were not.

5. I brought in well-written journals and asked course participants to identify aspects of real reflection in those journals.

Each of these techniques was used more than once throughout a period of 44 hours of training. My goal was to work on microskills that would lead to the development of a more general skill: critical reflection.

In addition,

6. I asked participants to focus in general on three questions when writing their journals, namely: What helped your learning and why; what did not help your learning and why; and what suggestions do you have for the betterment of the classes and the program?

7. When responding to their journals, I would always begin with a positive comment. For example, the first extract quoted above was actually the participant's entire journal entry! The response I gave to her was "Don't worry about not having much to say! That's completely natural! The first time I had to write a journal, I remember how difficult it was for me to come up with one single line! You've written much more than a single line. I'll help you do it, all right?"

8. I did not correct language mistakes they made in their journals.

9. I made journals part of their portfolios, and thus they became an assessment tool in the sense that they felt an external motivation to become involved in keeping a journal, and they were required to submit evidence that they had done so.

◈ OUTCOMES

In order to analyze if the use of the techniques had led course participants to be more reflective after 44 hours of work, I compared their most recent journals to the first ones written. I highlighted with red whenever I saw one of the problems worked on, and I used blue whenever I saw a reflective trait gained. This way, I could compare whatever subskills they showed they had learned, what they had not learned effectively, and who needed extra help. Below, I show excerpts of the most common reflective traits found:

1. At the discussion, as everybody wanted to speak at the same time, Eliana asked us to raise our hands if we wanted to talk. . . . At that time I got very frustrated, because I was raising my hand since the beginning of the discussion, but Eliana would never call me, and whenever I started talking Eliana asked me to wait for my turn. I was mad! Well, on the other hand, I could imagine how my students feel when I don't let them talk, or when I let one talk more than the other.

2. Do you think it is possible to use the writing of journals when teaching English at a regular course? I think that journals are a great idea, but elementary students will find them too difficult to write. An option would be to allow elementary students to write it in their L1. But wouldn't that be against the general idea that we should communicate in the target language? What can I do about it? Should I postpone journals until students have reached intermediate levels?

3. Do you remember that every time we evaluated ourselves or made comments during this semester you would ask us to say why, to give reasons? That has helped me in my personal life, and it made me grow as an individual. I've learned that nothing happens just because it does, but there must be a reason! I only wanted you to know that you've helped me analyze my life better!

4. I hadn't realized how important it was in a learning environment to create a comfortable atmosphere within the classroom.

5. In my opinion writing journals is hard, and sometimes boring, but it is a very useful way for students to remember their classes and for teachers to have feedback from their audience. It's also a way teachers have to evaluate themselves. I must confess I will miss it!

6. When I got here I was eager to know techniques I could immediately use in my classroom; now I am not that anxious for techniques anymore. I keep looking for the ideas behind them and I love reflecting. It helps me see beyond the concrete. I love it!

7. Eliana, when you talked about our journals, I decided to be more reflective while doing mine. The problem, though, is that I am very used

to make descriptions. I must admit that, during my education, I wasn't taught on how to be critical. I've been learning it by myself and it's been a very slow process. I hope to be a thinker by the end of this course.

8. I don't want to accept made ideas anymore! I want to create my own ideas, to produce new things, and, who knows, maybe, in the future, I could give my contribution to the language teaching process!!!

When a teacher works with her own students, it is impossible to know for sure how much praising the teacher is built into what they say, and I am aware of this possibility here. It would be quite ironic if I were to set out to teach critical thinking and then not apply it to myself. As a bare minimum, then, we might say that the work has been successful as an awareness-raising exercise. At the same time, as Elbow (1986) puts it, there are times for doubting and times for believing:

> Doubt implies disengagement from action or holding back, while belief implies action. When we doubt, we tend to pause; and by pausing—by disengaging or standing on the sidelines—we doubt better. When we believe fully, we tend to act; and by acting (for example when we can no longer wait and collect evidence) we often discover beliefs we didn't know we had. (p. 265)

On this basis, I want to claim more than the bare minimum. In Extracts 1 and 5, course participants were prepared to mention negative feelings toward something I did and to say how that affected their own teaching. Another change is that participants were raising ideas to be used in their classrooms and not expecting the trainer to come up with everything (e.g., the possibility of first language journals for elementary students, mentioned in Extract 2). Many have stated that reflecting on what they did had become a habit, which was affecting them as an individual as well as a teacher (e.g., Extract 3). The value now given by course participants to reflection is also shown in Extract 4. It is an example of the participant paying attention to, and reflecting over, his feelings while in class as a learner and analyzing it as a teacher as well. A change in attitude that was commonly found is exemplified in Extract 5. This teacher learner mentions the use of journals as an important tool for self-evaluation. That shows the realization of the importance of awareness in his practice.

Another typical behavior that was very much present at the beginning of the program and that was overcome through the use of journals was the demand only for techniques (recipes). Extract 6 shows that the student teacher now realizes the importance of going beyond the level of technique, and he also analyzes how reflection has been an important tool in raising his awareness of this point.

Another pattern frequently found when course participants struggle to change their ideas concerning education is shown in Extracts 7 and 8. One can sense the frustration with past educational experiences, as well as the excitement about the future and the desire to value oneself as a professional.

This analysis showed me that I could now find many more traits of reflectivity in course participants' journals. Participants had gone a step ahead in their learning of a reflecting process, and they had become aware of its importance in language teaching. However, two drawbacks in these techniques are worth mentioning.

Some students developed one or two skills better than the others. My solution was to write in the response what they were not doing and ask them questions whose answers would guide them to do what they had not. Time was the other concern.

Many course participants complained that writing dialogue journals was very time consuming, whereas others did not think so. After talking to all of them individually about it, I realized that those that were complaining would write at least two drafts before handing their final draft to me. We decided that the journals would be written either in pencil, or using a computer, and no drafts were necessary. Time was also a concern to me because I needed to read all their journals and respond to them. At first, I would write a response on a sheet. Then I began to respond in their own journals. They would leave enough room for it either in the sides or between lines so I could write my comments.

The starting point of this study was the need for building an updated TESOL certificate program. To proceed, I brought together my experiential knowledge of the social setting, my intellectual knowledge of the professional literature, and my professional values and beliefs. Looking back over this piece of action research, I believe that I see some indicators of success in terms of improving the quality of experience available to everyone involved, including myself.

◈ REFLECTIONS

At the beginning of my studies to become a teacher educator, I came across reflective teaching and different opinions on it. For example, it might be argued under some circumstances that beginning teachers need to be taught the basic techniques, whereas more experienced teachers can benefit more from reflective practice. This is what I understood Nunan (1998) to be saying in the interview referred to above. When working with inexperienced teachers, he felt it was in order to tell them what to do, whereas "with more advanced teachers, I advocate the use of reflective teaching which is teachers themselves thinking about teaching, analyzing teaching, collecting data on their teaching" (p. 5).

Although I fully see the logic of this, my own experience has made me sensitive to the opposite possibility. Some in-service teachers in my institution convinced me that they were not able to reflect, although they were experienced. My attempts to help those specific individuals become reflective practitioners were painful, and sometimes not effective. It was difficult to get them out of the old habit of seeing language teaching as a set of techniques to be memorized and applied. Therefore, that made me think that good teaching habits can and should be acquired from the beginning of the process of learning to teach and that reflecting on learning and teaching is one of them.

While my experimentation was going on, I continued investigating results of studies that would shed some light on the topic. It was then that I came across Richards's (1998a) study on critical reflection with in-service teachers. He concluded that

> Journal writing can improve an opportunity for teachers to write reflectively about teaching, though in itself it does not necessarily promote critical reflection. Teachers differ in the extent to which they can write reflectively, and some initial training in reflective writing may well be necessary as a preparation for journal writing. (p. 167)

After reading my course participants' first journals, I realized that asking teacher learners to write journals in order to make them become reflective practitioners was not enough. Course participants needed to be guided on how to engage in real critical reflection so the writing of journals could become an effective tool in teacher education. If I had asked them to keep writing journals, would they have acquired reflective skills by themselves? My study suggests that among all the students, one of them was very reflective from the beginning. That may have happened for reasons that I did not investigate, but the other 17 students did not have the same ability. Therefore, the guidance they received helped them change.

At the end of the first semester of the TESOL certificate program, when contrasting course participants' journals, I could see that the initial goals at the metacognitive level had been reached. Thus, my study convinced me that it is important not only to engage teacher learners in critical reflective practice from the beginning of their process of learning to teach but also to show them how to do so. This guidance needs to be given in a way that respects individual differences.

The result of this work has also affected the way I think about education in general. I have begun to think about how critical reflection could be taught at elementary and secondary schools, and how teachers of those schools could be educated in a way that promotes critical thinking in their classrooms. If critical reflection is not easily acquired, then it should be taught as other skills are so that the accompanying attitudes develop.

Finally, I am left wondering to what extent other teacher educators believe that reflective skills simply arise from teaching experience or that they should be taught only to experienced teachers. Or how many feel, as I do, that language teacher education programs should include, from the beginning, an explicit introduction to the skills of critical reflection so that they can be worked on and developed from the first days of a teacher's career? Here, I find that the perspectives available to me from experiential knowledge and received knowledge still need to be reconciled in my development as an action researcher into my own practice.

◈ ACKNOWLEDGMENTS

I would like to thank the course participants, for trusting me and letting me research with them; the academic coordinators and director, who honored me by inviting me to be part of their team; the board of CCBEU-Belém, for their support on the changes that were seen as needed; and especially Rita Costa, Tatiana Macedo, Walquiria Magno e Silva, Celia Jacob, Gilda Chaves, and Livia Sa, for their great suggestions and for sharing their wisdom with me.

◈ CONTRIBUTOR

Eliana Santana-Williamson has taught EFL in Brazil and ESL in the United States. She has also worked as a teacher educator. She is currently in an EdD program with a TESOL specialization, in California. Her interests are teacher education and brain-based research.

◈ APPENDIX

Survey

1. Name (optional): _____

2. Age: _____

3. Are you a teacher?   YES   NO

4. If yes, how many years of experience do you have? _____

5. Have you had any previous training as a language teacher?   YES   NO

6. If YES, describe your previous experience:

   _____

   _____

   _____

   _____

   _____

7. Have you ever had any experience writing class journals as a student or a teacher (consider elementary and high school)?   YES   NO

8. If YES, how difficult was it?

   VERY DIFFICULT   DIFFICULT   NOT EASY   EASY

9. Do you think that writing journals helped you somehow?   YES   NO

10. If yes, how?

   _____

   _____

   _____

   _____

   _____

   _____

CHAPTER 5

Process Courting Content: Action Research Meets Learner Education

John Rogers

⬦ INTRODUCTION

During the past 10 or 15 years, the concept of action research has been defined in many different ways, and about as many procedures for carrying out action research have been put forward. This chapter does not attempt to redefine the concept or suggest an innovative procedure. It is rather a straightforward and uncontroversial account of a medium-scale experiment in which 691 students and 25 teachers were involved, all from different primary and secondary schools throughout Slovenia. I hope that this account will provide further evidence that action research can be carried out by regular teachers in regular schools and, consequently, be a further encouragement not only to all teacher educators who hold that belief, but first and foremost to the teachers themselves to start or continue experimenting with action research for the sake of those who ought to be its ultimate beneficiaries—the students.

After a brief description of the context in which the action research was carried out, I explain the purpose of the investigation and provide full details of the tasks (questionnaires) used by the teachers involved. I then document the responses to the tasks, as well as the students' and teachers' reactions. I look at a number of outcomes, including learning outcomes for me and questions arising from the response and the procedure used. Finally, I attempt to summarize the main issues and outline some possible future developments. At various points, I explicitly invite readers to relate some of the issues arising to their own context and situation.

⬦ SITUATION

Primary education in Slovenia currently lasts 8 years (age range 7–14) and secondary education 4 years (age range 15–18). Primary education consists of lower primary (age range 7–10), where pupils usually have one teacher (except for subjects such as gym, arts, music, and English); and upper primary (age range 11–14), where each subject is taught by a different teacher. In the past, English was taught from the fifth form (age 11), but a few years ago most schools embraced the change introduced by the Ministry of Education and started offering English in the third or fourth form (age 9 or 10). So early English language learning is becoming increasingly more widespread as part of a broader reform of the school system whereby primary education will last 9 years. Some major changes have also recently been made to the curriculum with a view to making it more student centered.

Every year, the Slovenian Board of Education and the British Council jointly organize two 1-week summer schools for serving primary and secondary teachers of English. The summer schools have become the most popular In-Service Teacher Training (INSET) event in the country, with as many as 120 teachers attending. Participants are issued a certificate of attendance upon completion of a course project. For the 1998 summer schools, the board decided that the central themes would be learning styles and preferences and learner autonomy and that the project title would be "Creating Materials for Classroom Use."

The project was thus a course requirement, which means that the initial momentum for the action research came from the teacher educator and not from the teachers themselves. The teachers did not start from a classroom problem, nor did they have a hypothesis they were trying to test. Consequently, it might be argued that we were not doing proper action research. Clearly, the emphasis was much more on the action aspect rather than the research one, which is in fact the position proposed by Wallace (1993), who goes on to say, "This view of action research suggests that it is a means whereby teachers can improve their professional action by reflecting on it *in a more structured way* than would normally be the case" (p. 92).

As will be seen, teachers were invited to comment in a fairly structured way on their own and their students' reaction to the questionnaires and on insights they felt they had gained into what is happening in their classrooms. Finally, by making public their written reports, they are allowing others to comment and make further observations. These last two steps certainly make their project action research in my understanding of the term. Let us now turn to the more specific focus of the research itself.

◈ FOCUS

Having accepted the aim of teachers creating materials that would take into account their own learners' needs, interests, and preferred learning styles, it seemed appropriate to me as course director to create an opportunity for participants to engage in some form of classroom-based research that would focus on learning styles and strategies. Thus the idea of a dual project was born, with, on the one hand, the materials design part catering mostly to the *what* (i.e., what is learned/taught), and, on the other hand, action research in the area of learner development emphasizing the *how*. Nunan (1991) sees work on learning strategies as "part of a more general movement within educational theory and practice which takes a learner-centred view of pedagogy" (p. 178). The rationale is that by exploring their own beliefs and attitudes, by reflecting on their learning strategies, learners will become more aware of the range of choices available in language learning and, through classroom discussions, be in a better position to make informed choices (Nunan, 1991; Oxford, 1990 [in Lake, 1997]). Such an approach acknowledges the relevance of the learners' views and is in stark contrast with the top down, teacher-as-fount-of-all-knowledge approach. It therefore seemed entirely in line with the changes proposed by the board.

Furthermore, not only the content (i.e., learner development), but also—and maybe more importantly—the process (i.e., doing action research) contributed to making the classroom a more learner-centered environment and ensured that a short summer course had some impact on what actually goes on in the classroom. So the project had another kind of duality built into it—engaging the learners with learner development tasks on the one hand and, on the other, involving the teachers in action research by having them reflect on the results and the process, and encouraging them to share their reflections with others.

Learner development and action research seem to share a common philosophy: Both are person centered; both invite and enable individuals to take more responsibility for their own development. These two characteristics probably make action research—whatever its focus—one of the most effective forms of teacher development and the one most likely to foster student centeredness.

An account of what actually happened follows, beginning with the three learner development tasks from which the teachers could choose.

◈ RESPONSE

The learning-to-learn tasks were administered in more than 50 different schools. Most of the participants carried out their action research between mid-September and mid-November and had returned their reports to the board by mid-December. For the purposes of this chapter, I have selected those 25 teachers' reports in which all figures were properly recorded.

Before you read the learners' actual responses to the three tasks (see Figure 1), I urge you to take a little time to think about your own situation.

- Which task would you prefer to work with?
- Which task do you think your learners would choose?
- Do you have any predictions as to how they might answer some of the items?

Of the 25 teachers involved, 2 used the "'Good' Language Learner" task with their 16- to 18-year-old learners. Seven teachers chose to administer the second task, and 16 teachers chose the third, the latter two being answered by a majority of 13- to 14-year-olds and a small number of 12-year-olds. The apparent lack of popularity of the first task (which originally was not designed as a questionnaire) may be due to the fact that the way it had been set up made it rather time-consuming. What is more, the language used is much more sophisticated than in the other two tasks, which would mean that primary school children (i.e., the majority of the respondents) would probably have needed a full translation.

What Makes a Good Language Learner?

Altogether 39 students (nineteen 16-year-olds and twenty 17-/18-year-olds) from two different schools answered this questionnaire. In the first stage, the students themselves agreed on the three most important characteristics without referring to the printed questionnaire. A wide array of features were mentioned, of which the salient ones were the following.

- Good learners are interested in languages.
- Good learners read books or watch films in the target language.
- Good learners travel or study abroad, and communicate with people from other countries.

Summer School for English Teachers–Bled, August 1998

Course Assignment

Part B: Classroom-Based Research

Introduction: "A learner-centred approach to language learning is based on a belief that learners will bring to the learning situation different beliefs and attitudes about the nature of language and language learning and that these beliefs and attitudes need to be taken into consideration in the selection of content and learning experiences" (Nunan, 1991, p. 178). Learners can easily be encouraged to reflect on their attitudes, beliefs and preferences by completing short surveys or questionnaires such as the ones below, the results of which can then be used as the basis for classroom discussions.

Do ONE of the following "learner education" tasks with one of your classes in September:

Task 1: The "Good" Language Learner

What are the characteristics of the "good" language learner? What do "good" language learners typically do?

Stage 1: Ask your pupils those two questions. Individually, they jot down a minimum of three characteristics. Get them to compare and discuss their lists in pairs or in threes. Each group ends up with what they have agreed are the three most important qualities, which they write on a piece of paper to be handed in.

Stage 2: A couple of days later, give them this list (Rubin & Thompson, cited in Nunan, 1991):

1. Good learners find their own way.
2. Good learners organize information about language.
3. Good learners are creative and experiment with language.
4. Good learners make their own opportunities, and find strategies for getting practice in using the language inside and outside the classroom.
5. Good learners learn to live with uncertainty and develop strategies for making sense of the target language without wanting to understand every word.
6. Good learners use mnemonics (rhymes, word associations, etc. to recall what has been learned).
7. Good learners make errors work.
8. Good learners use linguistic knowledge, including knowledge of their first language in mastering a second language.
9. Good learners let the context (extra-linguistic knowledge and knowledge of the world) help them in comprehension.
10. Good learners learn to make intelligent guesses.
11. Good learners learn chunks of language as wholes and formalized routines to help them perform "beyond their competence."
12. Good learners learn production techniques (e.g., techniques for keeping a conversation going).
13. Good learners learn different styles of speech and writing and learn to vary their language according to the formality of the situation. (p. 171)

Get them to select, on their own, the three most important characteristics. They then work in the same pairs/groups as in Stage 1, compare and discuss their answers, and

Continued on p. 49

agree on the three most important characteristics, which they write on a piece of paper to be handed in.

You can then assess to what extent their original list overlaps with the second one. Or are they completely different? Does one provide you with more valuable information than the other?

OR

Task 2

How and where do you like learning? Number the following from 1 (best) to 7 (least):

Learning at home by yourself. _____

Learning at home with a friend. _____

In class, listening to the teacher. _____

In class, working in pairs. _____

In class, working in groups. _____

In class, working alone. _____

Working in the self-access center _____

Talk about your choices with your teacher and the other students. (Nunan, 1991, p. 180)

OR

Task 3

Do these statements describe the way you learn? Circle the appropriate response.

1. It doesn't matter if I don't understand every word.   yes   no
2. I try and use new words as soon as I have learnt them.   yes   no
3. I plan what I am going to say before I speak.   yes   no
4. If someone doesn't understand me, I try and say it another way.   yes   no
5. I try to find out my own problems in learning English.   yes   no
6. My way of learning is different from the rest of the class.   yes   no
7. I always ask people to explain things I don't understand.   yes   no
8. Out of class I always try and practice my English.   yes   no
9. I try not to use my own language out of class.   yes   no
10. It doesn't bother me if I make mistakes.   yes   no

(Nunan, 1991, p. 181)

Whichever of the three tasks you choose, make sure that the results are discussed in class. The next step is for you to prepare a written report. Make it as long or as short as you find appropriate, but make sure you include:

- a description of the class you did the survey with
- some statistics, focusing on significant results
- a few words about your pupils' reaction to the task
- any insights gained as a result of doing this task (e.g., Did it confirm your predictions? Will it affect your teaching, or your relationship with the class?)

FIGURE 1. Three Tasks

In the second stage, which took place a few days later, the students responded to the task as shown in Figure 2.

There appears to be a good deal of consistency between the two sets of students' responses, as the second and third features they mentioned are largely covered by Characteristic 4 in Rubin and Thompson's list (in Nunan, 1991), which was chosen 27 times.

About the learners' reaction to the task, Valerija has this to say:

> At the beginning they did not feel at ease, partly because of the sophisticated language of the questionnaire, but mostly because it was difficult to select the three most important characteristics from the list, many of which are really

	Total number of students who consider these items to be among the three most important characteristics:
4. Good learners make their own opportunities, and find strategies for getting practice in using the language inside and outside the classroom.	27
3. Good learners are creative and experiment with language.	24
1. Good learners find their own way.	12
6. Good learners use mnemonics (rhymes, word associations, etc. to recall what has been learned).	12
5. Good learners learn to live with uncertainty and develop strategies for making sense of the target language without wanting to understand every word.	11
13. Good learners learn different styles of speech and writing and learn to vary their language according to the formality of the situation.	8
10. Good learners learn to make intelligent guesses.	7
2. Good learners organize information about language.	6
12. Good learners learn production techniques (e.g., techniques for keeping a conversation going).	6
8. Good learners use linguistic knowledge, including knowledge of their first language in mastering a second language.	4
9. Good learners let the context (extra-linguistic knowledge and knowledge of the world) help them in comprehension.	4
11. Good learners learn chunks of language as wholes and formalized routines to help them perform "beyond their competence."	4
7. Good learners make errors work.	0

Figure 2. Action Research Characteristics

important; sometimes they also felt that the statements express the same idea. . . . Half of the Ss expressed their preference for choosing from the list of 13 characteristics, while the other half felt more independent while expressing their own views with their own vocabulary when answering the two questions.

As for Gordana, she found that, on the whole, the answers confirmed her predictions, but she "was surprised nobody chose 'Good learners make errors work,'" which she explains in the following terms: "[It may be because] most teachers still use the traditional style of teaching and therefore believe that students should not (or maybe even must not) make mistakes."

Elsewhere, however, another teacher attributes the students' general reluctance to try and use mistakes to their own advantage to the fact that the whole curriculum is too examination centered.

How and Where Do You Like Learning?

Altogether 212 students (twenty-four 12-year-olds, ninety-one 13-year-olds, and ninety-seven 14-year-olds) from seven different schools responded to Task 2, as shown in Figure 3. (The last option was usually left unanswered [or systematically awarded a rating of 7] as most schools do not have a self-access center.)

As regards the pupils' reaction to the task, all teachers reported that it was positive. The pupils expressed interest in the results, and some asked to do "another survey about learning." Others said they were "astonished and honoured at the same time" to be asked about their feelings and opinions. Finally, a class explained that "home learning is best because that's where the conditions are most favourable (we can have peace, or we can have music in the background, we can be loud or quiet, we're used to the place, and we've got all we need at hand)."

More often than not, teachers reported that the answers confirmed their predictions, although some were surprised that group work did not rate higher. As a result, some said they would start doing more pair work rather than group work, and one said that in future when setting up group work she would "try and organize the groups differently, taking into account for instance pupils' abilities."

	Points awarded	Rank order
Learning at home by yourself	437	1
In class, listening to the teacher	538	2
Learning at home with a friend	801	3
In class, working in pairs	813	4
In class, working in groups	905	5
In class, working alone	996	6

FIGURE 3. Results of Task 2

Do These Statements Describe the Way You Learn?

Altogether, 440 students (forty-three 12-year-olds, one hundred and fourteen 13-year-olds, and two hundred eighty-three 14-year-olds) from 16 different schools responded to Task 3, as shown in Figure 4. (The last option was usually left unanswered as it is not relevant to the situation of students learning English in a country where it is a foreign language.)

The pupils' reaction to the task is reported to have been unanimously positive: They were "eager to do it," "took it seriously," and "encouraged each other to talk about it." Some also told their teacher they had "too few opportunities for feedback like this."

Teachers generally said the answers confirmed their predictions. Mojca's comments throw some light on how surveys can be (mis)interpreted:

> My personal feeling [about the sixth statement] is that the number of "different" language learners in this class is much bigger. My students [were using] the expression "wrong way of learning"; after discussion they realized it is a "different," not necessarily a "wrong" way of learning.

I now invite the reader to compare how you think your own students would answer the three questionnaires with the answers from Slovenian learners.

- What are the similarities and differences?
- What might account for those differences?
- Did you find anything surprising in the Slovenian learners' answers?

Such were the answers given to the three questionnaires, but what are the implications for all those involved—learners, teachers, and teacher educators? What have they learned?

4.	If someone doesn't understand me, I try and say it another way.	yes	358	no	82	440
2.	I try and use new words as soon as I have learnt them.	yes	318	no	122	440
3.	I plan what I am going to say before I speak.	yes	317	no	123	440
5.	I try to find out my own problems in learning English.	yes	317	no	123	440
7.	I always ask people to explain things I don't understand.	yes	297	no	143	440
8.	Out of class I always try and practice my English.	yes	250	no	190	440
1.	It doesn't matter if I don't understand every word.	yes	196	no	244	440
10.	It doesn't bother me if I make mistakes.	yes	201	no	239	440
6.	My way of learning is different from the rest of the class.	yes	128	no	312	440

FIGURE 4. Results of Task 3

⬥ OUTCOMES

How successful was this modest piece of action research? As a teacher educator, my main aims (which I had not explicitly described to the participants) were twofold:

1. to ensure that a short training course had some tangible repercussions on what goes on in the classroom

2. to make action research accessible (in the sense of being teacher friendly) to a large number of teachers who might possibly develop a taste for more action research in future as a tool for professional development

The first aim was clearly achieved as, through an exploration of learning styles and strategies, the concept of learner centeredness was taken into a large number of schools. As to the second aim, an obvious precondition for it to be achieved had to be the pupils' reaction to the tasks. Had they found them uninteresting, the future of action research might very well have been doomed as far as those teachers were concerned. Fortunately, as the pupils' comments interspersed in the previous section make clear, their response was overwhelmingly positive and so was the teachers'. Because teachers had been asked whether the task would affect their teaching or their relationship with the class, let us hear some teachers' voices:

> I did not expect the pupils to think so much and so seriously about learning English. (Meta)

> We have become closer and respect each other more. The results can help me in directing and stimulating them how to learn. (Valerija)

> I am really pleased I have done this survey—it made me critically look back at my work, my teaching style and my relationship with the pupils. I have realized how important it is to give pupils more autonomy, to talk to them as people [...] and I am sure that they appreciate that. (Tanja)

> It opened my eyes. I need to give them more questionnaires like that. (Gordana)

> We have decided to adapt the questionnaires for later use, and also to design our own. (Mojca)

> I think teachers should do surveys more often to see . . . if the pupils feel the same way as teachers think they do. (Nidja)

Such statements of enthusiasm and intent do not, of course, guarantee that more action research has taken place in more classrooms in Slovenia since this particular research was conducted, but what matters is that a fairly large number of teachers now have at their disposal a usable tool to help them along the path of self-directed professional development.

For pupils, teachers, and teacher educator, therefore, it seems reasonable to claim that the quality of action available to them was increased by this piece of action research.

As a teacher educator, I have established in my own practice a way of working that serves the mutually emancipatory aims that I espouse. Conceptually, perhaps the most powerful insight I gained as a result of coordinating this work is how well suited the action research approach used is to the object of the study—learner education.

Before you have a look at Figure 5 below, please reread the preceding sentence and jot down as many similarities as you can think of between action research and learner education.

◈ REFLECTIONS

Ideally at this stage, all parties concerned should have the opportunity to get together and dialogue. As interesting as our answers and outcomes are, it is fairly obvious that the more closely one looks at them, the more questions emerge. This should not deter teachers and teacher educators from engaging in action research—quite the contrary! Answers, or parts of them, often lie hidden in questions, and reformulating a question can lead to an answer. This is, in fact, the essence of teacher development itself: keeping up a spirit of enquiry, asking oneself new questions and reformulating old ones, looking at learning and teaching from different angles.

Consider again the content of the questionnaires—learner development. What are some of the questions that emerge here? As regards the good language learner, is it not somewhat surprising that those teenagers seemed to know intuitively what qualities the good learner possesses? Also, their answers tally with those given by subjects on large-scale, sophisticated research carried out in other parts of the world, as reported in the literature (see, e.g., Nunan, 1991). Two of the factors learners find most helpful in learning another language are indeed interest/motivation and communicative language use outside class.

How about, then, creating more opportunities for students to make their voices heard, and teachers and teacher educators listening to their voices? How about probing their intuitions more often, as these seem to be such fertile ground for information about learning and teaching?

Next, the results of the second survey, "How and where do you like learning?," seem to indicate clearly that Slovenian teenagers like "learning at home by themselves best of all," and also "in class, listening to the teacher." Pair work in class lags behind, while working in groups and working alone in class are the least preferred ways.

What are the implications of these results for the teacher and the teacher educator? As teachers reported, students took the surveys very seriously, so their answers mean something important. Questions abound. How did those teenagers

Action Research	Learner Education
• aims to empower teachers	• aims to empower students
• aims to develop teaching solutions at the school/classroom level	• aims to develop learning/teaching solutions at the classroom level
• works bottom up	• works bottom up
• increases the number of options available to teachers at various stages in the teaching process	• increases the number of options available to learners at various stages in the learning process
• as such is a tool for teacher development	• as such is a tool for learner development

FIGURE 5. Similarities Between Action Research and Learner Education

understand *learning*? Do they really believe that learning a foreign language is essentially a solitary activity that is best carried out within the confines of one's room, complemented by the teacher's explanations at school? Why do the teenagers prefer learning at home by themselves? Follow-up questions would be necessary in order to gather the kind of information that could enable teachers to take effective action on the basis of their research.

As to the third task, some of the teachers' comments point to the danger of dumping on the students prepackaged learning-to-learn tasks or surveys without creating a proper opportunity for all to discuss potential difficulties and pitfalls. A teacher very pertinently remarked how difficult it can be to process double negatives even in one's mother tongue. "It doesn't matter if I don't understand every word." Yes? No? The extent to which this point was discussed in class is unknown, so there is no knowing whether "Yes" means "Yes, that's what I think" or "But yes, it does matter." The same applies to "It doesn't bother me if I make mistakes." Consequently, these particular statistics may not be valid.

What the above makes clear is that, in order for action research to be more meaningful and effective, all parties concerned should get together and scrutinize the instruments that are going to be used. This seems to be particularly important in the case of instruments available from external sources (e.g., English language teaching handbooks), and may be an argument in favor of homemade instruments.

What it also makes clear is that ideally provision should be made for all teachers and teacher educators involved to get together after the research in order to explore ways of acting upon the findings. Action research, after all, is supposed to lead to a better understanding of the classroom, which in turn can lead to change and development. As regards the particular piece of action research that is under scrutiny in this chapter, the feedback from both pupils and teachers seems to indicate that an obvious follow-up would be to involve learners in more systematic learner education, possibly based on Wenden's (1990) model.

In process terms, I feel strongly that doing action research, in the sense of teachers and pupils investigating learning and teaching together, in itself brings about change, even if no action is taken as a result of the research. Involving the learners in such investigations affects the balance of power in the classroom (Kenny, 1993): Pupils experience themselves as learners, and the classroom becomes a reality that can be talked about and in which the tyranny of the correct answer gives way to personal experience, thoughts, and feelings.

Starting from the specific action research/learner autonomy parallel that I have suggested above, then, one might want to move on to a broader conclusion: To the extent that any part of our language education work, from classroom teaching to large-scale language policy planning, seeks to involve the informed choices of the people concerned, it is difficult to see how this work would not be enhanced by some elements of participatory action research. Where, in detail, might this lead each one of us in terms of the focus of our next investigation?

◈ CONTRIBUTOR

John Rogers has worked as a teacher and teacher educator in Britain, Slovenia, and Hungary, and as a freelance ELT consultant and materials writer in Yugoslavia. He is currently working as ELT and INSET advisor for the British Council in Yugoslavia.

CHAPTER 6

Two Kinds of Becoming: The Researcher's Tale and the Mentor's Tale

Kasamaporn Maneekhao and Richard Watson Todd

◈ INTRODUCTION

This chapter tells the story of an experienced teacher who was inexperienced as a researcher and of her first piece of educational research. It is also the story of another teacher, experienced as a researcher, who acted for the first time as a research mentor. The story, then, is one of two kinds of becoming.

◈ SITUATION

The story is set at King Mongkut's University of Technology Thonburi, a well-respected Thai technological university where most students are engineering or science undergraduates.

As there was general agreement that the skills-based English for science and technology (EST) support courses provided by the Department of Language needed a complete overhaul, senior members of the faculty proposed a revised curriculum moving from task-based courses, through large-scale projects, to content-based courses (see Watson Todd, 1999; 2000, for details).

In developing the proposed curriculum, several problematic aspects requiring further investigation were identified, including using the Internet as a resource. In order to involve the language teachers fully in the process of curriculum renewal, teachers were encouraged to conduct action research projects into these problematic areas. Support was initially provided through workshops and later through mentoring. The action research that is the focus of this case study, then, is one of several projects conducted to provide input into curriculum renewal and for staff development.

◈ FOCUS

We have not focused on the actual research and its outcomes (see Maneekhao, in press, for details), but on the experiences of the researchers. If research, and especially action research, can be seen as a multilayered phenomenon (Woods, 1996), then the story told here tries to unpeel some of these layers in order to examine the deeper effects of events on the characters involved.

Another important aspect of the story is that it is told in the first person. Among the various characteristics of action research, the one we believe to be most important is that action research is participatory and involves insider, or emic, perspectives (Somekh, 1993; Watson-Gegeo, 1988). It is now time, therefore, to introduce ourselves in a little more detail.

The Teacher Researcher: Kasamaporn Maneekhao

When I first spoke to Richard of my desire to conduct action research, he suggested that I should write a diary explaining my background and my initial beliefs. In writing the following extracts, I envisaged Richard as the reader, but I hope it helps all readers understand where I was before conducting the action research.

> I got a Bachelor of Arts in English from Silapakorn University. In the university I studied only the skills of language. I had no idea what research is like, how it is useful and did not want to know either.
>
> Not until I studied for my Masters degree at Chulalongkorn University did I have my first experience in doing research. I studied pure linguistics from which I learnt many aspects of the nature of languages. In the second year my friends and I studied about the Mien language which is a hilltribe language and were made to believe by a teacher that one duty of a linguist is to conserve minority languages.
>
> There was no course in research methodology in the MA program. So I did not know what to do with my research and just blindly followed the advisor's suggestions. . . . Unfortunately, my experience of my MA thesis made me sick of research.
>
> Now I am working for the Language Department at King Mongkut's University of Technology Thonburi. Nobody wants to think about research since we have to teach so many classes and at the same time have so many other things to do.
>
> Throughout the five years that I have worked here, I feel that I have learnt many things about teaching and enjoy my career very much. Then last year the university was changed into a semi-autonomous university. The administrators have developed a new working system focusing on the efficiency of the employees. The vision of the university is now to be a learning organisation in which every teacher has two main duties, teaching and conducting research. There is also evaluation to judge the teachers' efficiency by looking at the academic products they produce each year. There is also a threat that we may lose our jobs if we do not have an article or a book published in a certain period of time. This is very scaring to most teachers in the Language Department. None of us has ever done research, except for their MA thesis, and I, especially, have never done anything about educational research. I feel that doing research is a big deal and it is too difficult for me to think about.

From these entries, I believe that three main points emerge. First, I had a very negative view of research deriving from my previous single experience of conducting research and from my perceptions of what research is. Second, I had strong external motivation for conducting and publishing research as my job was at stake. Third, although I had tried to develop myself, I had never considered research as an option for developing and improving my teaching.

With the external motivation of being evaluated, I felt that I should conduct some research. In a workshop introducing action research, a lot of possible topics for research were generated, and from these I chose to investigate using the Internet as a resource and how to use it efficiently. It is at this point that I see my action research beginning.

The Mentor: Richard Watson Todd

For this case study, I did not keep a journal (something I now regret), so the following is a retrospective description of my background.

The first point to make is that the teacher researcher and I had very different attitudes toward, and experiences of, research. I viewed research as a goal that is readily attainable with some hard work and a central part of my duties alongside teaching. I have conducted several pieces of research and have been fortunate enough to see them published.

I have worked at King Mongkut's University of Technology Thonburi for more than 7 years (longer, in fact, than Kasamaporn) and am familiar with the courses and with the attitudes and outlooks of my colleagues. My relationship with Kasamaporn is one of mutual respect, though I generally advise her on academic matters rather than vice versa.

The role of research mentor to a colleague was a new role for me. I have, however, had extensive experience of supervising theses on the MA program we run, but I realize that there are differences, especially in the nature of the relationship, between mentoring a colleague and supervising a student. Although it is very clear now that I was acting as a mentor, I did not realize that I was acting in this role when I offered to help Kasamaporn with her research. For this reason, I did not read any literature to guide me as a mentor, and much of what I did was impromptu.

A further role I am playing in this case study could be termed *action research evaluator*. I have been working closely with the dean of the faculty in leading curriculum renewal and general staff development. The faculty hopes that the action research undertaken by the language teachers will

- provide valuable input into the curriculum renewal
- help teachers in their personal and professional development
- raise teachers' professional status and the faculty's profile by being published

In working with Kasamaporn on her action research, then, I also looked at the extent to which the faculty's goals were being achieved.

◈ RESPONSE

To know what really happens in the messy world of actual research, rather than the neater picture presented in most articles, we need to be able to see the research process through the researchers' eyes, to understand how they perceive problems, and to follow the rationales of their decision making. To see the impact of the research on the researchers, we need an immediate account of events, the researchers' relationship with these events, and their emotions and reactions to them.

The teacher researcher, therefore, kept a diary throughout the research process (and is still keeping it). We draw on 14 entries with a total of about 5,000 words kept regularly over a period of 7 months. The diaries contain information about events and immediate reactions to events. To investigate the long-term effects on the teacher researcher, we can compare the diary entries longitudinally, and we can see how she now reacts to their content. In addition, the mentor comments on the same diary entries as they relate to his mentoring and to the goals of the faculty.

The research presented here, therefore, is "polyvocal" (Woods, 1996, p. 78). In the following subsections, for each diary entry, Maneekhao comments first, concerning her current thoughts on her previous views. Watson Todd comments second from his perspectives of mentor and action research evaluator.

Initial Feelings

As we have seen, the teacher researcher had decided to conduct action research on using the Internet. This would involve her in teaching students about using the Internet, collecting information concerning the effects of this on the students and on herself, and later, she hoped, disseminating this information. Faced with such a task, how did the teacher researcher initially feel?

The Diary

15 November 1998

How I feel with working on this project:

1. Confused. When I first talked to Richard, I felt I understood what I was going to do. But now it is a blur. So it is perhaps not true that I understand it. This might be because I have no experience in doing research or even thinking about such a difficult thing.

2. Fear. I am afraid that I do not have enough time to spend on doing this project. I am not a genius. I badly need time to think and prepare things. I am afraid that I do not have enough knowledge about using the Internet. I am afraid the students feel that I asked them to do hard work just for my own sake. So far no other teachers assign their students to use the Internet. And when I assigned them this task, some of them looked so worried.

The Teacher Researcher's Comments

I still feel that having no experience in doing research is a problem for anybody who starts doing it. The feeling of confusion normally happens at an early stage (Cf. Prendergast, n.d.). It is rarely possible to have a clear picture of the whole process from the beginning. But the state of confusion does not stay forever. The ideas will become clearer on the way through the end. Especially if we have someone (in my case, my mentor) to help gear us to the right way. We will feel more comfortable and confident. I always became less confused and had a clearer idea about my research every time I talked to Richard.

I discovered later that all fear was the result of the feeling of uncertainty and lack of confidence in dealing with a new thing. It has gone now because I have nearly finished my research. The challenge, which was very high at the beginning, gradually decreased after I started collecting the data. I was also often worried and bored with my research, especially when I was busy doing other jobs. However, I had fun with it most of the time. I enjoyed designing the questionnaires and interviewing the students. I can say that now I have a better attitude toward action research and my own ability and that I would like to conduct further research.

The Mentor's Comments

Confusion, or in Prendergast's (n.d.) terms *fog*, appears to be a normal state for teachers new to research. As the mentor, it is my duty to help clear some of the confusion, but with Kasamaporn, my help was not effective. As a research mentor, I need to find ways other than just talking to the researcher to effect a longer lasting clearing of confusion. If I decide to rely primarily on talk, I will need to ensure understanding by asking the researcher to paraphrase (Johnson, 1986). Fear is a more worrying characteristic than confusion. Kasamaporn's fear was a fear of the unknown, and her experiences in conducting research will, I hope, make her less fearful when she starts her next project.

Experiences of Teaching

The teacher researcher decided to introduce using the Internet as a resource to two groups of her students (called Group 1 and Group 2 in her diary). Both groups were taking a course called Basic Study Skills, which is a preparatory English for academic purposes (EAP) course. She planned to teach two main methods of using the Internet: using a search engine such as *Yahoo!* (http://www.yahoo.com) and going directly to useful pages such as those of the *Encyclopedia Britannica* (http://www.britannica.com).

The Diary

27 November 1998

A boy from Group 2 came to show me a piece of information he got from the Internet. That was before I taught his group how to use the Internet. I hope he can help his friends. In the other group there is also one student who has used the Internet before. I also hope he will help his friends. I believe that for some things a friend can be a better teacher because they are close to one another and have more time for each other. Besides people always feel free to ask their friends more than the teacher.

6 December 1998

One more thing. I feel different about the two groups of students. The first one asked me to teach them how to use the Internet. The other said "No" when I asked if they wanted me to do so. For the first group I feel more certain that they are going to use it properly. At least they have learned something from me. I'm really curious which group will be more successful.

5 January 1999

I feel that the Internet is very useful and a fun way of learning/teaching. Now I do not fear the Internet anymore. When the students explained how they used it, it seemed they felt they were teaching me. They looked so happy and proud of themselves. However they did not feel that I was inferior or more stupid. They just wanted to show me how well they worked and that's great. So now I realize that I don't need to be shy or feel guilty that I know something less than students or fear that they will look down on me when I don't know anything. I don't need to always teach students knowledge but I can just tell them how/where to find it. My teachers never taught me like this. It's a pity. I'd like my friends who are afraid of this way of teaching to know that it's not that difficult.

The Teacher Researcher's Comments

This confirms what I have heard—that learning does not take place only in class and that the students learn more outside the class, especially from their friends. However, I believe that the students still need me to prepare some background knowledge and resources and guide them in how to learn. I intend to look in detail at what/how much the students can help each other and what/how much they need from me. So from now on I will try to ask my students to help one another more in learning. But I still have to make sure they are going the right way and achieve the objectives of the lesson or the course completely.

I am surprised that the group I taught how to surf the Internet did not work any better than the other group who learned by trial and error. This also shows that learning with a teacher is not always the best way of learning. My students can really learn from friends or by themselves. Now I have more confidence to encourage the students' autonomy. I feel more comfortable letting the students go and work on their own because they have fun and feel proud of themselves. Finally, I will try to develop my role in this situation to become more of a facilitator who prepares the resources and aids the students' readiness in self-study.

The Mentor's Comments

Rather than looking at how Kasamaporn taught, I would like to examine the amount of reflection in her diary as an indication of her development. Sparks-Langer and Colton (1993), focusing on how reflection in teachers' diaries is expressed, suggest a classification of seven levels of reflection:

1. no description of the education event
2. simple lay person description
3. labeling of events with pedagogical concepts
4. explanation using only tradition or personal preference
5. explanation using pedagogical principles
6. explanation using pedagogical principles and context
7. explanation with moral/ethical considerations (p. 18)

Kasamaporn's search for possible reasons for her feelings and her awareness of rationales and implications mean that these extracts are an explanation. The explanation is pedagogically grounded, and Kasamaporn's worries suggest ethical considerations. The diary extracts here therefore show high levels of reflection suggesting development.

Writing the diary on her teaching as part of her research, then, has encouraged Kasamaporn to reflect deeply on her teaching. Reflection is a prerequisite of development (Wallace, 1991), so conducting action research has allowed one of the faculty's goals, namely development of teachers, to be reached.

Research Procedures

In addition to teaching, the teacher researcher's diary also provides insights into how she viewed the research. Her attitudes toward conducting action research are one of the foci of this chapter. Action research differs from exploratory teaching in that the effects of the implementation are more closely monitored. This means that data need to be collected and analyzed in conducting action research (Arends, 1989; Hopkins, 1985). Indeed, this collection and analysis of data form the core of the research part of action research (Wallace, 1998). For the teacher new to research, we might expect these aspects of action research to be the most worrying, as they resemble normal teaching less than the implementation stage. In this section, then, we look at the teacher researcher's views concerning data collection.

The Diary

14 January 1999

I have no idea about the next step. Now it seems that I have to wait. But I don't know what I'm really waiting for. I'm afraid of losing information. I'm afraid that at the end I'll find that I haven't collected some information nor done something that I should or must do.

27 January 1999

I keep thinking that I will certainly miss some important data. So I must try to collect as much data as possible. Perhaps I may need to design one more questionnaire. I perhaps waste time doing this thing; that is, it might not be useful or used at all. But too much is better than too little.

Richard said yesterday that I don't have to do anything much now. I'll have many things to do at the end of the semester. Does "anything much" mean I still have something to do? What is that thing? One thing I can think of now is preparing myself for hard work and trouble.

15 February 1999

I have decided to collect more data by using another questionnaire in Thai and also interview them in Thai. As for the questionnaire, I've kept thinking for a long time whether I should make it in Thai or English. English is good if they can understand it properly since this is an English course. Besides it is perhaps convenient if I have to put it into an article. I don't have to translate it into English. However when I consider the purpose of using it, I found that the correct data is more important. It is too risky to have them guess what each question means. And it is not fun to be deeply afraid that the data is not valid.

I plan to record the interview. It will be in Thai. I'll do it just because there is something I would like to know and that is not included in the questionnaire. (Poor kids!) I believe that I am collecting too much data and most of them might be useless. But it can't be helped. I feel fun with it. Ah! is it what a new researcher should be aware of?

I have just studied the students' first questionnaire. I found that they didn't understand the questions properly. I was so worried that I ran to see Richard and told him that the data was not valid and perhaps useless. He didn't seem worried at all. (How cool he is! I think.) He asked me a few questions to make me look at the questionnaire closely. He pointed out that the questionnaire can be divided into two parts. The rating scale can be used for collecting quantitative data, the Reason part is for qualitative data. And I can just only use the second one. This made me feel more relieved.

However to analyze such data is hard. Besides, not every student gave reasons for every single item. I don't know how to interpret such data. It seems horrible. Why is doing research so difficult? I'm trying to tell myself that it is not that difficult, instead it is challenging. . . . Anyway why it must be so challenging?

9 March 1999

I was right to create a few more questionnaires and to organize the interview. None of the students had completed the record sheet. They told me that they had just written some sentences a week before meeting me. I learned now that it's impossible to hope that the students realize the importance of the data we need. I tried to find the reason for this. Perhaps I didn't emphasize its importance and the steps to complete the record sheet often enough.

As for the recording, at first, I intended to use just only 3 cassette tapes. But after recording the first interview I was so afraid of making a mistake and erasing the data, I turned it to the other side. How nervous I was! All these things taught me that in collecting data I had to plan everything carefully but not nervously. I should also be aware of technical problems that can happen anytime.

The Teacher Researcher's Comments

The feelings when doing research always change. I felt so delighted when I discovered a way even to do just a small thing, such as how to use a Walkman for recording. On the other hand, I was so worried when I could not think of how to deal with problems, such as how to manage a large amount of data. I was always afraid that what I was doing was not correct according to a theory. But I finally found that there is no exact rule of how to conduct research because the factors involved in each person's research vary. However, reading books and articles written by people describing their research is very helpful (which suggests that the approach in Wallace, 1998, is effective). Having read Woods (1996), I know the importance of my background or past experience and how it becomes a part of the finished article. Moreover, talking with Richard and colleagues is extremely useful. They looked from the view of the outsiders and could often see everything more clearly. Their suggestions provided me with a shortcut to success because I did not have to waste time thinking all by myself or blindly reading every book in the library.

The Mentor's Comments

In contrast to her teaching experiences, where Kasamaporn could reflect and reconcile herself to classroom events, her research and reflection through diary entries led to more doubts. Kasamaporn believed that there was one correct way to conduct research and that the research process should be clear-cut. In practice, research is a very messy process that frequently involves making the best of a bad job, and the need for correctness in research procedure depends on its purpose. In this situation, with the primary purposes of gaining some insights into the value of using the Internet and developing the teacher, experimental precision is not a driving force behind the research, which could be conducted in a variety of ways.

As Kasamaporn's mentor, I am afraid that I was not much use in assuaging her doubts. For example, telling her that she did not have "anything much" to do seemed to create more problems than it resolved. Having read Kasamaporn's worries about her research, I can see two ways in which I could have acted as a better mentor for her. First, I could have provided more support concerning data collection at a detailed level. For example, I could have given detailed criticism of each question included in her questionnaire rather than just discussing the overall purpose of the questionnaire with her. Second, and perhaps more importantly, I could have tried to change Kasamaporn's views concerning what research is and what it involves. Perhaps encouraged by the way research is usually reported in the literature, Kasamaporn has placed research on a pedestal far above its station. There is a place for professional, rigorous, carefully designed research, but for Kasamaporn's purposes, a messier and looser version of research serves fine. The image of professional research may be the cause of the fear felt by new researchers such as Kasamaporn and may be a deterrent to teachers considering conducting research. If this is so, preparation for research should highlight the potential value of messier, looser kinds of research and thus emphasize the practical attainability of conducting research.

After Collecting Data

If the collected data is to be of any value, it must be analyzed. Again, this may be a worrying stage for a teacher new to research, and it warrants close examination. The final stage of action research involves reporting the findings, both to sustain the research process (Hopkins, 1985) and to disseminate the results so that others can share and learn from the research (Arends, 1989). In this section, we look at the teacher researcher's feelings and reactions toward the data analysis and the writing up of the research.

The Diary

28 February 1999

I just thought of something. I'm reading this book because Richard asked me to, not because I have questions and read it to find the answers. And that makes me frustrated. I finished collecting data nearly two months ago but I haven't done anything with it. I just asked a person to transcribe the tape for me. I really don't have time. But most importantly I don't know what to do. I think I should start by grouping data since I have got too much now, and select only some that might be useful.

10 May 1999

I've been so worried about writing the article. I didn't want to get started because I didn't know what to write. I've read some articles. All of them referred to the ideas presented in many books. I know that I can not do so because I don't like reading a textbook at all, and after reading some articles I found that I could understand only 50% of the text.

13 May 1999

I learn something new about doing research today. Before seeing Richard, I gathered every piece of data I had collected, grouped them and tried to review what each of them is about. I didn't want to deal with the data because there's a lot and I really had no time to work on it. I was also afraid of wasting time doing unuseful things since I had no ideas about how to analyze it. Besides, I feel that many questions have been answered already (from working closely with the students and from the interview) so I have no motivation to spend time analyzing the data. Moreover, I have left it for a long time so I feel a little bored with it.

Richard asked me many questions to help me find out what kinds of information I have and what I really want to know. I don't really know what I want to know. Well . . . not exactly. I want to know many things but they are just small things and seem unrelated to one another. When talking with Richard about my research, I feel like I am a student and he is a teacher. I always believe what he says and try to understand every word. This might be because he teaches MA students, has done a lot of research, writes many articles, and seems to know everything. I don't know whether this is good for an in-service activity, when the ideas of one person have a strong influence on another's. However this is just a starting point. It's impossible for a new researcher, like me, to develop my ideas without some influence from an expert.

After the discussion, I felt much better and more willing to analyze the data because, with Richard's help, I now have clearer ideas about how to deal with the data systematically. It seems not too difficult for me to do. But it needs so much time. I really want to divide myself into two so that I can do both my routine jobs and the research.

The Teacher Researcher's Comments

Due to my lack of experience, I was too nervous in collecting data. The fear of losing information made me crazy, and, finally, I had too much data to deal with. This is a very good lesson. I now know that I should design and use the tools carefully but not nervously.

I had better feelings about reading books after Richard told me how they were involved with my research. What I discovered about myself is that I cannot bear doing anything without knowing exactly why I have to and how it is useful. I now know that reading articles and the book helped me understand my own research better—for example, the rationale behind doing this in-service activity. I also accept that the faculty's goals of encouraging this in-service activity of conducting research to develop the teachers in my department are valuable. Also, I am lucky to have a mentor to supervise me. He helped me do my research by giving me valuable suggestions and was always ready to answer my questions. I know that I would not have been able to finish my research without him.

In conclusion, I now have very positive feelings toward action research. I have no fear of conducting further research, but in fact I feel eager to try. I feel that doing action research makes me look deeper into my own teaching. This enables me to understand myself and to find better ways to improve my teaching. However, I know that I still have to learn a lot more about research and still need advice from the mentor.

The Mentor's Comments

In contrast to previous sections, the diary extracts here suggest that I am giving too much guidance to Kasamaporn and that a lack of rationales in my guidance may be hindering her potential autonomy as a researcher. For example, suggesting books for Kasamaporn to read without ensuring that she was clear about the purposes of reading may have detrimental effects on her willingness to read. More importantly, Kasamaporn's feeling that our relationship is one of teacher and student rather than coresearchers is worrying. My previous experience of guiding research has been with MA students, and this probably affected my approach as Kasamaporn's mentor. The mentor needs to provide guidance and help but at the same time should encourage the mentee to rely on her own resources.

The ultimate goal of the mentor is to lose his job! Ideally, from the process of conducting research, Kasamaporn will have learned enough to become an autonomous researcher in the future. Kasamaporn's positive feelings toward action research are helpful in achieving this goal, but she still feels she needs guidance in conducting further research. It is probably too much to expect that she could become completely autonomous after conducting a single action research project. Nevertheless, Kasamaporn's experiences and changed feelings toward research imply that she will need less guidance from a mentor in her future research. In the long term then, mentoring may proceed from fairly high support for new researchers and reduced support for further research. As such, mentoring can be viewed as scaffolding (see Rosenshine & Meister, 1993; Scarcella & Oxford, 1992) where the ultimate objective is researcher independence.

◈ OUTCOMES

Regarding whether the teacher researcher has fulfilled the faculty's goals in conducting her research, the answer is yes. The faculty had set three main goals.

1. The faculty hoped that the research would provide valuable input into the proposed curriculum. Although this chapter does not focus on the effectiveness of using the Internet in teaching, the results of the teacher researcher's research regarding this are generally positive.

2. Regarding teacher development, conducting action research has provided an effective stimulus for her development as a teacher, as a researcher, and perhaps as a person.

3. As this chapter is now published and Maneekhao (in press) will be, her status and the faculty's profile have been raised.

Although the mentor made several mistakes in his mentoring, reflection has turned these also into opportunities for learning. The teacher researcher's appreciation for him and the generally positive results, especially concerning her attitudes toward research, suggest his mentoring was effective.

The mentor was accorded an unusual opportunity to reflect on his own practice, as well as to gain access to the teacher researcher's retrospections on the experience. He is now better placed to support other novice researchers and has taken appreciable steps forward in his own personal and professional development.

◈ REFLECTIONS

The action research conducted here has fulfilled the faculty's goals of developing the teacher, raising her professional status, and providing valuable input into the proposed curriculum. These goals were not, however, achieved easily. Confusion, fear, and worry, especially during the initial stages of the research, were common themes in the teacher researcher's diary. For teachers new to research, then, action research is viable but should not be seen as an easy option. The teacher must be motivated to conduct and complete the research, and this motivation may initially come from an external authority (Fullan, 1993). In addition, a high priority should be given to arranging for another teacher more experienced in research to have the time to provide support. If this is done, teachers can conduct valuable action research, develop themselves, and feel the desire to conduct further research more independently.

We hope that you have enjoyed our story and that you may have learned something from our experience.

◈ CONTRIBUTORS

Kasamaporn Maneekhao teaches at King Mongkut's University of Technology Thonburi, Bangkok, Thailand. Maneekhao hopes to establish a role among the new generation of Thai teacher researchers at the tertiary level who will develop their educational culture with an insider's perspective.

Richard Watson Todd also teaches at King Mongkut's University of Technology. He has had several articles and a book (*Classroom Teaching Strategies*, Prentice Hall) published and has been engaged in research for some time. He and Maneekhao are keen to continue their professional development and see action research as an important means of doing so.

CHAPTER 7

The Road Runs Ever On: Research, Development, and Language Awareness

Tom Hales and Clare O'Donoghue

◈ INTRODUCTION

> The clever man will tell you what he knows; he may even try to explain it to you. The wise man encourages you to discover it for yourself, even though he knows it inside out. (Revans, 1980, p. 9)

Literature on action research makes frequent reference to the action research *spiral* (Kemmis & McTaggart, 1988), a metaphor accurately reflecting the recursive nature of the process or processes involved. We shall be taking several turns around the spiral until we arrive at our current situation. The main part of this chapter is a narrative of the events that took place as we attempted to address a perceived deficiency in our teacher education courses. For the sake of clarity, we have numbered the revisions of our situation (our turns around the action research spiral) Phase 1, Phase 2, Phase 3, and so on. The focus of investigation of each cycle developed in response to the results of the investigation in the previous cycle.

We go on to consider the process, looking at how the continued revising of our approach has affected us and the various cohorts of participants on our teacher education courses. In this evaluation, we use criteria identified by Atweh, Christensen, and Dornan (1998), which look at action research as a phenomenon with wide-ranging implications in broad contexts (their own context was not TESOL). This has helped focus our assessment of the benefit of the process for all involved in the broadest possible sense. We shall therefore be examining the extent to which the process was

- social (in terms of its exploration of the individual and the social)
- participatory (as a means of examining our and our course participants' own knowledge and interpretive categories)
- collaborative and practical
- emancipatory (in releasing teachers and teacher educators from unproductive and limiting social structures)
- critical (in releasing teachers and teacher trainers from the constraints of power relationships and exclusion)
- recursive

❖ SITUATION

Accounts of implementing action research often refer to projects of a defined and clearly delimited nature. However, for the purposes of this chapter, we discuss a project that encompasses most of our careers in teacher education. The constant motivation for it has been a desire to improve personal current practice in achieving our aims of helping our course participants develop as teachers. The courses we refer to were for British, North American, and Australian nationals with little or no teaching experience, and for European teachers of English with some experience. They were run in various public and private sector institutions in Britain and Greece. All of the course participants had elected to attend the courses.

❖ FOCUS

In particular, this project has focused on the language awareness strand of these predominantly preservice teacher education courses. Initially, our intention was to broaden course participants' experience of language study beyond the narrow confines of course book "TEFLese." Later, in addition to this, we became more concerned about helping course participants develop their own language analysis and research strategies, as well as confidence in their own abilities in this area.

❖ RESPONSE

Phase 1: A Small Beginning

In the context of comparing reflective practice and action research, McMahon (1999) observes, "reflective practice can be a useful precursor to action research. It is not identical to it. . . . Reflective practice can be used to identify problems, action research can seek to provide solutions" (p. 168).

Although not stated explicitly, this goes some way to explaining the identification of an initial concern or problem addressed by any piece of action research. We shall therefore assume a period of observation and reflection at the very beginning of the process.

Planning

Initially, it was O'Donoghue who wanted to make a change to an activity in a training session in order to broaden course participants' experience of language study beyond the narrow confines of course book TEFLese. The area of language concerned was reference to the future, an area of notorious complexity and one for which a certain fuzziness is acknowledged in its description in terms of such categories as *planned future, future intentions,* and *future decided at the time of speaking* so beloved of TEFL course books. She felt that it was unfair to allow novice teachers to go away from their initial training with the mistaken view that these categories were clearly defined and that any problems they might encounter in their teaching careers were due to their own deficiencies of knowledge rather than the very real difficulties of linguistic description.

Action

Two course participants were asked if they would mind taking part in a recorded interview about their plans for after the course. O'Donoghue asked the two course participants if she could use the tape in the timetabled sessions on future forms. She transcribed parts of the interview and prepared a worksheet to focus the course participants on different instances and uses of future forms. The tape was edited so that O'Donoghue could use sections of it in the session.

Observation and Reflection

The session was observed by the director of teacher training, who noted that although it was novel and interesting for the course participants to focus on contextualization in authentic language data rather than use TEFL course book material, and that it was good for them to see homemade materials tailored to the students being used in class, the use of the tape was quite time-consuming. The expected variety of future forms—the hoped-for benefit—had not materialized as the participants in the conversation, knowing the purpose of the recording, had tried to be helpful and made frequent and unnatural use of *will* forms.

The idea was put on the back burner for a while, and it was not until Hales joined the organization over a year later that anyone attempted working with dialogues generated by course participants again.

Phase 2: Beginning Again

Planning

From the previous experience, it was evident that, despite our desire to be transparent, we would have to resort to more devious methods to get what we wanted in terms of natural language. The question was how to record the course participants talking about their future plans without telling them what it was for. If we were not going to ask a few of them to give up free time to make the recording, we would have to find a legitimate way of using class time to make the recordings, and this in turn would mean involving the whole group. We also thought that the involvement of the whole group would heighten the course participants' involvement in the analysis of the project.

Action

The way we achieved this next stage was to use part of a session on developing fluency to record the conversations. The course participants were divided into groups of three or four, put in separate rooms with a tape recorder, and asked to discuss their plans for after the course. As was the case with the first group in Phase 1, the course participants were very anxious that the tapes would be used in the phonology sessions and that their pronunciation would be found at fault. They had to be reassured that nobody would listen to the tapes except the tutor and that the tapes would not be used in the phonology sessions. After the course participants had made their tapes, they were collected by the tutor for transcription. Doing the recording activity in a session on fluency allowed us to explore with the course participants the importance of setting up activities, the accessibility of the topic, and the influence of the tape recorder on their spontaneity. Most reported that after a while, once they had got into the conversation, they stopped worrying about being recorded. This enabled us to discuss with them the benefits of recording EFL students, something that we both incorporated into our own EFL teaching on a regular basis. The tutor then had the fairly arduous task of listening to and transcribing sections of the different conversations for use in class. We found that it was best to select smaller extracts from all of the conversations rather than transcribing completely only one or two conversations so that no group would feel left out, and student interest would remain high.

This was how the project was run for several courses.

Observation and Reflection

The original desired objective had been attained: A wide variety of forms materialized in conversations, and novice teachers could be made aware of the difficulty of classification in the area of future forms. Understanding of the forms was much less of a problem than with created examples as the course participants themselves had been involved in the conversations and fully understood what had been meant by those involved.

On the negative side, anybody who has transcribed conversations knows how time-consuming this is. It should be remembered that this work contributed only to one session in one thread of a whole course. Also, on courses when recording was not practicable, such as those offered during busy periods of the year when there were no spare rooms or tape recorders, it proved unsatisfactory to use tape scripts from earlier courses. As the course participants examining the scripts had not been involved in the conversation, they tended to focus on the apparent "broken-up" nature of the language and made comments along the lines of, "How come these people are out there teaching English?" This alerted us to the sensitization of people who had been recorded to the untidy nature of real conversation. On most courses, participants would comment on how fragmented the conversations seemed, and how this must make following conversations among native speakers very difficult for students. This was a definite advantage for those teachers who were not themselves speakers of a foreign language and had not therefore experienced the frustrations that can be felt by a language learner.

As part of the standard quality control mechanisms, course participants gave written feedback at the end of the course, in addition to any informal feedback that occurred as the course progressed. Overall, comments from course participants were very positive. Some mentioned that as they had enjoyed the fact that they had been using their own conversations as the basis of activities, they could see how this kind of approach would also motivate students. Thus their own learning experience was demonstrating the benefits of a particular kind of student-centered classroom practice.

The most notable benefit from the point of view of teacher development, however, seemed to be the fact that quite complex concepts could be introduced and discussed very early in the development of language awareness of novice teachers who had not previously studied the structure of the English language in any great detail. Also, for course participants from mainland Europe, the experience was reassuring for several reasons. For example, they were well-versed in what grammar books said should be the case, and could therefore assume a knowledgeable role on mixed British, North American, and European courses. This helped give them status in groups where they often perceived themselves to be at a linguistic disadvantage compared with their British and North American peers. The examination of real language also helped to clarify for them why "things were not always as they should be."

It was the perceived benefit in terms of both course participant interest and enjoyment, combined with their motivation and engagement in complex language study, that motivated us as tutors to continue using this procedure.

The question raised here after several courses, though, was if this was successful in work on future forms, would it not also be successful in dealing with other areas of English?

Phase 3: Expanding the Scope

Planning

The next development came when O'Donoghue was doing an MSc in TESOL and wanted to do an assignment on materials development, looking at the way modals, especially *would*, were treated in course books and how this compared with every day usage (based on the ideas in Willis, 1990). Recording course participants seemed a good way to get at authentic data, which they could then compare with course book examples. However, different topics of conversation would be needed in an effort to bring out different usages. The topics used were

- what your plans are for after the course (for future forms)
- how your life would be / would have been different if you had been born a member of the opposite sex (for unreal past and present speculation)
- childhood holidays (for habitual past)

Action

At the suggestion of the MSc tutor, instead of the trainer transcribing the tapes, the course participants were asked to do it in groups, each participant taking a 5-minute section (about an hour's worth of transcribing). The transcriptions were passed to the tutor, who prepared worksheets, which were then used in class in the usual way. However, as each group had had a different topic of conversation to bring out different usages, all groups worked with each other's transcripts to look for and analyze different forms, contexts, and usages. Because the topics were different, there was quite a lot of interest in seeing what other people had talked about and much humor from the opposite-sex topic.

Observation and Reflection

In this phase, we discovered that in transcribing the tapes, the course participants had tidied up the language and written the dialogues in full sentences, losing much of the character of spoken language. This resulted in it being possible to discuss the use of modals but not features of spoken discourse. This was very interesting as we had perhaps not really fully exploited the fact that, when confronted with real language on the earlier courses, course participants had raised points on features they had observed. These features, for us as trainers, had been interesting but peripheral to our own aims. We had also discovered, by varying the topics of conversation, that more language forms could be studied in context and course participants were more interested in reading and working with each other's transcripts because of the change of topic. This came out in participants' comments, which were generally very similar to those at Phase 2. Perhaps, then, there was scope for using the impetus generated by the variety in topic to exploit this approach more, but with transcripts that were not tidied up by the course participants. This meant a return to transcription by the trainers.

Phase 4: Beyond Verbs and Parts of Speech

Planning

In the earlier phases, most of our courses had been on preservice teachers' courses for predominantly British or North American nationals with some European teachers of English. By now, our teacher education activity was much more varied and included a lot of work on in-service courses for Greek teachers of English in addition to courses involving British, North American, and Australian nationals. These courses were all run in Greece, and this presented us with the opportunity to see if our approach was as successful in a different context.

Action

The approach was successful, but we also wanted to extend the scope. So, in addition to setting language analysis tasks, we introduced a more discoursal element to the tasks by asking the course participants to compare their dialogues with course book dialogues or grammar book descriptions and asking them to account for the differences.

Observation and Reflection

The process had not only grown in terms of the traditional language areas covered (e.g., futures, conditionals, and various tense forms), but we were now dealing with features of discourse that would, perhaps in the past, have been thought of as inappropriate (i.e., too difficult) for preservice teachers. Course participants were asked to compare their transcripts with accounts in grammar books of ellipsis and thematic fronting, for example. However, as we said in the discussion of Phases 2 and 3, the fact that the course participants were a part of the conversation that produced the data for examination is of paramount importance. These are not examples of hard sentences taken from a grammar book or some devilish trainers' resource book; they are the participants' own conversations and, as such, interesting and valued and entirely comprehensible.

The participants themselves (as had happened previously in Britain) commented on how interesting it was to see conversation written down, and how complex it must be to follow for a learner. As the courses took place in Greece with groups of British, Australian, and North American participants, they were ideally placed to feel this and mentioned it. Some Greek teachers on other courses were initially worried about being recorded because they told us (later) that they felt that it might be used to highlight so called linguistic deficiencies. It was interesting for them to see that the disjointed nature of their spoken English was not in fact a linguistic deficiency on their part for failing to speak in complete sentences but a natural feature of spoken language. This in turn had ramifications for their views on the kind of oral language that their own students should produce.

This stage prompted some interesting thoughts about the nature of the treatment of language for teachers—particularly preservice teachers:

- Does the traditional approach in which the trainer or course designer selects areas considered worthy of study and within the perceived capabilities of the inexperienced end up underestimating the abilities of our preservice teachers?

- Does our urge to prepackage language on courses merely patronize participants and necessarily limit how far they can develop?

- What would happen if we did not limit participants in this way and gave them free rein to see how far they could go if left to their own devices?

This led to the next phase.

Pause

At this point, Hales presented the product of this process at a professional conference (Hales, 1996, and written up more fully as Hales, 1997). We have sometimes thought that this might have looked as if we had finished with the process, when in fact we were (and are) still reassessing it. In fact, writing it up led to reconsidering some of the questions above. It was very much an aid in taking stock of the situation and thinking about what might be a suitable future direction.

Phase 5: Letting Go

Planning

Back working in Britain, we decided to ask the course participants to prepare tasks for their peers based on their conversation transcripts. This was a first step. By chance we discovered the importance of a thorough precourse task in bringing the course participants up to a base of familiarity with terminology in order for them to go beyond form-naming in the preparation of tasks for their peers. When simply naming forms was itself a novelty (i.e., when simply the names of parts of speech, tenses, and other forms were themselves new knowledge), then that, rather than the way different forms were being used, became the focus of tasks.

By this time, Hales had become heavily involved in corpus research and was very interested in the way lexical phrases altered the way in which language could be described (see Nattinger & DeCarrico, 1992). However, none of these language developments seemed to be having any effect on the language study strand of teacher education courses that we were aware of. Visits to other centers confirmed that the tendency to study verb phrase chunks was as strong as ever. Developments in corpus software, specifically the very user friendly Wordsmith (Scott, 1996), the availability of separate corpora, and three personal computers able to run the programs enabled us to consider implementing an element of corpus research on the preservice courses.

Action

The corpus element involved instruction in the use of the software (we believe that this is only really possible with the kind of user-friendly software now available), and then groups of three or four people were given a word or pair of words to look at together (e.g., *when/while, quite/rather, that/if*). At this point, we made something of a wrong move. We asked the first group who undertook this kind of research to prepare 30-minute presentations with teaching materials. Unfortunately, we had not anticipated the preconceptions that go with a word like *presentation*, and the result was, essentially, a series of lectures. The emphasis on the pedagogical value of this work had been backgrounded, which we felt to be a deficiency in our own choice of outcome for the research.

We immediately changed the type of outcome we requested. The language awareness strand of courses now included the following elements.

- We now asked course participants to produce tasks for each other based on their conversation transcripts. Course participants now shared the task of transcribing a few minutes of their own conversations between them. We found that using a transcription of our own in an early session of the course and focusing on its apparently messy nature overcame the tendency to want to tidy up transcriptions.

- We asked course participants to produce teaching materials based on the concordance lines. This also involved using our own materials of the type found in Tribble and Jones (1990) based on the same corpora.

We also ran one course that contained only the element of corpus investigation. This meant that we had experienced courses with only one investigative element and with both. We did not repeat this for the reasons we mention below.

Observation and Reflection

Looking at the downside first, we learned very quickly that a focus on the pedagogical element must always be maintained. Also, we experimented with having courses in which only one element—either the concordancing or the transcript-based tasks—was used. We found that the quality of both elements was improved when both elements were included. That is to say, when most of the linguistic element of the course was based around research, the more there was, the better the overall quality. (A quantitative account of the differences is given in Hales & O'Donoghue, in press, as are some of the materials produced.) This surprised us as the areas of language studied in both tasks did not have any obviously clear connection, the methods used for collecting the data were very different, and the focus of research for each task appeared to be quite different. We had no explanation for this, but we took this finding seriously and ensured that both tasks were included in subsequent courses.

We were surprised at the quality of much of the work. The depth and breadth of analysis and the quality of some of the observations were, we felt, far beyond what we could have achieved using our early methods of *input* (still a term widely used in teacher education). Input, it seems, if taken literally, is very limiting—there is no room for teachers to grow. It is rather like the difference between watching and taking part in a football match: If you are watching, you do not have the opportunity to run with the ball and show what you can do. Novice teachers were producing work based on grammatical features, discourse features (as we mentioned above), and lexical phrases. The lexical element was something that emerged from course participants looking at the patterns in concordance lines and wondering if some of the expressions that stood out from the screen would be of use to students. From there it was a matter of producing the material to use in class.

Comments from participants have largely reflected what we felt about the courses but from a different standpoint. We were asking for written feedback on the specific activities involved in language awareness. The conversation/transcription-based activities were still being commented on favorably. Even the very act of transcription attracted more positive comment than we expected ("interesting," "worthwhile").

Devising tasks and doing tasks prepared by other groups were activities that attracted very positive comment indeed. The concordance-based tasks seemed to be much more sensitive to the make up of the language awareness thread as a whole. Where this was done alongside the transcription task and with the aim of producing pedagogical materials, the response was positive, and participants' comments indicated that they saw a reason for the process.

On the first course using concordances, comments were generally positive, but there were indications that some did not really feel that they had gained a lot from other group's presentations and some did not see the point of the activity. One person described it as "mildly interesting." Most comments were predominantly positive, however, including some indicating that we had achieved what we hoped. For example, one person reported learning from this that "'rules' are not as clear-cut as grammar books imply—useful knowledge to have when teaching." But the indicators of some degree of dissatisfaction reflected our view that the interpretation of the word *presentation* had been problematic (indeed, one person commented that it was "interesting to see how different groups interpret the word 'presentation'"). Later course participants, who produced pedagogical teaching material as the result of their concordance research, were generally much more positive not only about their own research and materials creation, but also about working with other groups' teaching materials.

The relevance of the research to classroom teaching was more clearly highlighted for them through the production of materials that could be given to students. The least positive reaction came from the group that had only had the concordance-based task. Stronger and more motivated participants commented positively, but others found it "alien" and could not see the point of it. We cannot be sure, but we would guess that the conversation-based activities are friendlier in form and more accessible in nature. Perhaps this gives a gentler introduction to the skills that are developed in this kind of language awareness activity. This may be a somewhat speculative conclusion, but we would think twice before doing only a concordancing task again. We do not know why the two types of activity work together as they do, improving the quality of work of each and improving the perceived benefit of each from the participants' point of view. At this stage, we simply accept that this is so and make sure we include both elements in our courses. It will be worth further examination.

◈ OUTCOMES

We have moved from a situation in which language was dealt with through input to one in which the greater part of language work on our courses involves investigation, often by people who have never been asked to think about linguistic features at all. The whole process has taken years, moving from a first tentative step to change a 20-minute activity, looking at the effect the changes could have, and then taking them a step further. Looking back, we feel that we have moved from a position where we felt that there was something wrong with language work as it was dealt with on our courses to one in which the work of our course participants puts into practice what we believe to be qualities of good teacher education.

Previously, the language element did not fit with other elements—particularly, for example, the teaching practice element—that were very much based around concepts such as *facilitation, empowerment,* and *reflection.* Language had still been a case of input. Even if input was achieved via discussion tasks that were superficially student centered in that course participants discussed, they only discussed what was on the prepared task sheet. The difference between awareness and analysis had been blurred. Previous course participants had been required to analyze examples of a predetermined canon of features (e.g., futures, conditionals, perfectives; see Kerr, 1993, 1996); now they could develop the more valuable quality of awareness that can be applied to whatever linguistic features they may encounter.

Our initial question was "How can we broaden course participants' experience of language study beyond the narrow confines of course book TEFLese?" Our initial response was to change an activity. After a series of revisions, we opted to change the whole nature of a course component. This was the final outcome, the product, but was there something in the process, too, that has affected changes over the period?

This is where the qualities and characteristics of Atweh et al. (1998), mentioned at the beginning, can provide a useful starting point for discussion. As we encouraged our course participants to be researchers on their courses, we also found that some of the benefits we were experiencing through the process of action research were being passed on to them. As we shall see, this seems to be particularly true in terms of the emancipation from a very limiting view of where knowledge about language comes from. Seeing this and other benefits manifest themselves in the teachers was one of the spurs that motivated us to keep working at this project.

The recursive nature of the process is evident from the account above. However, it is noticeable that there were times when we thought we should, in a sense, take a step or two back, for example on the issue of who should transcribe conversations, or, in the later stages, on the question of how much research is beneficial for preservice groups. This led us to withdraw one of the elements (conversational or corpus), to see what would happen. We concluded by reinstating both, but in the end with the knowledge that this was indeed beneficial. As with many metaphors in any field of study, perhaps the simple spiral, while providing a useful and powerful overarching image, does not tell the whole story in detail. We can take some steps back if necessary, and some sideways. Our progress may not look neat, and overall coherence may be something that we often supply in retrospect as we recognize where our spiraling found new purchase, but we continue working to become more aware and to respond sensitively to our context.

The critical and emancipatory qualities of the process are in a way the most striking and perhaps the most long lived. Action research is described as emancipatory in that it "aims to help people recover and release themselves from the constraints of irrational, unproductive, unjust and unsatisfying social structures which limit their self-development and self-determination" (Atweh et al., 1998, p. 120) and critical in that it "aims to help people recover and release themselves from the constraints embedded in the social media through which they interact" (Atweh et al., 1998, p. 120).

In the world of TESOL, there is a range of authorities who claim (or lay claim to) content and knowledge. For example, there are groups that stipulate the content of teacher education courses. The restrictions can vary in their rigidity, yet even when there is no direct stipulation, there can be an understanding of what is acceptable and what should be practiced (see Kerr, 1993, 1996). Linguistic elements of teacher development courses are often described in terms of parts of language: future forms, conditionals, perfectives, and so on. Questioning that this is the way things should be has very much removed the influence of these stipulations or understandings, which limited the nature of our course content and, therefore, we felt also limited the benefit of our courses to our course participants. In the specific context of developing language awareness, from our point of view as teacher educators, we know that there are huge gaps in the description of English, yet received wisdom dictates that we should pass on the canon as is, regardless of these deficiencies. The view of inaccurate simplification as a reasonable crutch for the uninitiated at first seems reasonable, until one considers what novice teachers do when they struggle with language in their work: Like the novice learner of English, they blame themselves for the difficulties they experience.

In our view, this exposes novice teachers to unjustifiable and unnecessary blows to confidence—and our dissatisfaction with this outcome (borne, incidentally, out of working alongside ex–course participants in our staff room) led to the impetus to expose novice teachers to true language with its resistance to easy, glib categorizations. The process also changes the role of the trainer away from that of the imparter of knowledge to supportive guide in an experience of research, discovery, and practical employment of findings. Despite the growth of this welcome trend in other areas of teacher education courses, the way in which language awareness and knowledge is developed still lags behind.

This approach has also released our course participants from an unhelpful hierarchy that dictates that carrying out research and taking a view on language is not possible at the beginning of their careers. It raises questions as to why this indeed should be the case—why novice teachers should be considered merely as ripe for input on language matters rather than as potential researchers, and why the valuable skill of research should be reserved until they are deemed to have enough knowledge rather than as a means of acquiring that knowledge in the first place. In this sense, the critical nature of the process is possibly more evident from their point of view. Grammarians are the experts, yet we know they do not tell the whole truth. The usual relationship and roles are here reexamined. Novice teachers can not only criticize the rules of the experts, they can also take on a role usually reserved for the most expert of experts: the researcher. In this they are the users, analysts, and teachers discussed in Edge (1988).

These are questions that arise out of this process and that are liberating in what they say about the accepted role of novice teachers in their own learning process and of trainers in their delivery of courses. The shift from input (albeit task-based) to research means a far more truly participatory nature in the process of learning about language. It has led to "people . . . examining their own knowledge" (Atweh et al., 1998, p. 120). We were continually reassessing what our own role in the training process was and what makes for effective training, and our course participants were also engaged in a process of reassessing what they knew about language and what knowledge about language is.

We learned from our course participants and from what they found—we clearly could not dictate what they would find or produce in the final stages of their investigations from the initial stages of data examination. In this sense, we could merely guide and help in a collaborative effort.

◈ REFLECTIONS

Every time we have spoken about the process in which we have been engaged, or have written down our process to date, we have found ourselves reflecting on what the next development could be. Our conclusion, in the sense of what we have learned, is that it is possible to avoid the common misfit between teacher education based on the qualities of facilitation, development, and empowerment on the one hand, and the input-based nature of much language awareness work on the other. We have learned not to do our course participants a disservice by imposing our limitations on their achievements. That is, we help them become language investigators from the beginning of their teaching careers.

As to the detail of what we record above, we hope that it might be of direct use to colleagues engaged in similar teaching. In more general terms, we have learned that we expect this process of research-based learning to continue and hope that it will.

◈ CONTRIBUTORS

Tom Hales is a freelance teacher and teacher educator.

Clare O'Donoghue is a lecturer in ESOL at Middlesex University, in England. She and Hales have taught English and educated teachers in Britain, Spain, Greece, Ecuador, and Thailand.

CHAPTER 8

Hearing Voices: A Robust and Flexible Framework for Gathering and Using Student Feedback

Phil Quirke

❧ INTRODUCTION

This case study looks at a program of systematically gathering student feedback on specific elements of my teaching and materials, both of which had been highlighted previously by students or me in my yearly evaluation. The case study also reviews ways I have used the feedback. I started the case study in September 1998 and originally gave myself a final deadline of March 1999, the date of the regional TESOL Arabia conference at which I wanted to present my investigation, share my findings, and encourage others to use their students' feedback as well. Following this and two other workshops, I continued the case study and involved other teachers, which led to new and unexpected outcomes.

❧ SITUATION

The case study is set in a women's tertiary education college in Abu Dhabi, one of the United Arab Emirates. There are restrictions on the type of teaching material we can use, and some teaching practices, which I would have considered part and parcel of my teaching persona before I came to the Gulf, are definitely unworkable here. To be more precise, there are some subjects that are taboo for a Western male teaching Arab women, and physical contact, a natural part of my teaching beforehand, cannot occur at all between a male teacher and female student. An early lesson that I learned, however, was that it would be a mistake to interpret such cultural conventions as being significant with regard to the potential availability of frank and useful student feedback. To do so would be to indulge in the blanket stereotyping of other people according to our own, external misunderstandings of what hangs together in a culture. To have practical experience of even this level of insight is a noteworthy personal and professional outcome for an exploratory, action-research-based approach to our intercultural work. However, I am getting ahead of myself.

I ran this investigation for 8 months with two regular classes I teach for 5 hours a week and with a variety of other classes that I taught on an occasional basis when I had to stand in for absent colleagues. The two 5-hour classes are part of the third year of study at the college. Students finish this year by sitting the IELTS (International English Language Testing Service) examination. Like the U.S. TOEFL

(Test of English as a Foreign Language), the British IELTS is used as a means of determining the English language proficiency of nonnative speakers for university entrance in English-speaking countries. These students are expected to get a minimum Band 5 score, and the majority of them are at a Band 6 level.

I had taught many of the students in previous years and was able to build rapport with them very quickly. As they were my regular students, I was able to negotiate the syllabus with them to a certain extent, within the confines of the course outline and goals set by the curriculum. The students grew quickly used to the idea that they would be asked for feedback and, as I point out later, were at times ruthless in their honesty.

The other classes were often at a much lower level, with the majority in their first year of study at the college. The students come from a very traditional rote learning, teacher-centered, secondary school system and take some time adjusting to the system of teaching and learning at the college, with its emphasis on student-centered and independent learning. To my surprise, these students were also very candid in their responses. I say surprised because I had expected many of them to reply with what they thought the teacher wanted to hear. The case study details my search as to why they felt they could answer so honestly, and it is from this search that some of the most important outcomes are drawn, not least the model of Explain Ask Collate Reflect Act, which I put forward in the section on outcomes.

◈ FOCUS

The purpose of the investigation was to give students a voice in my teaching, and thus help me adapt it to accommodate those students. I believe most teachers do this in most of their classes in an informal, unstructured way. Many teachers I have talked to have agreed that they do ask their students for feedback, but it tends to be orally at the end of a lesson with questions such as

- Did you enjoy this class?
- Did you find this class useful?
- What part of this lesson did you find most useful?

Out of 48 teachers at three different workshops I held on this topic, 22 said that they asked students for feedback. Of those 22, only 8 had an approach that differed from oral questions at the end of the class, and most admitted that they did not always follow up on that feedback. Although I do not wish to generalize from such a small sample, I invite readers to judge for themselves whether they recognize here a fairly accurate reflection of how most of us approach feedback from our learners. The reasons for this reticence are many and range from a belief that the students will only tell us what we want to hear, to a fear of what students might say and of our own inability to deal with it. Personally, I wanted to look at what would happen to me as a teacher if I formalized, systemized, and documented this process.

The problems that I originally identified were based on a couple of comments from my students on the formal student evaluation forms from the previous year. One student said that the readings I had used with the class were too complicated; a second had said that the journals I had had the class write should not have been compulsory; another said that the class as a whole needed more lessons on writing summaries and noted that the others would not tell me this, and a fourth said that she liked the way that I taught, but was not sure why we did what we did in the classroom.

This feedback and the perceptiveness of the responses made me wonder why I had not been asking them for their feedback and input during the course. As Leather (1998) says, it is better to know when things are going wrong. It also made me think that I could improve not only the specific materials and techniques that I use in these classes but also myself as a teacher.

Drawing on the above, I set out a list of initial questions:

- Can I get feedback on my performance as a teacher, the techniques I use, and the materials?
- How can I get reliable feedback from my students?
- How should I react to this feedback?
- Will the above have any effect on my ability as a teacher?

With these original questions in mind, I determined to start off my new teaching year in the spirit I have always tried to instill in the candidates I tutor on Teaching Diploma courses: Risk is growth.

❖ RESPONSE

Perhaps we could most usefully start with the learners, by bringing them properly in at the start of our explorations. (Allwright & Bailey, 1991, p. 200)

The first problem for any teacher gathering feedback from their students is how to ensure that the feedback the students give them is honest, reliable, and valid. This obviously requires an element of trust on both sides.

Making a Start

One of the first steps I took was to partly negotiate the syllabus with the students by providing them with a 16-week blank timetable and asking them to each fill it in with how they would like to cover the work. I collated these and by the next class 2 days later returned a completed timetable. I spent a lesson going through it and showing them where I had included their input and where I had imposed my own ideas and explained why. These first two classes were important for two reasons. First, they clearly showed the students that I would not just get their input and then do what I wanted, and, second, they demonstrated that I would spend time talking to them about their learning and their opinions.

The third class was a reading lesson run a bit like a test in that the students worked alone and in silence on a text with different types of questions to answer (five each of comprehension, true/false, reference, multiple choice, and paragraph headings). The students had 5 minutes to answer each type, and then they broke into groups and discussed their answers. At the end, I asked the students which types of question they had found most difficult and what they had liked about the class. I was confronted with a mix of "we liked everything," "nothing was very difficult," and "type 2 questions." Nothing very useful to either the students or me.

Thereafter, I began by quite openly telling students that I did not want positive feedback. I took a leaf from my tutoring on Diploma courses and told them that every class can be improved , but that the next time I taught this lesson, it would only be as good as the feedback they gave me. I told them that I could improve the lesson only by hearing their opinions about the parts of the lesson that they did not enjoy, find useful, or understand. By beginning with this largely negative outset, I have found it easier to come back to a more balanced analysis later.

I still found students saying that they would not change anything, but that was addressed by showing them how the lesson or material had changed thanks to the critical input of the others. The ways I did this I will leave until later in the section on methods. Students began quickly to take pride in the fact that they had some input into my teaching, and the feedback became more and more insightful.

By now the original four questions I had listed had expanded into a more detailed and wide-ranging set:

- Can I get feedback on myself as a teacher, the techniques I use, and the materials? Should I just aim for one thing at a time? Can I realistically get feedback on so many different elements? Should the feedback be guided, or can I leave it totally open?

- How can I get reliable feedback from my students? My preliminary investigation had shown me that the students would respond positively and give me detailed feedback, but was it just this class? Could I get the same type of reliable feedback from classes I taught only occasionally as a substitute? Was it necessary to demonstrate that the feedback would be used and how it would be used?

- How should I react to this feedback? How can I demonstrate that I am using the feedback? What should I do if I am not able to use it? Do I always need to react?

- Will the above have any effect on my ability as a teacher? And if yes, what would it be? Is it an effect I want to see?

At the same time, I began to realize that my whole research effort was aimed toward testing one simple hypothesis: that my teaching would improve if I could find an appropriate balance between having a robust framework for dealing with feedback, while maintaining a flexibility of response in order to deal with different situations.

Moving Toward Robust and Flexible

In this section, I had originally intended to lay out my approach to gathering student feedback as in Cohen and Manion's (1985) stage four: plan intervention, which is subdivided into methods, questions, and response. However, I found that the examples needed to be narrated as they happened because the method and questions used initially changed, depending on the student feedback I received. I discovered that action research is long term and flows from one stage to the next in the same way as we hope our lessons do. Therefore, I will detail two specific cases where I looked at one aspect of my classroom teaching and then, in the final section on collaboration, show how other teachers drew on my work and developed it. This section on collaboration is dear to my heart as it highlights key elements of action research that I was not aware of when I set out on this project. These key elements are, first, that action research is long term and continues long after even the publication and reporting stage is completed because action research affects what we do in our daily teaching lives. Second, action research is cyclical, moving from problem identification through intervention to outcomes (Cohen & Manion, 1985), which in turn expose new angles to the problem that need intervention and lead to further outcomes, and so on. Third, collaboration is a must in all good action research, which truly changes us as teachers in a positive way.

The examples I will draw on are approaches to reading and forms of presentation. The review and selection of the examples was made based on the variety of interactions between the student(s) and me. In other words, I have not written up two examples of the same kind of feedback. I will attempt to focus on the response from the students and how intensely involved they became in giving me their personal feedback. In one case, a student waited for me for 2 hours after her final class to give me her feedback.

Approaches to Reading

This first example is taken from a strong second-year class who were all expected to score around Band 6 on the end-of-year IELTS. The group included many students I had taught before although they were studying together as a group for the first time. Around the fourth week of study, and after I had already introduced the idea of their giving me regular feedback on my teaching, I set out to look into their reactions to different approaches I use to teach reading.

We had already agreed to focus on reading every Monday, and I started the first in a series of classes by listing the different approaches I would use. They were jigsaw reading, long text question cards, silent reading for pleasure, group reading, analysis of test questions, clap reading, prediction, question writing, and paragraph matching. As the object of this chapter is not to go into different approaches to the teaching of reading, I will not give any detail about the above methods, but I hope that the student responses still come across clearly. I told the students that over the following 9 weeks, I would be using these nine different approaches to the teaching of reading and that I would ask them to complete the same questionnaire (see Figure 1) after each class before completing a table at the end. I did not explain the rationale to the students, and their answers surprised me in that they clearly show the understanding students have of the classroom process and the techniques we use in our lessons.

At the end of the class, I gave the students 10 minutes to complete their forms, which they then handed in to me. During these 10 minutes, they could ask me any questions they wanted to although I did not give any answers to questions on the approach. I explained to them that I needed to see their responses and opinions first and that if they wanted to discuss the outcome, we would do so after the final lesson.

Figure 1 shows the handout in its final form. I originally included the final comment line to see what would come up. During the first 3 weeks, students regularly added comments on their enjoyment of the lesson, so I then added this question in its own right for the remaining weeks. After that, many students left the final comment line blank. It was also interesting to note that most students left the "Why" line blank at the beginning but, from about the third week on, began to enter reasons. The final week saw all the students bar one complete every line of the form.

Please complete the following honestly.

I will use your responses to plan our approach to reading classes next semester.

Week _____

Title of text _____

Approach _____

What was the aim of this class? _____

What did you learn during this class? _____

What did you enjoy most about the class? _____

Why? _____

What did you find most difficult? _____

Why? _____

Other comments: _____

FIGURE 1. Handout 1

The questions asked became more and more specific, and I often just needed to tell myself yes. For example, one that I noted after a lesson was "Can I say, 'because there was too much difficult words'?"

At the end of the 9 weeks, I asked the students to complete the following table to try and summarize their opinions.

Before the students filled in the table, I gave them back their original questionnaires so they could refer to them while they were completing the table. I collected everything and collated the results. The following lesson, I gave them the collated table of their opinions, and we discussed the whole 9 weeks.

TABLE 1. FEEDBACK ON READING APPROACHES

Please complete the following table with numbers.

    1 = the most (e.g., the most enjoyable, the most useful)

    9 = the least (e.g., the least enjoyable, the least useful)

Week	Approach	Useful	Difficult	Interesting	Enjoyable
1	jigsaw				
2	question cards				
3	silent				
4	group				
5	analysis				
6	clap				
7	prediction				
8	question writing				
9	paragraph matching				

Their responses were extremely perceptive. All the students were able to note that the analysis, question writing, and paragraph matching were directly aimed at exam preparation. Eight of the 11 students noted that the clap technique was aimed at improving their reading speeds, and 4 students noted that jigsaw reading was aimed at helping them understand how good writers organize their writing. I was surprised to see that the interesting and enjoyable columns were very different, and in the discussion, the students told me that *enjoyable* depended on the activity and my involvement as a teacher, whereas *interesting* depended on the text. Six students said that they found group reading "uncomfortable," "unhelpful," or "distracting," but the 2 weakest students said this approach was "the most useful" and "very good because the other students show me ways of read I do not know." Finally, 9 students said that the silent reading "was not good for class," "a waste of time," or "boring."

Presentation of Grammar

This example was based on a lesson and six-page handout on the present perfect that I have used for years. It is a handout that was originally designed and adapted by high intermediate students, and I was interested to see how I could use the same worksheet with lower levels depending on my presentation technique. The handout clearly divides the present perfect into three concepts using time lines and involves the students in discussing the concept behind different sentences.

During the year, while substituting in all eight of our intermediate classes, I presented the handout in lessons of an hour and a half, with the class teacher agreeing to follow up with the pages of the handout I did not succeed in covering. Their support and agreement were vital to this case because without it, I would have had to cut the worksheet down and realign my aim, and this once again reinforces the collaborative nature of action research. In much the same way that we do not teach at our best in isolation, neither is it advisable to attempt action research in isolation. We need the support and input of our colleagues to do our research justice.

For the purposes of gathering feedback, I decided to use graffiti boards, which I had only ever used before in Venezuela, or in teacher training sessions. I brought two large cards into the classroom and put them up on either side of the door. The first group I tried this with was the strongest; they were aiming to sit for the Cambridge First Certificate English examination in 6 months' time. I decided to present the tense with three paired sentences: one in the past and one in the perfect, with each pair relating to a different concept. The students then tried to decide why I had separated the three pairs, and we finished with a class discussion, featuring teacher input and explanation, using the time lines. After a break, they went on to the exercise where they decided which sentence expressed which concept.

But before leaving the class for the break, I gave each of the students a board marker and told them that I wanted them to put up on the graffiti boards anything they wanted to express about this lesson. I said that I was going to teach another class the same lesson next week, and I wanted their opinion. When I came back 10 minutes later, only six students had written anything so I asked all of those who had not written to add something even if it was only the words *good* or *bad.* I came back after 5 minutes to find 10 instances of *good* and 4 of *nice.* The original six had also only written comments such as "I like your way of teach," "I have fun," and "Thank you. It was good and I learned a lot."

Disappointing though this was, it was also one of the most important learning experiences I had over the months I looked for feedback. If I wanted reliable feedback, I had to give the students guidance, and I had to involve them more in the process, explaining clearly how their feedback would help me. The second class I presented the material to was an almost equally strong class. I used exactly the same technique as with the first class but began the class by telling them I was going to use material and a presentation that I had developed thanks to the input from my classes over the last few years. I explained that I would use the graffiti boards to gather their opinions of the lesson at the break. In this way the students actually participated in the class knowing that they were going to comment on it.

After the time lines explanation, I left the class and asked each student to write on the graffiti boards one thing they had not liked about the lesson and one thing that they had found particularly difficult. When I came back after the usual 10 minutes, they had not finished writing and asked for another 5 minutes. Some of what they produced is shown as Figure 2.

The comments were insightful and again showed me the usefulness of starting from negative prompts. With 36 comments, I found that I could group them into three main points: time lines, original sentences, and explanation. The comment that summed up the time lines was surprising and interesting: "We know this lines from our teacher, but I do not understand your lines. I want to make my line."

The original sentence point can best be made by summarizing three comments:

Why do you give the past sentence with the perfect one?

We have heard the perfect but are not sure when we can use it.

The past sentences made it confusing.

Finally, the comment on explanations made me kick myself: "I like you explain the meaning but it would more clear when we write our sentences with you."

For the next class, I planned to present the material using just three sentences in the perfect, with another three perfect sentences to match them should the students have problems. I decided to see if the students could come up with their own time lines and finally, before the break, would elicit a third example sentence for each

What I DIDN'T like about the lesson.	What I found MOST difficult
I don't like your lines.	
You give me sentence but I don't give you one.	The different with the 3 consepts
The sentences and examples are not clear.	
I get confused with the past and perfect together — why you do this???	The draws for the lines because they are not cleer.
Why your line so confussing?	
What concept??	
	I cant see the connection to now which you always say.
This all two difficult for us level.	

FIGURE 2. Sample of a Graffiti Board

concept. I went back to the second group and thanked them for their feedback, showing them how I had adapted the lesson based on their feedback. They received this without much enthusiasm, but when I sought their feedback in other cover classes after that, they showed me how important it was to follow up in this way. The feedback I received from this class thereafter gave me some of the most comprehensive and detailed comments I have gathered.

The third class I introduced to the idea of feedback in the same way, but one graffiti board I headed "What I Did Not Like" and the other "One Thing I Would Change." The feedback on the "Did Not Like" board clearly indicated that they did not like producing their own time lines and that some were still unclear about the difference in the concepts.

The solutions came from the other board, for example: "I want an example of time line." In response to this, I planned to do the first time line with the class, before asking them to produce their own.

In response to the comment "What we call this concept for 'I've eaten camel'?" I decided to elicit a name for each concept and give the students time to take notes.

The fourth and fifth classes gave similar feedback, but questioned as to why I did not give them more sentences at the beginning, so by the penultimate class, I had an overhead transparency (OHT) with three sentences for each concept, which the students discussed. For the final two classes, I sought the feedback at the end of the double period with two boards now titled "What I Found the Most Difficult" and "One Other Comment." This second board allowed students to say what they had liked about the class with 28 out of the 31 comments being positive.

By the end of the eight classes, I had a presentation of specific material that was very different from when I had started. It was better aimed at the lower level students, was more clearly staged, and gave the students more space. Equally, I had learned the importance of clearly explaining why I was looking for feedback, the importance of guiding students as to the type of feedback I required, and the importance of responding to that feedback by showing the students the difference their input had made.

Collaborating

In another case, I shared the student feedback from one class with their Critical Thinking teacher, and he began to use student feedback in all his classes. He pointed out later that as his aim was to improve the critical capacities of these young women, he often spent as long as 15 minutes at the end of his classes discussing the lesson with the students. He also suggested some forms of gathering feedback that he had begun to use and that I had not considered. These included e-mail, journals (which I had used but not specifically for feedback), a suggestion box that he kept permanently by his desk and that any of his students could put feedback into about anything to do with his teaching, and the 1-minute feedback slot at the end of class in which all the students talk at the same time and during which he notes as many points as he can.

This experience of seeing another teacher take the investigation I had been working on for 3 months and come up with so many novel and exciting methods I had not even considered convinced me of the importance of sharing and working together with others on our classroom research. From that point, I decided to get others involved, and I gave an in-house presentation on what I had done so far to the teachers in the English department. Although many reported that they asked students for feedback, no one had tried a systematic approach. Three teachers came to me afterwards expressing an interest in working on this with their own classes, and one even had a handout he wanted to start using with his classes to investigate how the students felt about working in different groups.

This last teacher had a particularly problematic class, with several apparent animosities among the students. The sheet asked students to comment on how they felt during the class when they were working together, how well they had worked as a team, what they had learned from the other students and, finally, how this group experience compared to that of the previous lesson. After 15 classes, during which every student had worked with every other student, the teacher presented his results to the class and suggested they try and work in one particular seating arrangement for a week.

The teacher himself commented that the class seemed far better able to work together and he had few problems thereafter. I also taught the group a couple of times after this and found them much more homogenous. The teacher was not sure if this was due to the final seating arrangements or to the process of 15 classes and the constant reflection he had required of the students during that process. So, he asked the students, and 15 of the 17 attributed it to the process of having to comment on how they had worked as a team.

I also presented my work at the TESOL Arabia conference in March and again at a local secondary school in April, and although I have had little feedback at this point, it has been an impetus to my own research. One teacher from the secondary school contacted me recently to let me know that he had adapted the graffiti board in a truly original way. He lets students write their feedback on his lab coat as long as it refers to the lesson he is teaching. If he receives any glib comments on the coat, he simply refuses to let them give feedback, and he has found that this (combined with threats of extra homework) has kept the feedback focused and useful.

These are just three examples of how other teachers have developed methods of collecting feedback and helped me clarify my own reflections and assumptions about both gathering and using student feedback. They also emphasize the importance of collaboration with colleagues and the long-term, cyclical nature of the action research process, which goes deeper and deeper into what we do in the classroom, and which ultimately changes for the better what we do as teachers.

◈ OUTCOMES

The outcomes of this year of action research were many, and I can perhaps summarize them best in terms of my students, my teaching, and me.

As far as my students are concerned, I am satisfied that these experiences of having their opinions sought, and seeing them respected, did indeed help students develop their critical thinking skills.

In terms of my teaching, I now have a model that I developed and that I believe facilitates the effective gathering and purposeful use of honest student feedback. It is based on both my experience and the experience of the others around me who came to share in this investigation in ways I had not foreseen.

The model can be stated very clearly as: Explain Ask Collate Reflect Act:

- **Explain** to the students why you are gathering feedback and that you need criticism in order to help you improve.

- **Ask** for the feedback you require with specific questions aimed at the area you are investigating.

- **Collate** this feedback into a series of manageable points you can work on.

- **Reflect** on how you are going to react to these points and what changes you need to make, or, equally what changes you cannot make.

- **Act** on this feedback and tell the students how you are acting on their feedback. This also means telling them when you cannot act on their feedback and why not. Involve them in the process because this will motivate increasingly reflective and useful feedback.

This is a simple model that does not state anything revolutionary. It is all common sense, but common sense that we may forget to apply in our busy teaching lives. For the present, at least, it gives me the robustness and flexibility that I was looking for in this area.

As for me, the outcomes vary from a growing awareness of how intelligent and probing the analysis of students can be, to a realization that this was the most rewarding year of teaching I have had in many, and during which I have both felt and seen my abilities stretched. I feel that I have developed as a teacher, learned to respect my students in a light I had never done before, and allowed my students to grow with me so that we could together build a better learning environment. That is undoubtedly the main outcome—a personal one.

◈ REFLECTIONS

My final reflection will doubtless have many readers nodding sagely that they were aware of this all along. For me, however, it was a striking realization and an extremely important one—one that I do not believe can be stressed enough. Good action research works best when shared and investigated collaboratively with colleagues.

I would just like to conclude my reporting by saying that this chapter has been successful in its aims if it encourages any of you to attempt to use student feedback explicitly to influence your teaching decisions, or if it persuades you to form an action research group to work collaboratively in an investigation of your classroom teaching.

◈ CONTRIBUTOR

Phil Quirke has been teaching and educating teachers for 13 years in Germany, Venezuela, Spain, and the United Arab Emirates (UAE). He is currently head of general education at Abu Dhabi Women's College, in the UAE. His previously published work includes articles on observation, face, and group work. He is currently investigating potential roles of Web sites in teacher development.

CHAPTER 9

Beverage Assassination and the Making of Appropriate Requests

Christopher Nicol

❧ INTRODUCTION

How often have ESOL teachers stood in front of a class, course book in hand, expounding language about which they feel more than a little uneasy, wondering when last—if ever—the particular item in question crossed their lips? And in a broader speculation, wondering to what extent the language taught in course books reflects the language actually used by competent speakers in a situation-specific context? Williams's (1988) doubts as to the adequacy of a repertoire of grammatical exponents to perform certain functions and speech acts appropriately in a business context are never far from my mind when planning work for students:

> Language is so complex, and our understanding of it is so far from complete, that perhaps authentic language is the only safe starting point for teaching. More real data is needed about what language is used in different situations before we as teachers and coursebook writers can begin to select what to teach for different situations. (p. 53)

It would be facile, however, as Williams above is careful to avoid being, to single out course books as being responsible on their own for the gap that may exist between language taught and language used. Teachers, too, in the worthy aim of rendering new language manageable for second language learners, may reduce language to a diminished and oversimplified list of grammatical formulae.

How often, for instance, does the teaching of the common speech act of requesting center itself on the modals *Could you . . . ?, Can you . . . ?,* or *Would you mind . . . ?* without fully considering the strategies and language used by competent speakers around these exponents and, indeed, sometimes in place of them?

❧ SITUATION

These thoughts were foregrounded recently when discussing with French students newly returned from studies in the United States and Britain how they had fared abroad linguistically. There was a fairly general consensus that, though adequately prepared at an English for academic purposes level, they often felt disadvantaged socially when involved in many of the daily speech acts required for social survival. They felt they were speaking more or less correctly, using the expressions they had been taught at school and beyond, but they felt at the same time that they were employing language that often sounded remote from the expressions used by their friends and colleagues in their social encounters.

The above experience, taken in conjunction with the seeds planted long before by the Williams article, motivated me to carry out an action research inquiry into the issue. I hoped for beneficial, practical results for students in real-world situations—indeed, for their teachers, too.

◈ FOCUS

As a focus, I decided to take the already mentioned speech act of requesting because it had always seemed to me (as an Anglophone living in a Francophone world) to be one of the trickier ones to negotiate successfully in a second language, the danger being to miss the appropriate level of formality, given the context, the speakers, and the weight of the imposition.

My purpose was to examine the language of requesting by comparing British and North American approaches to requests in certain common circumstances with the language used by my French learners. I wanted to establish the extent to which the latter's strategies and language paralleled the former's. The aim was not to criticize course books or teachers, for the above modal exponents frequently do form the head of any request. I wanted to find out for myself how native speakers of British and North American English actually request and to discover to what extent my French learners follow any requesting strategies that might emerge here.

Even more interesting in the long term, for me as a practicing ESOL teacher, I wanted to determine if and how action research could be of practical use to me or other busy classroom teachers. Personally, satisfying my curiosity about these potentially different approaches to requests would be of obvious linguistic interest, but was there a way to achieve this that would in itself provide pedagogically constructive data for any necessary classroom follow-on program?

◈ RESPONSE

Identifying Informants

In the search for empirically sourced data, I managed to interest 15 students at the university where I teach in the south of France in taking part in the project. The Euro American Institute of Technology provides freshman and sophomore courses for French students intending to complete their degrees in the United States, Canada, and Britain. My small investigation, as already indicated, was an attempt to help them socialize more naturally into their new linguistic environment. If successful, it could, I felt, be expanded into a broader internal program of language studies based on naturally occurring data. When alerted to the aim of the project, the students, who had at this time not studied abroad, were quick to support the idea. When asked why, interestingly, they indicated a preexisting apprehension about their linguistic fitness for nonacademic matters. Already my learning process had begun.

The other members of the data-gathering team were drawn from a mix of ESL teachers and exchange students at the same institute, with a fairly even balance of North American and British participants. They, too, showed more enthusiasm than I had at first expected, the teachers in particular warming to the subject of language as it really is used, some spontaneously volunteering areas of inquiry that they thought particularly relevant. Here was another aspect of my own learning process, for some of those teachers I had—to my shame—never suspected of nurturing the linguistic curiosity they were showing. Action research was already teaching me things about my students and my colleagues before the linguistic inquiry had even started.

With regard to terminology, I shall henceforth refer to the first group of informants as French speakers of English, and the latter as Anglo speakers of English. I do so partly in order to avoid any discussion here of the concept *native speaker* and also to particularize my findings.

Raising Awareness

As I indicated earlier, I selected the speech act of requesting for closer study for the perhaps mildly selfish reason that I, myself, had sometimes found it awkward to negotiate in my own second language, French. If I found it occasionally troublesome, there might be grounds for suspecting my students would find something similar in English. My suspicions as to the trickiness of some English requesting approaches were confirmed in the days following this decision. With my thoughts more closely focused on requests than previously, I had begun consciously to note requests that Anglophone colleagues and friends made in my presence.

One colleague had stuck her head round my office door, saying, "I don't suppose you would have any change for the machine?" Installing himself in an armchair, a friend who had come for a meal said, "I wonder if I can bother you for an ashtray?" These, although not using the requesting exponents previously referred to, followed a strategy familiar to ESL teachers and would form part of any enriched "requesting" program.

But what of the colleague who, approaching a closed door with both hands full, wailed, "Do you have a hand, Chris?" Or another friend who, eyeing my coffee percolator, volunteered in his Scottish accent, "I could murder a cup of that coffee."

True, these latter two requests (a questioning of a felicity condition [Searle, 1969] and an off-record hint) conform with the "lack of fit between form and function" to which Nunan (1988) calls attention:

FUNCTION	FORM
Request	May I have a drink, please?
	Thirsty weather, this.
	Looks like an interesting wine.
	I'm dying for a drink.
	Is that a bottle of champagne? (p. 31)

But, although familiar in approach to ESL teachers, the surface structures of my own latter two examples are sufficiently strange to merit some pause for reflection. They are indeed items of empirically sourced data, but they are so idiosyncratic in their realizations that their utility in a repair program might be a matter of some doubt.

Nevertheless, a fairly general pattern of indirectness was already being mapped out in my preinquiry note-taking. Why this preoccupation with indirectness? Why do native speakers tend to couch requests in rather roundabout ways, sometimes with, sometimes without requesting exponents? Leech (1983) has an answer:

> Indirect illocutions tend to be more polite (a) because they increase the degree of optionality (for the hearer) and (b) because the more indirect an illocution is, the more diminished and tentative its force tends to be. (p. 108)

But other questions were now beginning to pile up. To what extent would French speakers resort to the conventionalized *Can I . . . ?, Could you . . . ?* forms? To what extent would they share the Anglos' alertness to this generally indirect approach discussed above? If alerted, to what extent would they be familiar with the various approaches that might make up a speech act set for requesting? Would we see examples of cross-cultural breakdown? And turning to the Anglos, would their realizations provide a rich mine of pedagogically useful data, or would the famous, or perhaps infamous, linguistic richness of English prove rather a minefield of linguistic idiosyncracy, offering at times a barrier to communication?

If I had originally had any doubts about the need for an action research inquiry to look into these areas that, after all, come close to the heart of many important sociolinguistic and sociocultural issues, they were now rapidly disappearing. I moved on with increasing motivation.

Checking the Literature

Before getting started on the inquiry itself, I needed to inform myself further on the speech act of the request. Searle (1969), following the pioneering work of J. L. Austin, lists the request under *directives* in his typology of speech acts. It is glossed by Levinson (1983) as "an attempt to get Hearer to do something" (p. 240). The word *directive* frequently surprises, so accustomed are we to hearing polite requests realized in question forms, such as these further examples collected during my preparatory careful listening phase:

> Could you open the window, Hubertus?
>
> Would you like to sit down?
>
> Will you just reach over and switch that off?
>
> You wouldn't have any change, would you?
>
> Any chance of a lift?
>
> How about a drink for an old pal, then?
>
> I hate to bother you, but could I have another?

Leech, as we have already heard, offers a convincing explanation for much of this strategy. By offering the hearer an out, we reduce the risk of our request sounding like something much more brusque, a plain unvarnished directive.

In their studies of the pragmatics of politeness, Brown and Levinson (1978, 1987) explore this area further by developing Goffman's idea of *face*. Brown and Levinson attribute two aspects to face: positive and negative. Positive face concerns itself with the individual as someone of worth, deserving of approval. Negative face relates to the individual's right to act as a free agent, unhindered by others. Mutual self-interest in conversation requires both participants to respect and have respected these dual aspects of face.

Our area of interest—the request—immediately poses a threat to the hearer's negative face. By asking something of our addressee, we are presenting a potential threat to that person's freedom of action. There are several ways to defuse this potential threat, as the examples, above and below, show.

One way is to sound pessimistic about the outcome, thus giving the hearer an out (and the speaker, too, because it sounds as if nothing was expected in the first place): *You wouldn't have such a thing as a lighter?* Another way is to hedge the request in some manner by questioning the chances of something happening: *I wonder if there's any chance of seeing you tomorrow?* Another still is to question the capacity or willingness of the hearer to do something: *Could you pour me a drink? Would you like to pass that hammer?* (This latter approach is one favored by course books, as we have already noticed.)

We have spent some time on this subject because so many requesting techniques flow from various politeness strategies based on the concept of preserving negative face. All those versions that question the capacity or willingness of the hearer to do something, or appear pessimistic about a positive outcome, or hedge the request in some way—or sometimes a combination of all three—derive from this principle. What unites them all is the desire to cultivate a respectful distance and to avoid any suggestion of encroachment on the hearer's negative face.

Other politeness strategies attempt to neutralize threats to the speaker's positive face posed by a possible refusal. Here, utterances are typically prefaced with apologies, inviting the hearer to bolster the speaker's positive face: *Excuse me, but can you tell me where they live? I'm sorry to bother you, but is this yours?*

More informally, they may emphasize the idea of camaraderie and in-group spirit via intimate ways of address: *How about a drink for an old pal, then?*

As we have seen, indirect requesting techniques using negative and politeness strategies offer vast choices that can be bewildering to the second language learner. Although Brown and Levinson (1989) point out that "strategies for making indirect speech acts appear to be universal" (p. 36), Schmidt and Richards's (1980) comment is equally valid and perhaps more immediately relevant: "Even if speech act strategies are to a certain extent universal, learners of a new language still need to learn the particular conventionalized forms in the new language" (p. 140).

So, to what extent would my learners know the conventionalized forms of requesting? Which of the negative and politeness strategies, if any, would French speakers of English use? Which would be used by Anglos? Would any other strategies appear? The time had come to start getting some answers. But, first, the implementation details of the inquiry itself had to be devised.

Categorizing Requests

My focus was sharpening: I had already established the speech act for investigation, who were to constitute the participants, the broad approach to a format (a comparison), and some of the potential strategies I might encounter. What was still lacking was the detail of the inquiry itself.

First, to whom were these requests to be addressed? In an attempt to probe second language participants' awareness of a range of norm-appropriate forms of request, the targeted audience was split into three groups:

1. figures familiar to the speaker (three examples)

2. figures quasifamiliar to the speaker (three examples)

3. strangers/authority figures (three examples)

The selection of these figures appeared to offer speakers a variety of possible approaches, paralleling a range of encounters fairly typical of daily life. The interest was in ascertaining if—and how—requesting strategies might differ in the three areas.

But what of the requests themselves? And in what contexts? A worthwhile point of departure seemed the many minor requests that occur in daily life: asking for change, help with a door; asking for a glass of wine, a lift home. Brief scenarios were created around the following requests: (a) a request for minor assistance (three versions); (b) a request for a minor item (three versions); (c) a request for minor action in a potentially sensitive situation (three versions).

The first request area (a) was prompted simply by its frequency and utility in daily life. The second area (b) was suggested by the examples cited by Nunan (1988). The third area (c) was the subject of a study by Cohen and Olshtain (1993), who found that this kind of request could involve second language learners in some difficulties.

Gathering Data

Empirical evidence was my target, but how to collect it? On reflection, I realized that certain speech acts in naturally occurring contexts are problematic and time-consuming to set up. Requesting falls under this heading. Sending out 30 participants to record themselves making requests in English to a variety of people in certain specific contexts seemed rather impracticable, doubly so in a largely Francophone environment.

Eavesdropping on a variety of naturally occurring requests in real-life contexts (e.g., cafés, train stations, shops) would be enormously time-consuming even in an Anglophone world—and in a Francophone one, well-nigh impossible.

Discourse completion tasks allow the rapid collection of data in context-specific situations without undue difficulty, but as I discovered in a previous inquiry (Nicol, 1998), the fixed nature of one side of the exchange is not really conducive to spontaneity on the other.

What seemed to be needed was a readily realizable method with a speaker approach that approximated the spontaneity of a real encounter. In an attempt to produce this, I drew up the requesting scenarios in the Appendix.

Re-creative Engagement

The nine brief scenarios in the request-induction document are based on the three types of figures and three situations already mentioned. Participants were invited to record what they might say in these contexts. The word *request* was avoided throughout the document in an attempt to forestall—or at least minimize—any Pavlovian instincts on the part of the participants to reach for routine requesting exponents at the word's mention, which might well have reduced the opportunities for other strategies and surface structures to come into play.

Rather than leave the participants in the rather dead environment of an office with only an audiotape recorder for company, the following procedure was adopted:

- I invited the participant to study one scenario at a time and to indicate any difficulties with regard to meaning.

- I then attempted to bring each scenario to life, using voice and actions to re-create the scene as far as possible. For example, in Scenario 2 the approach was: "So here we are. It's 7:45 in the morning. We're alone in the building. Just you and I. You're dying for a coffee since you haven't had any breakfast. You've only got a 50 franc note and the machine only takes coins. Along I come. Now you know who I am but you don't really know me. But thinking of that coffee, you stop me, smile and say: . . ."

- The utterance was immediately recorded.

Now, although seeking in no way to minimize the element of contrivance here, I felt that this technique of re-creative engagement produced a request that was the result of a genuine face-to-face encounter, with participants required to record their request at the point they would have been obliged to make the request in a real-world situation.

I avoid calling this role play because it usually demands that both participants enter fully into the scenario. Here, one participant re-created the scenario by animating it, and the other produced a request from its periphery, as it were. Role play per se was avoided because it is a procedure with which I have had only mediocre results with French students, who seem somewhat self-conscious in this context. The relative ease and readiness with which the speech act was here performed suggested that the re-creative engagement had gone some way to eliminate this obstacle.

How effective this technique was can perhaps best be judged by the requests discussed later in this study. Personally, I felt that this face-to-face encounter produced in Anglos and French speakers alike something very close to a spontaneous response, with some participants in Scenario 2 adding the name of a new member of staff, as if directly addressing that person.

Researchers reluctant or unable to bring their own personalities into the inquiry would, of course, find difficulty with this technique. And, indeed, for some longer, reactive speech acts like rejections and refusals, turn taking would enrich the procedure and help assure context-sensitivity, a key element in obtaining varied levels of empirically sourced data.

Analyzing the Findings

The action research project was a modest one, but when the findings began to come in for transcription, their interpretation gave rise to one of the major challenges of the investigation. Thirty participants with nine requests each produce 270 items for analysis, no light undertaking for the research novice. Once into the analysis, however, the sheer fascination of the variety of requests put aside all doubts I may have had as to the worthwhile nature of the project.

Three points stood out. The French speakers used significantly fewer words than the Anglo speakers. But more important than the length of utterance was the quality of their requests. Their general abruptness set them apart from those of the Anglos (and abruptness is not a characteristic of speech best calculated to get speakers what they want when requesting). The absence of many of the Anglos' multiple strategies (see below) among the French speakers' requests was the third striking feature of the findings. Indeed, it is the inclusion of these strategies that largely accounts for the extra length and less abrupt nature of the Anglo requests.

A few examples give an idea of the differences:

French Speakers of English

> Please, can you open the door?
>
> Excuse me, could you lend me your map?
>
> Could you give me a glass of wine, please?
>
> Excuse me, could you please drive me home?
>
> Please can you give me the book?
>
> Could you not park in my place, please?

Anglo Speakers of English

> You wouldn't like to give that door a kick, would you?
>
> Would you mind if I had a quick look at your map?
>
> Now there's a welcome sight! (eye on wine bottle)
>
> Would it be bothering you too much to ask if you could maybe give me a lift home?
>
> I hate to trouble you, but do you think I could have my book back?
>
> I don't know if you realize, but you've been parking in my parking space.

Now, our French speakers are not lacking in an awareness of the need to be polite, as all those *excuse me*s and *please*s bear witness. But as well as a fairly general unawareness—or failure to use—the full range of negative politeness strategies, there is a widespread lack of encoding for context specificity. That is to say, they did not seem to differentiate between familiars and nonfamiliars, or the relative weights of the imposition involved. There was a fairly general undifferentiated politeness on offer here that paid little heed to context. The French speakers were perhaps at their weakest in dealing with familiars, often treating peers as nonpeers, and to do so, as Ervin-Tripp (1976) reminds us, is to be "cold and distancing" (p. 63). Even their generous use of *please* and *excuse me* with strangers and authority figures did not always strike quite the right emollient note to achieve their desired end.

So, the first of the questions I had asked myself at the beginning of this action research project had been answered: My French learners did not use the strategies employed by Anglos here, and they were often at a distinct sociolinguistic and sociocultural disadvantage when attempting to produce requests.

But what was it that Anglos actually did when requesting? Could analyzing their requests help my learners? What emerges even at a casual reading of this study's findings is that approaches to requesting (discussed far less in course books than their tactical exponents) are multiple in number, various in strategy, and far richer in exponents than even Anglos probably consciously realize. Moreover, most of the data recorded by the Anglos did provide a rich bank of highly useful, idiomatic expressions and recurring strategies that could easily be integrated into a repair program.

For the purpose of assisting French speakers of English toward Anglo-type appropriateness, the following elements of a speech act set for requesting emerged:

- Off-record hints/explanations. Used extensively in all three familiar scenarios by Anglos: "Now there's a welcome sight!" (eye on wine bottle). Also useful in requesting in delicate situations: "I'm sorry about this, but you're parking in my space."

- Pessimism/hedging. Present in five Anglo scenarios and in none by French speakers. Least popular in potentially sensitive situations. Most common where the risk of refusal was slight: "You don't have the time, by any chance?"

- Imposition minimization. When imposition was inevitable, Anglos sought to reduce it, a strategy often detectable in the lexis. In borrowing a map, they wanted to "have a (quick) look/look for a moment/take a look/glance at . . . ." No Anglo *borrowed*.

- Imposition orientation. Paralleling the need to minimize the imposition is the desirability of steering it away from hearer. Fourteen out of 15 Anglos in requesting a map began with "Could I . . . ?" Not one of them started with "Could you . . . ?"

French speakers' alertness to using the above elements was embryonic. There was no pessimism and no hints at all and only 7 instances of hedging in 135 requests. Absent, too, was sensitivity to imposition minimization and orientation. All too present, however, was an overreliance on modal-based requesting exponents untuned often to context- and addressee-specificity.

Could there also be problems involved with richly idiomatic Anglo responses? On balance, it seemed that much of the data could be used most profitably in a repair program, but there were exceptions. Two participants produced

I could murder a glass of wine. (a participant previously cited who was clearly fond of this particular variant)

I couldn't half go a glass of that stuff.

Whereas another volunteered

Whew, this heat's done me in. I'm parched.

Here, as a practicing ESOL teacher, I felt that idiomatic richness may have its limits. The obfuscatory nature of the lexis here certainly created an in-group spirit of camaraderie, but in-groups presuppose the existence of out-groups, and language teachers should perhaps be more concerned with breaking down communication barriers than with erecting them. We recognize here, perhaps, a distinction between language that one might wish to make available for recognition purposes and language that one might wish to teach for active use.

◈ OUTCOMES

Given the multiple demands on the time and energy of ESOL teachers, can an investigation of this kind be justified? In my opinion, the answer is an unqualified yes. It has given me lots to think about with regard to my classroom approach.

For a start, the wealth of information revealed about the rich complexity of Anglo approaches to requests can be used to underpin any future action with real authority. Teachers using the results can be certain that the weaknesses they are attempting to repair actually do exist and that the surface structures and surrounding strategies suggested actually do feature in real-life language and not just in the heads of course book writers and teachers.

At a practical level, the data bank provided by the Anglos, as well as being empirically validated, was substantial in quantity, offering the raw material for many repair lessons.

There was also confirmation that an element of caution has to be exercised in the Anglo realizations used. Whereas native speaker richness of expression is to be prized, it should not be at the price of nonnative speaker bewilderment. The global explosion of interchanges in English in which no native speaker is present should caution us against an English that does not travel well across Anglo national borders—wherever these borders may happen to be.

There were unlooked-for outcomes, too. Until this action research project, I had never found for myself a data collection method that really seemed to serve my needs. Re-creative engagement turned out to give me the spontaneity that had eluded earlier attempts and will now form part of my research methodology.

Furthermore, in approaching colleagues for their ideas on what to put in the request document itself, I discovered I was tapping into some interesting questions that they had often posed themselves about requesting—not simply with regard to odd turns of phrase they had noted in native speakers, but about some of the semantic structures offered by course books. The strengthening of professional and personal links with some colleagues I barely knew was considerable.

As for the difficulties of my students themselves, they were thrown into sharp relief. Although they regularly managed to communicate their request intentions, they often did so without an acceptable appropriateness of language. The request, imposing as it does on the hearer's negative face, is a particularly sensitive speech act. Success depends not only on the hearer's ability to respond favorably but also on their willingness to do so. Hence the importance of politeness strategies and semantic realizations that encode the estimated threat to face and the appropriate redress.

Next Steps

As I contemplate the devising of a repair program, I see the need to sensitize students to the ways in which the nature of the social relationship and the imposition involved colors the final selection of language form. At the same time, this work highlights the dangers of relying too heavily on modal-based exponents.

I foresee consciousness-raising activities grouped into three types as a way of starting the sensitization process:

1. Diagnostic assessment: I edit recordings to give a combination of six French and six Anglo requests in certain scenarios and invite groups to award acceptability ratings, commenting on what they feel are strengths and weaknesses.

2. Contextual analysis: I first tape longer exchanges between Anglos that are to be halted before the actual item or assistance required is articulated,

and students presented with multiple-choice answers to (a) the item or aid required and (b) the social distance between speaker and hearer. For example:

I'm really sorry to bother you like this, but would it be inconvenient if I asked you . . .

(a) the time?

(b) for a glass of wine?

(c) to give me a lift home?

Is speaker talking to a familiar person or an authority figure?

List the points that tell you this.

I then record two Anglos in a brief social situation ending in a request and invite students in groups to suggest the relationship between speakers.

3. Creating requests: Using television soap opera clips long enough for the establishment of social relationships between interlocutors, I stop the clip and invite groups to formulate any request that one character might suddenly make of another, respecting both the apparent relationship between them and the scale of the imposition. Then, provided with highly specific request scenarios in which the relationships between interlocutors are firmly established, students are invited in groups to record at least four different ways to approach the request.

❧ REFLECTIONS

At a linguistic level, I now know a lot more about the making of appropriate requests, in which social distance and imposition-weight demand as much attention as any semantic surface structure. I also have a greatly heightened awareness of the dangers of viewing any speech act as a discrete item, rather than as an integrated component of an ongoing conversation or social event. Failure to appreciate this is to misunderstand seriously the place of speech acts in the larger conversational framework.

As an action researcher, I feel validated in my efforts not only by this increase in knowledge and awareness, but also by the development of the re-creative engagement technique, which I regard as a useful investigative instrument in its own right. My own sense of professional empowerment is thereby enhanced.

As a developing ESOL professional, I am preparing myself to take the next, more directly pedagogic, steps in the cycle I have here in part described. I also see in this a chance to strengthen the unexpected collegial links to which I referred earlier. In this sense, I feel myself engaged in increasing the quality of action available to my students, my colleagues and myself in our own educational environment.

❧ CONTRIBUTOR

Before moving to France, where he teaches English for academic purposes at the Euro American Institute of Technology, Sophia Antipolis, Christopher Nicol taught

English at Cheltenham Ladies' College, in England. He has published a study on the playwright Willy Russell and is currently working toward a PhD on the teaching of academic writing.

◈ APPENDIX

Life's Little Problems

Imagine yourself into the following scenarios. Try not to reflect unduly before recording the response that seems to you to be the most natural in the circumstances.

1. You are carrying a cassette player in one hand and a heavy bag in the other. As you approach a closed door, a colleague, whom you know well, joins you. Looking at the door, you say:

2. You arrive early at work before people are about. You would like a cup of coffee but you have no change for the machine. A colleague, whom you know only slightly, arrives. You say:

3. You are leaving work. Your car will not start. You see the Director getting into his car. You know he lives near you. There is no other car left in the car park. You say:

4. You drop into a neighbor's kitchen after delivering home their children. On the table is a well-chilled (open) bottle of wine. They are talking to the children and do not notice that you do not have a glass of wine. It is hot. You are thirsty. You say:

5. You are working in your garden. You have left your watch inside and need to know the time. Your next-door neighbor, who has only just moved in, goes past. You say:

6. You are sitting on a train going to Marseilles. You do not know the town or where to find a certain small street. Opposite you is a woman who has a map of Marseilles on the table in front of her. She is not using it. You say:

7. The girl with whom you share an apartment has woken you up at 2 a.m. several times recently by playing loud music. She is doing it again. You get up, go to her door and say:

8. For the third time this week, a new colleague has occupied the parking-space reserved for you. You would like this to stop, so you go to his office and say:

9. On the first day of your new course, your English teacher, whom you have only just met, borrows your text. He leaves the lesson, forgetting to give you back your text. You follow him to his office and say:

CHAPTER 10

Mind the Gap!
Noticing in Real Time

Karen Adams

◈ INTRODUCTION

Every year, many thousands of learners of English come to Britain to improve their language skills. The commonly held view among these learners is that, by being exposed to language in a target language environment, their level of English will improve dramatically. However, many learners in language teaching institutions express disappointment with their rate of progress, particularly in understanding and using English outside the classroom. The aims of the research project reported in this chapter were to investigate why, with the amount of exposure to English that these learners receive outside the classroom, uptake appears to be limited and to suggest possible methodological frameworks that might encourage more effective links between learning strategies used within the classroom and those used outside.

◈ SITUATION

Imagine the ideal situation for learning and teaching English. For many learners and teachers, I am sure that this would involve small groups of motivated adult learners, most of whom have set aside a period of time (perhaps 1 or 2 months) for intensive study to improve their language skills. They are studying in London, where they have access to a wide range of language-based cultural events and activities, in a group where the only common language is English. After 3–5 hours of lessons each day, they meet with other members of their group, none of whom share their first language and, after visiting a museum or watching a film, they have dinner in a restaurant and then go home to their English-speaking host family. Homework, which might involve them in reading that day's newspaper or interviewing their host, is followed by a television program; then the go to bed, ready for the next day's language lesson.

At first glance, a program of study that allows almost constant exposure to the target language, combined with a need to communicate in that language, might seem to provide all the necessary elements for successful language learning to take place. However, during 10 years of teaching in a situation similar to the one described, it has become increasingly apparent to me that exposure to language does not guarantee success in learning that language. Throughout this time, many students have complained that, although they understand everything in the classroom, they continue to have difficulty in understanding and communicating effectively outside the classroom.

A solution to this problem seemed to be offered in recent methodological developments in the area of task-based learning based on a lexical approach to language (e.g., Lewis, 1997; Willis, 1996). Combining a focus on real-life tasks with the use of materials that reflect a more authentic use of language, these developments have been seen as providing a more effective bridge between the classroom and real world language exposure. Activities are designed to enable learners to notice salient features of authentic language use rather than have isolated structures or vocabulary items presented to them. It is argued that this approach to language will allow learners to access the language they hear outside the classroom more effectively.

One key feature of this development in methodology is the emphasis placed on learners working on extended pieces of text to identify features that they find interesting or for which they have some need. For classroom practitioners, the difficulty has been in adapting existing methodological frameworks to facilitate this approach to language focus activities.

Perhaps the most accessible framework to date has been that suggested by Willis (1996), in which students perform a cycle of tasks and then hear or read a similar task as performed by proficient users of English. Learners follow up this listening or reading stage with analysis of the text to isolate lexical features that might have made their own performance of the task more effective. Willis's task-based framework requires teachers to select texts that reflect authentic language use and to direct students to process those texts, first for content and then, in what she calls *noticing activities,* for language use.

It is interesting to note, however, that although this framework encourages teachers to increase learners' exposure to authentic language in the classroom, the listening and reading procedures are very linear. This more traditional approach to receptive skills work stresses the need for learners to move in stages from general understanding to more detailed analysis of language. A second important feature of these procedures is that, in the analysis stage, learners are often asked to analyze a transcript of the text they have heard. In effect, therefore, noticing activities are very often reading activities.

As a teacher working in London, where learners are constantly exposed to spoken language outside the classroom, I began to question the effectiveness of reading-based classroom activities in enabling learners to process and learn from that exposure. In an effort to promote noticing outside the classroom, I adopted van Lier's suggestion of an "entry ticket" system (1996, p. 44), which required each student to bring to class a new word or phrase they had learned by listening to someone outside the classroom. This system met with limited success, with some students choosing words from a textbook or bringing phrases that were incomplete or half-understood. The focus of the research described below was, therefore, to find a way to enable my students to benefit more effectively from the language they heard outside the classroom. As an initial investigation, it was necessarily evolutionary, responding in stages to students' needs as they became apparent.

◈ FOCUS

The impetus for the research project stemmed initially from frustration. In autumn 1998, I was working with a group of early intermediate learners, many of whom arrived late to class due to problems on London's notoriously problematic underground transport system (known as *the Tube*). When questioned as to why they were late, it became clear that none of the students could understand the reasons for the delays despite the fact that problems are announced repeatedly over an intercom system and displayed on digital sign boards. These announcements and displays are repeated at regular, short intervals using a very restricted pool of language items; therefore the amount of exposure to the language was not an issue. However, many of the students commented that they did not listen to the announcements because they knew they could not understand them. This was a clear demonstration of a process that I recognized from my own experiences as a language learner, that of the learners excluding themselves from interacting with the language data around them because they assume that they will not understand.

This is particularly interesting when one considers language data in terms of lexis and grammatical structure. An announcement such as *Trains are delayed due to signal problems* should not prove particularly difficult for a learner at an intermediate level. If we view language data as input, we might expect the learner in question to understand with few problems. However, when the learner assumes that this piece of language data is not accessible, she or he opts out of the process of comprehending.

Successful interaction with language data, therefore, depends on two distinct elements. First, the learner must be open to accepting new data and, secondly, the data themselves must be perceived to be accessible. Van Lier's (1996) view of exposure to language in terms of its *affordance,* that is, that which can be usefully accessed by the learner, found practical expression in my students' unwillingness to engage with the language of the platform announcements. In turn, it was this unwillingness to engage with exposure to language outside the classroom that caused me to examine the relationship between the ways in which students are expected to process language in class and the processing of language in real time. Three issues appear particularly salient.

Safety Versus Access

It is usual in classroom listening tasks to prepare students to listen. Much time is often devoted to clarifying items of vocabulary, to discussing the topic before the listening text is introduced, and to replaying the text should it prove difficult. All of these procedures are designed to make listening easier for the students. However, in playing safe in the classroom, we often forget to focus on the strategies needed to enable learners to access the spontaneous and unpredictable. Students' comments indicate that an important factor in being able to process the language that they hear around them is the knowledge that they can in fact access it. In the case of the underground announcements, it was clear that the students did not listen because they felt they could not listen. They therefore ruled out any possibility of engagement with the language before the announcements began.

Choice Versus No Choice

Outside the classroom, it is reasonable to assume that a learner's engagement with the language data that surround them will be defined not only by what they feel confident about accessing but also with what they perceive to be interesting or useful. In class, however, much noticing is done through teacher-selected texts and tasks, with decisions of what is and is not useful also made by the teacher. As a result, little time is spent helping the student develop strategies to enable them to identify and select useful language from the text they hear.

Interpreting and Decoding

As mentioned above, classroom approaches to the processing of listening texts usually follow a linear path through interpretation of content to the decoding of linguistic form. However, when processing language in real time, the listener needs to understand the interaction of meaning and form on a single listening. For learners, this is not an easy task, and, on many occasions, they achieve only one part of the process.

It is possible, for example, to understand vaguely the meaning of what has been said without being able to identify the words used in the message. The inverse is also true. One entry ticket brought by an elementary student to class bore the words "Mind the Gap!" a phrase often heard on the underground to warn passengers of the space between the train and the platform. All of the students in the class recognized and could repeat the phrase, yet none knew what it meant. It would appear, therefore, that in order to help learners maximize the value of their engagement with language outside the class, consideration needs to be given to how classroom activities might focus on strategies that enable students to use their knowledge of form to understand the message and vice versa.

Having considered the difficulties that my group of students were facing, it became clear that it was not exposure to language that was lacking, but rather strategies for accessing and engaging with it. Furthermore, although classroom-based activities often required them to analyze a piece of language data, it was not clear that they were fully aware of the need to transfer these learning strategies to the language that they heard outside the classroom. The aim of the research study, then, was to explore ways of accessing language outside the classroom and to promote an awareness of strategies that might facilitate independent learning through listening. The following section is a description of the processes that we adopted.

I have since worked in this way with other groups, but I restrict myself here to an account of the early intermediate learners already mentioned. My intention is not to produce generalizations, but to show how this specific research experience has led to outcomes that have, in turn, triggered continuing exploration.

◈ RESPONSE

The first stage of the investigation was held with the early intermediate class over a period of 3.5 weeks (17 days of teaching). The group of students was made up of eight young adults from South Korea, Japan, Italy, Switzerland, and Brazil. Of the eight, three hoped to go to university in Britain, and one wanted to stay in London to work as a designer. All but one had been in studying in London for a period of between 4 and 8 weeks prior to this study beginning.

Step 1: Tube Language

Our specific purpose was for the students to understand the information given in underground announcements. If the students were to feel that they could access language data in a real-world environment, it was necessary to consider how I might put to positive use some of the element of safety that is often present in listening activities in the classroom. The most obvious way to do this was by providing the vital lexis that would provide a key into the language that they heard, and this, in turn, meant considering how to restrict the field of data in order to ensure that the key of vital lexis was appropriate. So, we began by focusing on collocations that are used frequently to describe the causes of delay. The first classroom activity required the students to attempt to match collocants:

signal	failure
earlier	delays
security	alert
defective	train
broken	rail
passenger	action

Once the meaning of each phrase had been clarified, this "Tube Problems" language was displayed on the wall. With this key of collocations, a listening task was then set. As a group, we agreed that, if a student arrived late due to a Tube problem, he or she would have to let the class know the cause of the problem. By setting a clear but restricted task, the students had a framework for selecting information from the data around them. In effect, by narrowing the field of listening and providing a framework for repeated listening, a classroom task was set in a real world environment.

The result of this approach was very encouraging. By the end of the first week, the majority of the students in the class could identify the reason for their delay either by saying the phrase (e.g., "It was a broken rail") or, for the less confident, pointing to the phrase on the wall. When the more confident students began discussing the problems that they had had on their journeys home after class the previous day, I realized that their confidence in accessing this language pool was definitely growing. This development in the students' ability to begin to key into a hitherto inaccessible source of language seemed to indicate that, by adjusting classroom procedures to link overtly with out-of-class language processing, it might be possible to encourage the students to view the exposure they received to language outside the classroom in terms of the language learning opportunities it provided.

Step 2: Promoting Noticing

The next step was to encourage the students to become more independent within a restricted range of language exposure. My initial experiment with entry tickets had highlighted the potential problems of setting relatively unstructured noticing tasks as homework. The field of noticing was restricted, therefore, to "phrases or words you see or hear in the Tube." This framework allowed the students to work with written as well as spoken language. The aim of the task was to discover if the participants in the task could both decode the form and interpret the meaning of what they heard or read. In feedback to this task, the first phrase contributed by a student was "SEEK ASSISTANCE," a phrase that appears on ticket barriers when a faulty or expired ticket is put in.

Giorgio, who suggested this phrase, did not understand the meaning, although all members of the group recognized the form. This ability to decode and remember the form of the language, while not understanding the message, highlighted the need to raise the students' awareness of the type of discovery strategies that are often used as part of a guided approach to learning. Giorgio's failure to work out the meaning of the phrase suggested that, although he might be used to answering a teacher's focused questions aimed at leading the learner to meaning, he was not aware of the need to pose those questions for himself.

Therefore, it became necessary to work with the students to establish a number of interpretation questions that would enable them to discover the meaning of the language they had heard or seen. As the students were accustomed to classroom activities that required them to guess the meaning of items in written text from context, we began by discussing how they worked out meaning. We agreed that the most important elements were an awareness of the general context of the text and the ideas or information that immediately preceded and followed the unknown item. To enable the students to apply this approach to what they heard, I provided the following five questions:

1. Where did you see (hear) this phrase?

2. Who said it to whom? (for spoken language). Did these people know each other?

3. What happened before it was said (or shown)?

4. What happened as a result of it having been said?

5. What do you think the phrase means?

Working through these questions, Giorgio was able to find that "SEEK ASSISTANCE" on a Tube barrier means "ask a ticket collector for help." After we had used these questions to analyze "SEEK ASSISTANCE," we discussed why the questions had helped. By stating overtly the purpose of these guiding questions, the students were able to recognize their use as a tool for discovery of meaning. The students then copied these questions into their notebooks with a reminder to use the questions as an aid to understanding.

By guiding the students to create their own hypotheses about the language they had heard, I intended to highlight a framework that they could use for their own noticing. This approach of heightening cognitive awareness of learning strategies that facilitate comprehension—a process that van Lier (1996) terms *language learning awareness*—underpinned the next stage of the project, which was to enable the students to extend beyond the restricted field of Tube language to noticing any language items that they found interesting and introducing them to the group.

Step 3: Door Poster

To highlight the importance of accessing language outside the classroom, a variation on the entry ticket system was incorporated into the work of the class during the last 10 days of the course. An area in the classroom was set aside to display contributions that students brought to class. This consisted of a large poster that covered the back of the door bearing the title, "I've noticed that people in Britain say. . . ."

Unlike in the entry ticket approach, the students were not required to bring a new word to class each day. However, time was allocated on 3 days each week for discussion of words or phrases that members of the group had picked up. During these discussions, each contributor gave a phrase or word, and then explained what they assumed it meant. In order to heighten the students' awareness of the need to make decisions about the importance to them of the language they heard, we then decided as a group what items might be most useful for everyone. The most popular items were chosen for display on the door poster.

During this door poster phase of the project, I became aware of three important issues. First, the range of items that students introduced varied markedly. Some chose, initially, to work with language that they heard in conversations in their hosts' homes. As a result, the range of items brought to class often reflected the type of family structure in which they were living. Those living with families with children brought to class examples of things parents said when annoyed with their children ("What a mess!"), while one student who was living with an elderly couple contributed idioms such as "I'm tickled pink," a fairly archaic expression of delight. The discussions that followed their introduction to the class often allowed for exploration of issues relating to the appropriateness of use of such items. It was important for the students to realize that because it was they who had heard the word or phrase and they who knew the context, they could interpret meaning to a level beyond that of simple definition.

Second, there was a marked increase in the students' confidence in their ability to understand. Initially, only the more confident students contributed to the door poster activity, but by the third lesson, I found that some of the less confident students had begun to bring in lists of items they had heard. This was particularly true of Tomoko, a Japanese student who had complained at the beginning of the class that understanding what she heard, even in classroom listening tasks, was difficult. This increase in the amount of language that was being noticed seemed to indicate a growing willingness to interact with language outside the classroom.

Third, the language items that the students chose to put on the door poster were not always predictable. I had assumed that they would choose items that they themselves could use at a later date. However, looking at the list (see Figure 1), it is clear that some were chosen for their recognition value (e.g., "Let the passengers off the train first please" is a regular announcement on very crowded Tube trains) and some simply because they made the students laugh (hence the inclusion of "I'm tickled pink"). I felt that this last point was particularly interesting as very often the language preselected by teachers for inclusion in classroom teaching, particularly at lower levels, is chosen on a strictly utilitarian basis, forgetting that we often retain information simply because it is funny.

As my time with this class drew to an end, at the close of a 4-week program, I realized that the students had consciously picked up a range of idiomatic language

SEEK ASSISTANCE

It's a deal!

What a mess!

I'm going bananas!

PENALTY FARE

I'm tickled pink.

I wish!

Let the passengers off the train first please.

I'm just popping out.

I need an early night.

Would it be OK if I come in?

FIGURE 1. Poster 1

that I had never, in 15 years of teaching, introduced into class. I also realized that the way in which the students and I worked with their contributions in class had evolved into what might be a transferable methodological pattern.

Throughout the period of the study, individuals had brought to the class some items that were either incomplete in terms of form or that they had not wholly understood. Initially, in both cases, I would write the (incomplete) phrase on the whiteboard and, for items that had not been wholly understood, ask the series of guiding questions mentioned above. By the final week of the study, these questions were being asked by the other students in the group, who had come to realize that the questions played a strategic role in enabling them to understand the language item.

Items that were incomplete or incorrect in terms of form proved to be more problematic with this group of students, however. In some cases, writing the phrase that the student provided on the board (e.g., *I____ just popping out.*) and highlighting some aspect of the grammatical form (in this case the present participle) would enable them to complete the idiom by using their knowledge of structure. However, being at early intermediate level meant that their knowledge of grammar was relatively limited and, as a result, their ability to analyze the form of what they had heard was restricted. A subsequent study with more advanced learners (not reported on here for lack of space) demonstrated that the usefulness of this approach does increase, as teachers might expect, when used with higher level students.

◈ OUTCOMES

The initial aims of the investigation were to examine possible reasons for the apparent limitations on the use that students could make of the exposure to language that they received outside the classroom, and the possibility of devising classroom procedures that could facilitate more effective understanding and noticing of the language around them. From initial conversations with the students, it was clear that the accessibility of the language was a key issue, and the first steps in the project were aimed at empowering the students to view the exposure they had to language in terms of its affordances.

As the work progressed, I became more interested in the extent to which their interaction with language outside the classroom seemed to be affected by the evolving methodology inside the classroom. In particular, given that much of the language on the door posters was idiomatic, I wanted to find out if there were any particular patterns in the language that the group had noticed. I also wanted to discover the extent to which the students themselves felt that they had benefited noticeably from the study.

Outcome 1: Language

Closer inspection of the door poster proved to be very interesting. One aspect that was particularly noticeable was that, when other teachers read the poster, opinion was divided as to the level of the participants in the study.

(Items are arranged in chronological order, with the earliest contributions appearing at the top of the lists. Items in block capitals were highlighted in class as written language. Items in italics were highlighted as either archaic or highly idiomatic. This was particularly important for this lower level as a "don't use" warning.)

Two comments seem permissible.

1. The items became more grammatically complex as time went on, moving from simple subject-copula-adjective to a mixed conditional construction at the end. This seems to suggest that, as the process of noticing went on, some of the students became more confident at keying into more complex language.

2. The items noticed were often more complex than language that might be preselected for teaching at this level, either in terms of structure (*Would you mind if I come in?*) or on the level of idiom (*I'm just popping out.*). This appears to suggest that, by working on noticing outside the classroom, the learners can extend their range of language far beyond that which might normally be taught in the classroom. This range of language also provides the opportunity for classroom discussion of issues of style and register that might not be afforded by items preselected to be taught at lower levels.

Outcome 2: Feedback

I held informal feedback sessions with the students, asking for their final reactions to the tasks involved in the study. Five of the eight students in the group, including Giorgio and Tomoko, were mentioned above, recognized a distinct improvement in the amount of language that they could understand outside the classroom. They focused particularly on the importance of using the guiding questions I had introduced to work out the meaning of what they had heard. The remaining three, however, were disappointed because, according to Kazumi, one of the Japanese students, "I still can't understand everything." All of the students, however, reported that they now paid attention to Tube announcements.

From this informal feedback, I considered three main points.

1. All of the students involved in the study recognized that they could now access, to a greater or lesser degree, the language they heard in the Tube.

If we accept van Lier's description of language exposure in terms of its affordance, it is important to consider how the language that the students heard in the announcements moved from being inaccessible to being comprehensible. I would suggest that just as a climber needs to see a foothold in an apparently sheer mountain face in order to climb it, so the learner needs to see an entry point into the language in order to feel that this language can be understood. For the students in this study, that entry key appears to have been the list of collocations that they could hear repeated in the restricted language field of the underground announcements.

2. The language items that the students contributed in class moved relatively quickly from items heard in the Tube to items drawn from a wide variety of contexts. This was particularly noticeable when students began actively to seek out interesting phrases. Tomoko began to keep a notebook for her interesting phrases, most of which came from her conversations with her elderly hosts or from conversations overhead on bus journeys around London. This appeared to indicate not only a growing confidence in their listening and understanding, but a marked increase in these students' motivation to engage with the language around them. It is possible that, having found a path into the language around them with their entry key, the students recognized that they could go further.

3. Within the 4 weeks of the study, the majority of the students involved recognized an improvement in their ability to understand and retain language that they heard outside the classroom. Those who expressed dissatisfaction were those whose personal objectives were very ambitious, aiming for perfection rather than improvement. This suggested that the learners who benefited most were those who recognized value in clearly defined goals. In following a goal-oriented framework that progressed through a series of stages and that could be applied to the language heard outside the classroom, these students seemed to become better able to assess and to further their own learning progress.

Areas for Further Study

My initial interest in this area stemmed from a perception that many students seemed to be unable or unwilling to transfer the strategies for understanding and noticing language that I hoped they were developing in the classroom to language that they met outside the classroom. Following this study, I felt that two main areas for further study presented themselves.

Real-World Processing and Classroom Processing

Although recent developments in language teaching methodology have aimed to bridge the gap between the classroom and the real world through a focus on task achievement and authentic language, little attention has been given to how learners actually encounter that language in the real world and how they need to process that language to understand and learn from it.

Teaching Strategies and Learning Strategies

One key feature that evolved during this study was the employment of aspects of classroom methodology in the accessing of language outside the classroom. These aspects included

- the identification of key vocabulary in a restricted field of language to provide an access key to that linguistic field

- the development of a clear series of guiding questions, coupled with an overt statement of the aims of those questions

- the development of a structured, goal-oriented framework that allowed the students to expand from a restricted area of language to a wider field

It is interesting to note that, although the students involved in this initial study were experienced language learners, it was only when regular classroom methods were applied to language that is heard outside the classroom that the students began to perceive the relationship between these classroom-type activities and real world exposure. One suggested reason for this is that, although regular classroom tasks may facilitate the learner's understanding of a text, within themselves they remain part of the teacher's toolkit. By sharing the rationale for these tasks, and by having the students bring in the language content, in effect, by handing control of the tasks over to the students, it might be possible to turn them into effective learners' tools.

◈ REFLECTIONS

Many language learners feel dissatisfied with their ability to understand and learn from the language to which they are exposed outside the classroom. The aim of this study was to examine possible reasons for these difficulties as expressed by the students involved. A further aim was to examine the possibility of devising a methodological framework that could facilitate more effective understanding of meaning and noticing of linguistic features of language heard outside the classroom.

The methodological framework that evolved during the study was based on attempts to enable the students to perceive as accessible language within a restricted field of exposure, and then to enable them to build on the confidence that the access afforded them. This included the creation of a framework for effective analysis of the language that had been heard and a forum for discussion of issues of form and use of the language that had been noticed.

The success of this initial investigation could only be measured by a noticeable increase in the number and variety of lexical items that the students were able to contribute from listening to language outside the classroom and the increase that they reported in their confidence in their own abilities. However, the study itself does suggest that a useful area for further methodological research would be into the area of the development of listening skills with a view to examining the extent to which classroom procedures can aid effective understanding and noticing outside the classroom.

From the bridging activities advocated by early proponents of communicative methodology (see Littlewood, 1981) to the use of noticing activities in class (see Willis, 1996) and van Lier's suggestion of entry tickets, much has been done to try to bring aspects of the real world into the classroom.

It may be, however, that in order to enable students to learn effectively from the language that they hear around them, we should also consider other ways in which the classroom/world interface can be more consciously explored in both directions. If, as van Lier (1996) suggests, language development is what happens between lessons during the time that individuals have to engage with language and make observations at their own pace, it seems reasonable to suggest that, as teachers, we need to examine how we can draw learners' attention to strategies that can make that engagement with language as productive as possible.

◈ CONTRIBUTOR

Karen Adams has been a teacher and teacher educator at International House, London, since 1990. Prior to this, she taught in Sudan, Egypt, and Yugoslavia, and she has also worked with teachers in Poland, Estonia, and the Netherlands. She is writer and copresenter of the BBC World Service radio series, *Grammar Girl*.

CHAPTER 11

Encounters: The Virtual in Search of the Intercultural

Heike Jackstädt and Andreas Müller-Hartmann

◈ INTRODUCTION

The potential of the new media for foreign language teaching and learning has been heralded for some time now, and the advent of the Internet promised a boost for intercultural learning with international learning networks. Although there has been an incredible pace to technological innovation, the integration of the new media into the classroom (along with concomitant issues of teacher pre- and in-service education) has proved to be a difficult matter.

In this case study, we outline our attempt at learning about and researching the integration of the new media into Year 11 and 12 EFL classrooms in a German comprehensive school (i.e., with 17- and 18-year-old students). For almost 2 years, three consecutive e-mail projects with partners in North America and Germany were organized on the basis of the common reading of literary texts in the field of young adult literature. Apart from the integration of an e-mail project into an EFL classroom context, we were especially interested in enhancing intercultural learning throughout the process.

Heike Jackstädt works at the Clemens-Brentano-Schule (CBS), Germany, the setting for the projects, but Andreas Müller-Hartmann had moved to the TEFL institute at the nearby University of Giessen before the project started. The situation at the university level in terms of integrating the new media into teacher education programs is as bad as, or probably worse than, at the school level. Hence, this action research project between two former schoolteacher colleagues (now turned into a teacher/researcher relationship) supported innovation in both contexts.

◈ SITUATION

The CBS, a comprehensive school of more than 1,000 students, is located near Giessen, about 80 km north of Frankfurt. Twenty-five percent of the student population is of non-German descent, originally coming from 18 different countries. Due to its multiethnic student population, the CBS's profile stresses intercultural learning, which finds expression in the teaching of several foreign languages, such as English, French, Spanish, and Russian, as well as a large number of international partnerships. More than 10 school exchanges are currently in operation with schools in Australia, France, Italy, Turkey, and the United States, just to name a few. At the same time, the CBS is a UNESCO project school, and also one of the designated "European schools" in the state of Hessen, which offer special programs to enhance European integration.

We are both teachers of English and French, and we have both participated (Jackstädt still does) in the organization of school exchanges with France and Australia. Consequently, the potential of e-mail and the World Wide Web for strengthening the foreign language program by having access to native speakers and authentic texts was immediately obvious to us.

After an initial in-service training session (a traditional one-shot event outside the actual classroom context), Müller-Hartmann tried out the use of e-mail in a 1-week project as part of the European Days activities organized by the CBS together with seven partner schools. In the workshop, students contacted other schools in Europe to find out what they think about the European Community.

But this was not the everyday classroom situation. After having talked repeatedly about the possibilities of intercultural learning through the new media, we decided to incorporate an e-mail project into a 12th-grade course that formed part of the EFL minors' program, and that ran for three 45-minute sessions (two of them in a block) every week. The two e-mail projects that came to follow this one were organized in an 11th-grade class, forming part of the same program.

Because the English curriculum for Years 11 and 12 prescribes rather broad themes, such as "the individual and society" or "society and minorities," it allows for the organization of longer running projects. At the same time, the teaching of literature has been strengthened in the new curriculum, allowing us to offer literary texts for young adults as a basis for discussion via the learning networks.

Müller-Hartmann's current position in the TEFL institute at the University of Giessen, which offers programs in teacher education as well as in English for specific purposes, provided an additional rationale for the project. One of the main research and teaching areas of the institute is the question of how to integrate the new media into the foreign language classroom. But this raises the question: How does one instruct student teachers in something that one has not really experienced oneself? One of the major problems with the integration of technology into teacher education is the fact that the university faculty are often afraid, reluctant, or unwilling to use the new media in their own teaching (Willis & Mehlinger, 1996). Another issue is the difference between teaching in a high school and a university context. Considering the obviously difficult integration of the new media into teaching practice, Müller-Hartmann had a strong interest in first experiencing the high school context himself.

◈ FOCUS

The foreign language learning process is intricately interwoven with intercultural learning, as Kramsch (1994) has pointed out. In her view, language learners should

- communicate appropriately with native speakers of the language;

- get to understand others;

- get to understand themselves in the process. (p. 183)

At the center of intercultural learning stands the intensive exchange between oneself and other people. In all this, affective aspects play an important role. Understanding develops most effectively when learners are ready to open up to others, discovering common fears and hopes, similarities, and differences. In the process of opening up to the other, one also risks changing one's own identity by incorporating new elements, and thus achieving fundamental changes of perspective. According to Byram (1997), the goal of such a learning process would be to become an intercultural speaker. These are people who have acquired "the ability to see and manage the relationships between themselves and their own cultural beliefs, behaviours and meanings, as expressed in a foreign language, and those of their interlocutors" (pp. 12, 38). This interplay between intracultural learning processes— those of the learners' own culture(s)—and those of an intercultural nature would mean for the teacher "to teach the boundary" of a "third place . . . that grows in the interstices between the cultures the learner grew up with and the new cultures he or she is being introduced to," as Kramsch (1994, p. 236) expresses it. By organizing the local and virtual contexts of the learning network, the teacher thus creates the grounds for this third place to evolve, a place that is personal to each learner. In Kramsch's (1994) terms,

> For each learner it [the third place] will be differently located, and will make sense at different times . . . . For most, it will be the stories they will tell of these cross-cultural encounters, the meanings they will give them through these tellings and the dialogues they will have with people who had similar experiences. In and through these dialogues, they may find for themselves this third place that they can name their own. (p. 257)

This process is obviously dialogic, and it is the teacher's role to facilitate this "complex interplay between students' greater familiarity with highly *contextualized*, locally produced writings of their classmates . . . together with their desire to understand the more *decontextualized* texts that they receive from distant partner classes" (Cummins & Sayers, 1995, p. 139).

Reflection on our practice of facilitating intercultural learning through e-mail in an EFL setting therefore centered around three foci:

1. finding reliable partners and developing writing tasks together that would allow negotiation of meaning on the intra- and intercultural levels

2. creating emotional access for the learners, in order to enhance tolerance, empathy, and understanding among partners

3. intensifying the intercultural learning process through intervention by the teacher at critical points

It is with the last point that questions of being more teacher or learner centered as well as aspects of classroom management are paramount, and it is here that we differed most.

◈ RESPONSE

The three e-mail projects were based on the joint reading of

- a play for young adults on the Northern Ireland conflict (Higgins, 1986, *Wednesday's Child*)

- a novel about different ethnic groups in the United States (Miklowitz, 1985, *The War Between the Classes*)

- a play about different ethnic groups in Canada (Taylor, 1990, *Toronto at Dreamer's Rock*)

We chose these texts because they fit into the general curriculum and because they were easily available in Germany in school publishers' editions. Most importantly, however, they seemed to allow for identification by our learners in Germany as well as by our prospective partners, and could therefore form the necessary basis for authentic communication, negotiation of meaning and, we hope, intercultural learning. We offered all three books as project ideas to possible partners, on the first two occasions via the well-known e-mail list services of Minnesota's St. Olaf College, and in the third cycle, having been fortunate enough to find very reliable partners in the preceding project, again to those same partners.

During the 2 years, access to computers changed dramatically. Although we started out by sending e-mail from one office computer in the school administration, later in the first project we could share a small computer room with another class so that groups of students could use five computers. During a lengthy phase of the second project, we did not have any access to a computer room, and the students gave us their handwritten letters, which we then typed in our private or office computers. During the last phase of that project, we had access to one lab. We were able to organize the third project with two computer labs at our disposal, whereby all of the computers had access to the Internet, allowing us much more freedom in organizing pair and group work.

By giving one example from each project or research cycle, we would like to show the stages of our learning process, highlighting the points of change in our reflection and planning, as well as some of the problems these changes entailed.

The Northern Ireland Conflict

The first project, about young people involved in the Northern Ireland conflict, tested our resilience right away. Both the organizational part and the intercultural learning aspect failed miserably at the outset. We had found U.S. partners, but after our students had written their introductory letters, the partners dropped out because of an unexpected absence of the teacher. Frustration ran high among students, and we tried to find new partners. A computer group of 12- and 13-year-old students in Belfast, looking for partners on the St. Olaf network that we were using, seemed to be a possibility, even though our students were 17–18 years old. Our first letter to them put our efforts concerning intercultural learning to the test.

We had started reading the play, having agreed on pursuing a student-centered approach that would allow students to develop their own questions about the book so that communication with the partners would not result in letters like "Our teacher told us to ask you . . . ." Questions of classroom management, which we both considered as decisive for creating the groundwork to allow students to produce their interests in writing, developed into a point of disagreement between us and followed us throughout the various cycles. Müller-Hartmann favored a strongly group- or pair-centered approach, whereas Jackstädt looked more for a mix of approaches in which the teacher, too, had her share of organizing question-and-answer sessions relating to the various topics.

At the outset, Jackstädt agreed to have students form groups and find aspects in the first two scenes that would be of interest. That did not work, and then the switch to Jackstädt's pointing out important passages and the students' discussing them did not produce the desired results either. We talked to the students and found out that, contrary to our expectations, they did not have any images of the Northern Ireland conflict in mind and consequently had difficulties finding emotional access to the characters and the topic.

We decided to change the approach. We formed groups, distributed pictures about many facets of the conflict, and had the students create collages. A discussion of the collages then produced a number of questions, and also led to intercultural comparisons between the conflict of Catholics versus Protestants and the situation of dominant society versus minority groups in Germany.

The students had found emotional access to the topic, and we felt that we were on the right path. Now we only needed the partners, and we decided to let the class design a letter to the above mentioned computer group in Belfast. The letter turned out to be a surveylike assembly of questions, such as "Does Sinn Fein distance itself from the violent actions of the IRA?" or "How do you imagine your future? Will there be peace soon?" We did not want to censor this and sent the letter off, but we never got a reply. There might be many reasons for this, but one likely reason could certainly be the survey nature of the letter, which may have been unsuitable for 13-year-olds. Müller-Hartmann's involvement with foreign students at the university finally allowed for some kind of exchange with four British and U.S. students, thus somewhat reducing the frustration about the earlier failures. With those partners, we also attempted different tasks, such as creative writing tasks that offered much more potential than what we had had so far. From a list of scenes that the author might have written but did not, the students chose two scenes that they found interesting and created the scene. For example, one of the protagonists becomes pregnant and has to tell her parents about it. Our students wrote versions of this conversation and when we compared them to the dialogues the university students had created, an interesting class discussion ensued.

We learned that we had to find a more balanced mix between student choice and teacher control to ensure that, first of all, the students would be able to establish personal rapport with their partners and not turn them off with a barrage of questions. Beyond that, we needed to devise ways of working with such learner texts so as to help students develop sensitivity to intercultural issues, such as the format of the letter, the tone, the appropriateness of content, and the fact that one does not just ask questions, but also tells about oneself.

From our first endeavor, we had learned that reliable partners are essential in establishing a satisfactory exchange. The emotional access of our students to the topic, as well as to their partners, was another ingredient in enabling intercultural learning processes. But these lessons, which had been created out of an intra- (different ethnic groups in our class) and intercultural (through the collages) discussion process, were only preliminaries, as our experience with the letter to Northern Ireland had shown. While planning the next project, we agreed that the letter should have been moved more into a central role, in order to work out aspects of intercultural etiquette and sensibility. Through our intensive planning and reflection sessions before and after the classes, then, we had been able to react to some of the instructional problems and to make changes as we went along, but our practice needed improvement.

Conflicts Between Classes and Ethnic Groups

Because our first project had been organized in the last weeks of the school year, we decided to move the next one into the fall to allow ample time for finding partners and negotiating the setup. We were lucky and found two reliable partners in Quebec, Canada, and in the south of Germany, a triangle that worked together on the next two projects.

In all of its organizational aspects—having reliable partners, reading the novel *The War Between the Classes* together over a number of weeks, and moving into interesting negotiations of intercultural aspects—this project proved to be a success. Based on a sociology experiment, the novel deals with issues of conflict and understanding among different classes and ethnic groups in California. After a creative introductory phase, including the exchange of pictures, students were matched on a one-to-one basis. Having experimented with a reading log at the end of the first project, we introduced this student-centered approach to reading from the beginning in all three classes, and used the products to enable students to engage in various discussion threads that grew out of their interests and questions. Not only did students follow the development of the protagonists in the novel very closely, but they also quickly related the situations in the book to their lives.

One group of ethnic Germans, for example, wrote about the social aspect of the book, pointing out that even though they have "problems with the integration of foreigners [Turks and Russians]," they stress that it is not their fault alone, but that "most of those foreigners do not have the will anymore to integrate." They closed with the assertion that "discrimination in Germany you can find in a few places, but the main population has no problem with intercultural understanding, they live in harmony with many different ethnic groups."

Reactions from a Turkish student in the other German classroom, as well as from students in Quebec, highlight the intercultural potential of such a learning network.

> I wouldn't call that living in harmony, as I am not sure what you meant by "harmony." There are serious problems between the so-called "foreigners" and German people. But this comes because both sides make mistakes. You mentioned some of them made by German people, though it is more than just settling the "foreigners" in ghettos . . . . On the other hand, non-German people are not open enough, especially the elderly ones. This is because they are so afraid of being assimilated, that they can't even tolerate the smallest integration, . . . whereas the problems of the young generation are mainly based on being between two cultures . . . . If you can say, you do not recognize many problems with ethnic minorities it is good for you in one respect, but don't you think so too, that it could also be because you don't have much to do with each other—I mean here personal relationships?

Here a process of negotiation has set in, students' authentic responses to their peers' thoughts and ideas. The multiple perspectives are strengthened through the learning triangle, allowing students and teachers in all classrooms to discuss similarities and differences, creating third places in the process. A student in Quebec compares the intracultural discussion in Germany to her situation:

> I found it surprising that there was a large social rift in your schools mainly between the Germans and the Turks. It is almost an exact parallel to what we have here between the French and the English. I would be interested in

knowing more about some of the types of problems that arise (if any do), and also if there are many Germans with Turkish friends or vice versa. I think that although there is a definite separation in our school here between the French and the English, it can't be all that bad because I have lots of French friends.

We decided to make the Turkish student's letter the center of a class session, but not having spent enough time on planning this session, we organized the class discussion in a teacher-centered way, which, even though some salient points were discussed, did not lead to dealing with the full potential of the letter. Our approach was not suited to making students particularly aware of the various aspects of sensitivity, and of carefully worded argumentation in this letter, which attempts not to insult or hurt the reader, while at the same time offering real-world solutions ("having much to do with each other"). At a certain point, we stopped the discussion because it began to turn ugly on the issue of ghettos in Germany. As one student correctly remarked, "We still need to understand each other outside of class."

The learning network had triggered an important discussion in the foreign language classroom (similar discussions took place in Quebec, the teacher informed us), but instead of leading students to issues of understanding and sensitivity in intercultural relations, we had ended up in an exchange of rather heated arguments.

Even though we were not satisfied with the discussion, it had obviously provided some food for thought because, in the following letters, the hard-liners did not use the word *foreigner* anymore in their letters to Quebec, but took up the student's suggestion of non-German. In general, our setup had proven us right, and evaluations by students from all three classes were overall positive and optimistic as to the intercultural potential of such a project.

We were satisfied regarding the levels of organizing the virtual exchange and involving our students on an emotional plane, but in trying to improve on our handling of the class letter to Northern Ireland, we had again not achieved our original objectives. We aimed to do better still in our next project.

First Nation Issues

Again we read a play, this time about three native boys from different time periods who meet in a sacred place and discuss their fears and hopes. Having a larger class, and following a suggestion from our Canadian partner, we decided to change the matching approach by having students form identity groups. By giving themselves an identity based on common interests and an interesting name, such as "Graceful Dancers" or "Metal Maniacs," and by matching up with similar groups in the other classrooms, the emotional bonding was intensified. At the same time, the circulation of letters received also increased because those written between individual students were made available to other group members as well. Although some of the groups proved too large in the long run (pair work eventually seemed most efficient, especially with regard to working in front of the computer and negotiating writing), this framework offered the possibility for even closer cooperation among learners.

Because the play was rather short, we all read it fairly quickly and resorted to a prompt system in which each participating class developed interesting statements or tasks that aimed to draw the partners into a discussion and negotiation of issues. Our prompt, a creative writing task, created a whole cluster of intra- and intercultural exchanges, which, having profited from our close cooperation and reflection, we were able to handle this time in a more satisfactory way. Three boys meet in the play, so our prompt read

> Do you think the atmosphere of the meeting would have been different if girls (the boys' girlfriends) had come together at Dreamer's Rock? Since the dialogues are just parts of possible conversations, my class would like your students to join their ideas. You may fill in some lines wherever you think it's necessary.

The creative dialogue by the "Computer Freaks" from Giessen, for example, was commented on and extended by the "Computer Group" from Ulm (marked *):

> Hello,
>
> The dialogue between Keesic's, Michael's and Rusty's girlfriends could be like this. The names of the girls are Betty (future), Sherry (present) and Nunghons (past):
>
> N.: Oh, where am I ?
> S.: Who are you, are you a spirit ?
> N.: No, I am Nunghons, I am an Indian and who are you ?
>
> * We think that Nunghons would not call herself an Indian because this term didn't exist in her time. One suggestion is:
>
> *N.: No, I am Nunghons, I am from the tribe of Odawa.
> S.: I am Sherry and I am an American girl.
> *N.: American ?
>
> N.: Oh yeah, a boyfriend. Very nice, HiHiHi. I also have a boyfriend, and he is the sweetest boy in the world. And he is the son of the chief, his name is Keesic, but we call him Red Bull with his flying horse, because he has a very fast horse.
>
> * (Hey, we like that one ...:-))
> B.: What does Red Bull mean ?
> N.: He is as strong as a bull and has red hair . . . .

On a cognitive level, students from Ulm criticized their partners' use of the term *Indian*, signifying that they had learned their cultural facts in earlier sessions. On an affective level, the wordplay around the name/drink *Red Bull* shows that students understood the joke and that they connected on an emotional level (notice the smiley emoticon in the third to last line). Cooperation in the creative writing task of the girls' dialogue thus led to multiple references to intra- and intercultural aspects. An exchange of letters ensued when male students in Germany speculated about what girls would do in such a situation, asserting that girls "often talk about fashion, make-up, music ('They are soooo cute!!!!!'), films ('Titanic-mania', horses)." Female students in Quebec reacted accordingly:

> We . . . find what you think girls talk about VERY insulting. You make it sound like women are narrow-minded and obsessed with superficial, materialistic bullsh*t. You are wrong. Girls that do that are immature and represent only a tiny percentage of actual women. Please do not stereotype! I NEVER talk about fashion and make-up.

Again we had a letter for an intensive class discussion, only this time we combined small-group and whole-class discussion. After having allowed groups ample time to closely read the letter based on the following questions, we had a very productive class discussion in which many different opinions were voiced, and we were satisfied that we had used the intercultural potential of this letter to its fullest.

- What is she angry about?
- How does she tell us?
- Can we accept her criticism?
- How would you answer this letter?

This potential proved itself even further when students left for the computer lab after the discussion. Due to the fact that we had two labs at our disposal, students could split up in pairs, and they used the free space of the open writing task (answering their partners' mails) by transferring the classroom discussion into the virtual mode, showing sensitivity in the process. Although the male students tried to improve relations again by pointing out that they "wrote only in an ironical way" because their "letter referred to a creative task," two female students, who had not had enough chance to enter the discussion because of their weaker oral skills, wrote a letter to the students in Quebec assuring them of their support: "We think that your reaction was right, we would react in the same way." And two other male students warned their partners: "Did you get the letter with the story about the three girls at Dreamer's Rock? I think it is funny and don't forget it's written by some boys!!!"

This had been a learning experience on all sides, as the Canadian teacher's comment shows: "I think the whole episode was a learning experience for Wendy's [a pseudonym] group . . . . Thanks for your patience and also for caring so much about what my students say."

Finally, we seemed to have been able to instigate positive change on all three levels. Profiting from a stable and cooperative relationship with our partners and having created an atmosphere of trust and collaboration among students, our creative writing tasks triggered processes of intercultural learning that we were then able to strengthen with more responsive decisions at the classroom management level.

⊗ OUTCOMES

Three foci identified earlier are discussed in this section: finding partners, creating affective access, and intensifying the learning process through pedagogic intervention.

The organizational aspect of such projects is obviously difficult. Teachers simply have to keep looking for appropriate partners even if early attempts fail. Although there are different organizational forms, we still prefer the personal negotiation process between two or more classrooms that organize the project according to their specific local contexts. As in action research, this is a process in itself. Often one has to go through an initial period of frustration, but having found reliable partners, one can replicate the projects each year, improving them in the process.

The choice of appropriate books allowed learners to identify with the characters and, supported by various attempts at strengthening the affective side of the projects, they eventually found common ground with their partners for discussion and negotiation.

Regarding our differences concerning instruction and classroom management, we came to realize several things. Müller-Hartmann's idea of student-centered classroom instruction, based on extensive pair and group work, broke down due to the different levels of proficiency of the various learning groups. Jackstädt, knowing her students, was much more in tune with what was necessary to secure the learners' understanding during the process of reading the book, which often meant close teacher-led text work with the entire class. A related factor, as Jackstädt pointed out repeatedly, was that time (three lessons) often proved just too short for longer group processes. At the same time though, we both realized that a good mix of group/pair work and teacher-led discussion was conducive to more intercultural learning. '

A clear distinction can be made between writing letters in the classroom and in the computer lab, where collaborative writing on the screen enhanced negotiation of content as well as language. Also in the lab, however, there were phases where teacher intervention proved necessary—most importantly to support a close reading of incoming messages in order to make sure that students were aware of decisive points of content, as well as to engender deeper intercultural learning, such as recognizing the tone of letters, the way questions are asked, or the choice of words. At the same time, of course, these are also not processes that exclude creative group/ pair work, as we have tried to show. This is the most difficult level of our practice, but we also believe that the greatest potential for the improvement of future projects lies in how we support the intercultural learning process here.

The last level, regarding questions of instruction to intensify intercultural learning, is closely related to the teacher/researcher relationship. Müller-Hartmann's move to the university did not have a negative impact on our working together. Although Müller-Hartmann was happy to have the opportunity to come back to the classroom, Jackstädt enjoyed the fact that Müller-Hartmann contributed certain skills she did not possess at the outset and that they could split the workload through team-teaching and by having Müller-Hartmann take care of the correspondence with the partners. This setup caused Jäckstadt a bit of anxiety when Müller-Hartmann moved out of the team-teaching arrangement during the last cycle and became an observer during the sessions. At the same time though, she cherished the experience of doing it "alone," taking on other aspects as well toward the end, such as the correspondence with the partners, thus preparing for the time when she would run e-mail projects by herself.

Although the teacher/researcher relationship certainly can be problematical (Carr & Kemmis, 1986; Ulichny & Schoener, 1996), we had well-established bonds that held us in a trusting relationship. Given that, the combination of teaching and research purposes found its organizational frame in an action research format that allowed both our interests to merge. Our research methods developed (to include the use of interviews, questionnaires, and audio- and videotaping) as we moved from our initial involvement in a single classroom toward Müller-Hartmann's growing interest in extending the project to include a number of other schools. At all stages, however, we found that our intensive conversations, whether maintained face to face, by phone, or by e-mail, were the perfect platform for reflection and revision of past and future practice. We thus affirm Tharp and Gallimore's (1988) assertion that "all intellectual growth relies heavily on conversation as a form of assisted performance in the zone of proximal development" (p. 25).

◈ REFLECTIONS

The above exploration has been at times contentious, but it has also been highly stimulating for improving our practice. Furthermore, the action research format as a way of innovating practice in the field of foreign language teaching and new technology has certainly proved its worth. The projects have clearly shown that, with the introduction of e-mail into the foreign language classroom, the complexity (and richness) of the classroom context in its local and virtual dimensions rises exponentially. Team teaching and the evolving structure of several action research cycles have been extremely helpful in instigating innovation in the classroom.

The change from a possibly more teacher-centered approach to a more learner-centered one, together with the need for acquiring computer skills, the increasing organizational demands of running a learning network, as well as the change to a new setting—the computer lab, where intensive advising of students is warranted—makes this kind of innovation especially receptive to a team-teaching and team-learning approach.

This kind of collaborative learning between teacher and researcher, or simply between teachers, holds out promise not only at the school level but also for in- and preservice education at the university. In-service education should move away from the one-shot seminar to a form of work where support is available for a longer period of time and teachers meet more often and work together more intensively, thus facilitating the long innovation cycles of introducing technology into the classroom.

As for preservice education, students could be involved in their own smaller scale projects of ethnographic research, visiting the classroom in order to experience teaching, and then reflecting on their experiences in university seminars. In all three research cycles, we often had students in our classroom who also participated in seminars on foreign language learning and technology that Müller-Hartmann was teaching at the university. Not only could students learn about the new media in the classroom through observation and conversations with the teachers, but they also had the chance to act as change agents, working closely together with the teacher, partaking in the actual teaching process for certain periods of time and contributing theoretical knowledge that they had acquired at university.

The integration of technology in the foreign language classroom, still a very new and powerful form of innovation, especially with regard to enhancing the potential for intercultural learning, makes the action research format a formidable approach to changing and improving practice. Technological innovation develops at a seemingly ever-increasing pace, making connections between cultures worldwide possible at different levels. Here it was just e-mail, but what will happen as we gradually introduce into our classrooms voice mail, videoconferencing, virtual 3-D worlds, application sharing, and other innovations to come? Teachers and teacher learners at all levels have to pool their resources to find out if, and in what ways, these innovations can actually help them in their educational endeavors. We hope to have shown with this case study that there is potential in the new media for foreign language learning and intercultural learning, but that it is a long process, and we have to depend on each other's knowledge and support.

◈ CONTRIBUTORS

Heike Jackstädt has been teaching English and French for 10 years at various state schools in Germany.

Andreas Müller-Hartmann, originally a teacher of English and French, has been working at the TEFL Institute of the University of Giessen, Germany, since 1996 as a lecturer and researcher.

CHAPTER 12

Constructions Across a Culture Gap

Gregory Hadley and Chris Evans

◈ INTRODUCTION

Understanding student expectations of teachers is becoming a pressing concern in Japan. The Japanese Ministry of Education is considering replacing the present tenure system for teachers with a contract system directly linked to yearly student evaluations ("Proposed," 1996). Ryan (1998) predicts that this change will have broad implications for foreign language teachers: "Culturally-determined expectations may lead Japanese students to judge their teachers against standards that are literally 'foreign' to their native-speaker teachers. However well these teachers teach in their own terms, they may not live up to their students' impression of a 'good teacher'" (p. 9).

This development has led to a growing awareness on the part of language teachers that more cross-cultural research is needed in order to better appreciate their students' culture of learning. Shimizu (1995) explains,

> Research on this topic is doubly important because not only are student attitudes towards them (as teachers) important, but also because they are representatives of the culture which speaks the target language. Viewed in this manner, attitudes towards foreign teachers could adversely affect student motivation not only in the classroom, but also in terms of a student's desire to continue learning the language. (p. 6)

Such research may also help to do something about the apparent rift that exists between many foreign teachers and their Japanese students. Foreign English teachers sometimes characterize their Japanese learners as passive, introverted, and unmotivated (Aline, 1996; Cohen, 1995; Paul, 1996). The same teachers, on the other hand, are themselves occasionally portrayed as insensitive, emotionally unstable, or ethnocentric in pedagogic approach and attitude (Akimoto-Sugimori, 1996; Kobayashi, 1991; Miyoshi, 1996). In such a climate, language teachers can greatly benefit from reflecting upon their teaching beliefs and learning how their views complement or conflict with those of their students. This can pave the way to discoveries that may help them frame their future pedagogic decisions and improve the affective environment of their classes. We report on one attempt to bridge this cross-cultural gap through action research.

Readers will notice a shift between *I* and *we* during the narrative of this case study. The first person singular indicates Gregory Hadley, who was the classroom teacher and primary action researcher. The first person plural signifies inclusion of Chris Evans, whom Hadley sought later on because of Evans's expertise in the type of research methodology and analysis employed.

◈ SITUATION

It was the spring of 1995, and I was at the end of my rope. After a year of teaching at college level, I was depressed, confused, and angry. Despite all of the activities and approaches that I had tried during the year, my learners would not actively participate in class. I felt as if I were floundering as a language teacher.

This state of affairs was very different from the zeal with which I had started. Through a fortuitous turn of events, I had been hired as a part-time lecturer at two universities on the northwestern coast of Japan. Most of my classes met at a private, 4-year Christian college that specialized in liberal arts. The rest of my classes were at the prefecture's most prestigious national university. All of the classes were required courses for first- and third-year students and met once a week for 90 minutes. Although the course titles differed, the classes shared the common goal of giving learners a chance to improve their oral communication with a native English speaker.

I had little experience with teaching college classes, but I had entered a distance MA in TEFL and was looking forward to applying what I had learned. As a new teacher, I rarely strayed far from the textbook, but I did develop supplementary materials to give the learners more practice in speaking. My classes were active for about a month, and then it seemed that the newness was starting to wear off. I observed my classes becoming unresponsive. Direct questions to students were met with impenetrable silence. Pair work and jigsaw activities were done mostly in Japanese unless I was literally standing over them. Listening tasks were left undone or completed by a few students who would give the answers to others who attended the class later in the day. Attempts to give homework also failed. Only a third ever returned their assignments on time. Most did not bother doing the work at all.

This situation was exacerbated by the practice of social promotion at these schools. The unwritten rule was that teachers were responsible for their students' grades. Only students who had not attended more than half of the course could fail the class. Otherwise, the teacher would be responsible for finding a way to pass the student. As a result, students were often given class credit based more on attendance than on test or homework scores. Grades were generally treated as pass/fail. A student receiving 60% in a class was considered by the administration as no different academically from a student who received 90% in the same course. I learned later that most companies do not consider the students' college academic performance when hiring. I was left feeling that, apart from actually attending the class, there was little within the system itself that would motivate students to do more than the bare minimum for passing my class or any other.

I spoke with other teachers to find out how they were doing with their learners. I was surprised (and slightly relieved) to find that even the experienced teachers were dealing with the same problems and were just as stumped as to how to improve the situation. I purchased teacher resource books and increased my participation in the local Japan Association for Language Teaching (JALT) chapter to get more ideas. This helped, but the students' response continued to be sporadic.

Over time, I became more frustrated with what I saw as my students' unwillingness to participate. As the year progressed, I became increasingly strict to coerce the students into complying with my wishes. This they would do, ever so slowly, and often with hurt or fearful expressions. This downward spiral continued to the end of the year, leaving everyone involved emotionally exhausted.

I hoped that things would be better the following year. Perhaps the problems of the previous year were due to my lack of experience, a bad group dynamic, personality clashes, or some other unknown factor outside my control. But after a couple of months, I began to see similar patterns emerging. I realized that I needed to find out what was happening and take steps to improve the situation before developing permanent teaching habits that would be very unhealthy for me and my learners.

◈ FOCUS

I wondered if the problems in class had something to do with differing cultural values and expectations. Instead of continuing my fruitless search for activities to coax students to speak, I embarked upon a quest to discover the students' expectations. I hoped that this would provide a starting point for understanding the students' classroom behavior and uncover clues about how to adjust my teaching. However, in my agitated state, I was not sure if I could develop an objective survey. Other observation tasks would also rest on my interpretations. Finding someone to come and observe my class was not possible; other teachers were either too busy or not interested in coming. I was on my own, and it was ultimately up to me alone to find solutions to my problems. I needed a research tool that could lower the risk of my own bias, allow the students to communicate in their own words, and organize the findings so they could be understood by outside observers. About this time, I found out about a promising research instrument called the repertory grid.

◈ RESPONSE

Repertory grids were developed 50 years ago by George Kelly, a clinical psychologist who created a branch of psychology called *personal construct psychology* (Kelly, 1955). According to Kelly, people behave like instinctive scientists. Based upon their experiences, they create theories to explain the world around them. Kelly called these theories *constructs*. Kelly believed that a people's future behavior and the interpretation of events in their lives could be predicted by the constructs they had formed from past experiences. To put it another way, after enough experience, people begin to see what they expect to see (regardless of what may be actually taking place) and act accordingly. Kelly believed constructs were bipolar, meaning that one could not define something as *good* without an implicit knowledge of what is *bad*.

The main strength of this technique is that the researcher does not select the content but merely provides a framework for individuals or small groups to express themselves in their own words about a set of issues important to them. To do this, Kelly would ask interviewees to think of examples of the domain he wished to explore. For instance, if he wanted to learn about a person's family life, he would start by asking them to list their family members. He called these examples *elements*. From a set of these elements he could then find out a person's constructs. First, he asked clients to choose three of the elements at random. Then they chose two of the three elements that seemed to them to have something in common. After choosing these two elements, the clients would then write down the aspect they felt the two elements shared. Then they would write in what way the third element was different from the other two. The result was a bipolar construct. This process was repeated about five to eight times or until the client wished to stop.

Repertory grids are used today in marketing, artificial intelligence, the social sciences, and educational research (Diamond, 1983, 1984; Feixas & Cornejo-Alvarez, 1996; Munby, 1982; Olson, 1981). However, except for a few papers written by psychologists on its statistical validity (Sakamoto, 1993, 1996; Sakamoto & Numazaki, 1989; Takagi & Sakamoto, 1991), there have not to our knowledge been any published accounts of repertory grids used in Japanese action research.

I administered the repertory grid to myself first so that I could better understand the technique and discover my personal teaching constructs. I then administered the grid in two sessions to all six of my college classes. A total of 165 Japanese college students (99 males and 66 females) took part. In both sessions, the instructions were given in Japanese and English and verified with several students before starting. Students were allowed to write their answers in either Japanese or English, but all opted to write their answers in Japanese. The first session involved the discovery of elements. The second used the repertory grid procedure to elicit bipolar constructs.

During the first session, I wrote the research question, "What is a good teacher?," on the blackboard. Students then brainstormed about eight or more qualities that they felt described a good teacher. I assured them that no part of this research was a test consisting of right or wrong answers and that no effort would be made to track the responses back to any particular individual. The students were asked not to misinterpret the question by writing what they thought of me. They were not to read between the lines and write elements that they felt I might like. They were also asked not to write down qualities they felt applied only to good foreign teachers.

After it seemed certain that the students understood the task, I let them go to work and did not wander around the room. When asked for clarification, I would explain the process again but declined requests for sample elements so as not to contaminate the data. All the elements were then collected and translated into English. More than 180 distinct elements were elicited. Out of these, 8 were chosen for the repertory grid (see Figure 1).

Experts say that samples of 5–8 elements are sufficient for a repertory grid. They also allow for the selection of elements when working with large groups if the elements are coherent, representative of the research domain, and understood by the subjects (Pope & Keen, 1981; Yorke, 1985). The elements were selected for their high numeric frequency or similarity to other less frequent elements. Although they may seem similar to each other in English, their nuances are distinct in the original Japanese.

"Kind" (*yasashii*) means one who is gentle, calm, and mild in his or her dealings with people. "Fun/entertaining" (*omoshiroii/tanoshii*) is a literal translation of the Japanese. "Caring/understanding" (*omoiyari no aru*) denotes one who can sympathetically feel the pain of another. "Friendly" (*shitashimi-yasui*) means one who is warm, open, outgoing, easy to feel close to, and easy to talk with. "Fair/impartial" (*kohei*) comes from two Chinese characters, one meaning "public" and the other meaning "normal," "standard," or "regular." Together the characters mean a sense of detached impartiality. "Understandable" (*wakari-yasui*) means literally, "easy to

やさしい   Kind

おもしろい　たのしい   Entertaining/fun

思やりのある   Caring/understanding

親しみやすい   Friendly

公平   Fair/impartial

わかりやすい   Understandable

興味深い授業・話   Interesting lesson or story

熱心   Enthusiastic

FIGURE 1. Eight Elements Used in Repertory Grid

understand." "Interesting lesson or story" (*kyomi-bukai jugyou/hanashi*) is also a literal translation meaning, "A lecture or story that is deeply interesting." "Enthusiastic" (*nesshin*) is translated as "zealous" or "passionate." It comes from two Chinese characters, one meaning "heat" and the other meaning "heart" or "spirit."

The elements were written in Japanese and English on a repertory grid sheet, which was then enlarged and photocopied on large sheets of paper to allow room for students to write their bipolar constructs (see Figure 2).

The second session took place the following week. The research question was again written on the blackboard. Students were again asked not to misinterpret the research question as stipulated in the first session. They were allowed to work either individually or in the groups. Students choosing to work alone were asked not to confer with others during this session. Groups were also asked not to seek consensus with others outside their group.

Some who had participated in the first session were not present for the grid procedure, and others who were present had not taken part in the element elicitation. Most of these students were members of existing social groups and had already been briefed about the research project. Three students with sporadic attendance and no group ties were given a complete briefing and encouraged to fill out their repertory grid sheets individually. Setting up this session took an average of 20 minutes for each class, leaving approximately 70 minutes for grid elicitation. I felt the first-time challenge of the repertory grid procedure would leave learners only enough time to write about eight bipolar constructs.

I drew on the blackboard a large repertory grid similar to the one the students were to receive. We discussed briefly the idea of elements and constructs, and then each individual or group received one repertory grid sheet and a set of cards numbered 1–8. I explained that each number corresponded to the numbered element on the grid, modeling the following method for eliciting constructs on the blackboard before allowing the students to start.

1. Each group or individual would turn all of the element cards (which were numbered 1–8) face down on their desk and shuffle them.

	やさしい 1 Kind	面白い 楽しい 2 Entertaining/ fun	思いやり のある 3 Caring/un- derstanding	親しみ やすい 4 Friendly	公平 5 Fair/impartial	わかり やすい 6 Under- standable	興味深い 授業・話 7 Interesting lesson or story	熱心 8 Enthusiastic	
+									−

FIGURE 2. Repertory Grid Used in This Project

2. They would then turn over three of the cards and write a circle or an X on the grid to show which elements had been drawn.

3. Each group or individual would then decide which two of the three elements had something in common with each other. They would then connect these two with a line.

4. The students described in writing what it was these two elements had in common on the plus side of the grid. Then they wrote what they felt was the opposite of this on the minus side.

5. They were to fill out the grid row by row, only moving to the next row after completely writing a bipolar construct.

6. In the case of drawing the same three elements as in a previous turn, the students were to reshuffle the cards and try again.

7. Students were not to write constructs that were the same as the elements. Most understood that writing something like "a kind teacher is kind" was unhelpful.

8. Students repeated the process until the repertory grid sheet was completely filled, or they ran out of ideas.

After the students began, the classes were monitored to verify that the procedure was being followed. Out of the six classes, only three groups in one class were discovered to be following a different procedure. I stopped them, explained the process again, and gave each a new grid sheet. Most finished their grids within 55 minutes. Others took the entire 70 minutes. An actual grid completed by a group of male students can be found in Figure 3.

After collecting and translating the grid sheets into English, I was now faced with the task of analyzing all this data. There are several ways to study grid data, from interpretive methods such as a content analysis of the themes found in the constructs and elements, to a full grid analysis involving statistical methods such as cluster analysis, principal analysis, or multidimensional scaling (Evans, 1998; Sewell, Adams-Webber, Mitterer, & Cromwell, 1992; Stewart & Mayes, 1998; Winter, 1992). Unsure of which was best for my situation, I searched for someone to help me analyze the data. I found Chris Evans, a psychiatrist and psychotherapy researcher who was an international authority in the repertory grid technique and willing to serve as a collaborator and second author on this project.

After putting the data though various computer analysis programs, we decided to use content analysis for the student data and a statistical analysis for my data. Content analysis is simple and powerful in discovering themes and terminology specific to the learners and an accessible method of analysis for EFL teachers who do not have the time and resources for other methods. It is often more meaningful because a statistical analysis of repertory grids from large groups can become muddy and difficult to interpret. When studying the grid created by one person, however, a statistical analysis is easy to do and often helps reveal issues with which the individual is currently contending.

We analyzed my grid using GRIDCOR (Feixas & Cornejo-Alvarez, 1996a, b), a software program specifically designed to analyze repertory grids. As I studied the readout, I was surprised to find out how much of an influence my own religious schooling had on my understanding of a good teacher. At the time of the research, I

+		1 Kind やさしい	2 Entertaining/fun 面白い楽しい	3 Caring/understanding 思いやりのある	4 Friendly 親しみやすい	5 Fair/impartial 公平	6 Understandable わかりやすい	7 Interesting lesson or story 興味深い授業・話	8 Enthusiastic 熱心	−
つきあいやすい			X		X				X	つきあいにくい
意欲的に教える			X				X		X	投げやりに教える
好印象		X	X			X	X			悪印象
親愛			X		X					卑劣
魅力的			X	X	X			X		魅力的でない
人情家				X	X	X	X			冷血漢
無差別			X						X	差別
仁		X		X			X			人間のくず

FIGURE 3. Example of Repertory Grid Completed by a Group of Third-Year Students

Translation of Terms in Figure 3	
+	−
Easy to get along with	Hard to get along with
Teaches eagerly	Teaches with neglect
A good impression	A bad impression
Affectionate	Mean
Attractive	Unattractive
Warm-hearted	Cold-hearted
Shows no discrimination	Shows discrimination
Humane (*jen*)	Human garbage

was spending most of my time teaching at the private Christian college, and I realized that the focus of this school had activated some constructs that might not have been as influential in my teaching decisions had I been in another teaching environment. As I reflected on the correlations of my elements and constructs, it dawned on me how perfectly the readout described my feelings about myself in the classroom. Many qualities that correlated highly with my present classroom behavior described what I remembered about some abusive teachers in my past. Qualities I valued highly correlated very negatively with what I was doing in class and marked how far I felt from this standard—a standard that, up to that moment, I had not consciously realized I was trying to live up to.

The students' grids were equally revealing. The data consisted of 62 grid sheets and 496 bipolar constructs. Because of the amount of information collected, only the most frequent constructs can be shown in this chapter. Even with this representative sample, much can be learned about the learners' expectations for teachers. Table 1 contains the most frequent constructs. Figures 4 and 5 place these constructs in a mind-map format connected to their converse positive or negative constructs. This allows for a fair and balanced presentation of the data and visibly displays the interconnected nature of the students' construct system.

TABLE 1. TOP CONSTRUCTS BY FREQUENCY

Construct	Frequency	Construct	Frequency
− Boring	24	− Silly	7
− Cold	15	− Narrow-minded	7
−Selfish	11	+ Attention to detail	7
+ Cheerful	10	+ Earnest	7
− Gloomy	9	+ Interesting	7
− Lazy	9	− Ignores students	7
− Unprepare	9	+ Understands students	5
+ Warm-hearted	9	+ Attention to students	5
+ Like a Loving Parent	8	+ Good speaker	5

Note. + signifies a positive construct. − signifies a negative construct.

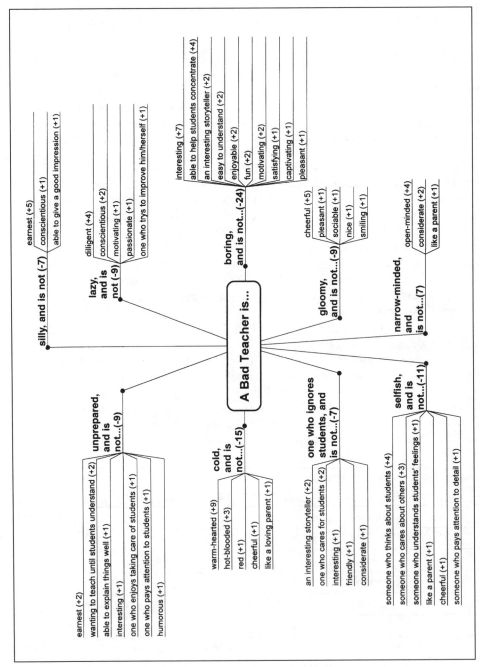

FIGURE 4. Japanese Students' Profile of a Bad Teacher

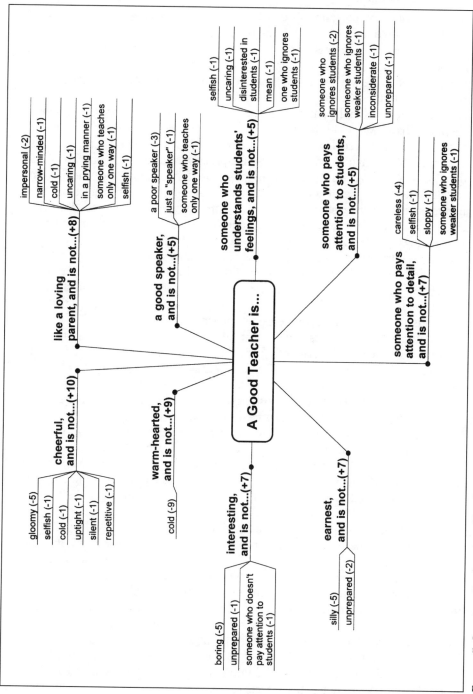

FIGURE 5. Japanese Students' Profile of a Good Teacher

We had not anticipated a high frequency of negative constructs. It suggested to us that the students could more easily verbalize the qualities of a bad teacher than those of a good teacher. Evans also noticed from his experience as a peer reviewer for university education programs some lack of development or complexity as compared to what he would have expected in the constructs.

For example, there was not a single construct addressing issues such as "a teacher who helps students see something new in himself or herself" or "a teacher who can change the way we see things." The responses of the students seemed more concerned with how a teacher made them feel than what he or she made them think, and more interested in the character of the teacher than in any pedagogic skills he or she might have. Many constructs elicited by the learners differed little from what might have been expected from a younger group of Western students (Eriksen, 1984; Erikson, 1968; Merrett & Wheldall, 1990), especially in the use of "loving parent" to describe a good teacher. Another concept diffused throughout the student constructs, but not explicit enough to include in the graphs, was characterized by numerous statements of students participating in class as a reward to good teachers and passively resisting bad teachers as punishment for ignoring their concerns. Discovering that many of the students viewed language study as something done for a teacher was troubling. It suggested a basic unfamiliarity with learner independence.

To find out why 18- to 20-year-old adults would write constructs such as these, we decided that I should show the findings to some Japanese teachers and students. Our Japanese colleagues were not at all surprised by the data and suggested that part of the answer might lie in Japanese Confucianism.

Confucius taught that fostering proper human relationships solved most of life's problems. The parent-child relationship was the most important and even had priority over one's obligation to the ruler. The key to maintaining harmony was through respectable outward conduct (*li*) and humane benevolence (*jen*). A person who loved his parents, maintained honest relationships with friends, practiced benevolent justice (*jen*) with those below him, and respected those above him might become what is usually translated into English as a "superior man" (Muller, in press, p. 4).

Confucius's superior man was characterized as a teacher, but not all teachers were superior men (Analects 11:20; see Muller in press). The superior man had the authority to teach others not simply because he was well educated, but because his life was characterized by *jen* (Analects 17: 6–7). In all things, he was to be fair and impartial in his dealings with others (Great Learning, v. 9). When teaching others, the superior man was open minded and careful to do everything tastefully. He was never boring or inflexible (Doctrine of the Mean: v. 10, 18, Analects 15:36), and could reach this moral summit because he had purged himself of the following faults: "imposing his will, arbitrariness, stubbornness and egotism" (Analects 9:4).

Confucianism entered Japan early in the fourth century, but it was soon modified so that government officials and educators were revered as parental figures that were to be obeyed even over the will of one's natural parents. Japan's national ideology and educational theory were largely called into question after the end of World War II, but despite their new freedom from direct government control, educators found it difficult to discard centuries of Confucian traditions and teaching styles. Fujita (1985) notes that, except for cosmetic changes in the national curriculum, Japanese schools remain essentially unchanged in form, function, and purpose since the Meiji Period. The role of the teacher is still compared with that of a protective parent, while the student is considered a child lacking personal responsibility. Japanese teachers frequently affirm these roles in the literature. For example, Okuyama (1996) reveals that a parent-child relationship between teachers and students is strongly encouraged, especially during the impressionable high school years: "It is perhaps less well known that Japanese high schools are also family-like and teachers often play more important roles in students' lives than their own parents do" (p. 89).

This relationship often continues for a lifetime, depending upon how well the teacher has cared for the students. Okuyama (1996) explains that, over time,

> the parent-children-like ties with their students become stronger, and these ties may last for many years, with invitations to weddings and regular visits from former students . . . [because] the students depend more upon their teachers than on their parents, who typically have little knowledge regarding jobs or colleges. (p. 92)

To further verify the accuracy of our growing understanding of the data, we shared the findings with a class of fourth-year Japanese university students who were training to become high school English teachers. They found the data very representative of their expectations for teachers. When asked why, one female student explained,

> It is simple. From our first day in junior high school to the day we graduate high school, we spend most of our time in the school. If we are not in the class, we are in club activities at school until late at night with the teacher. When we go home, our parents tell us, "go to your room and study hard," so we can go to a good university. Many of us hardly saw our parents. So we never talked about our feelings with them. But we talked to our teachers. Isn't it natural we want the teacher to love us and be a parent for us?

Whereas the influence of Japanese Confucianism is only one of many cultural patterns in the students' vast cognitive tapestry, it nevertheless appears to be a pattern that stands out clearly. Nozaki (1992) notes how, despite the Western veneer of today's Japanese students, their "core values remain traditionally Japanese" (pp. 27–28). Our findings suggest that Nozaki may be correct: Although a growing number of Japanese college students are "dyeing their hair yellow, wearing rings in their noses and crying into Kirins on the fringes of society" (Roche, 1999, p. 23), when these learners verbalize their expectations for teachers, their core values seem to have changed little from those of their parents or grandparents. This group of Japanese learners desire teachers to be dynamic, morally superior, benevolent figures who will prepare them for success in Japanese society. They do not want teachers to be only entertaining, permissive parents. Neither do they only want their teachers to be monolithic Confucian superior men (or women) whose lives are typified by *jen*. We conclude that the good teacher for this group of students is best expressed in the role of "teacher as superior parent."

Before acting on the data collected from the students, I first needed to consider the insight gained from my own grid. I sought out a trusted colleague and participated in cooperative development (Edge, 1992), a process in which one colleague works with another to reflect upon professional issues in a nonjudgmental manner. I came to realize that I was harsh with my students because they were not working as hard as I did when I was in college. This prevented me from respecting them. They were picking up on this and passively resisting my efforts in class to make them speak. Realizing that most of my focus had been on teaching rather than learning, I concluded that many of my teaching ideals were abstract, unrealistic, and judgmental. I decided to move away from these self-defeating teaching patterns and toward an approach of accepting others as they are.

◈ OUTCOMES

In response to the students' constructs, I was encouraged to find several things we agreed on, such as paying attention to detail, working earnestly, and being prepared. I found it very helpful to carry the mind maps of the students' constructs with me to class. They reminded me how the students might be interpreting my actions or the affective outcomes of certain language tasks. These attempts to pay attention to the students and understand their needs seemed to thaw the decidedly cool response of many students.

Most changes that I made were simple. For example, I tried to smile more in class while I was teaching and giving instructions. This felt contrived at first, but in time I learned firsthand about the positive power of a smile. I began to feel better about myself and observed the students responding more cheerfully. I went to my classes about 10 minutes earlier, and, starting from the back of the classroom, I chatted with students in simple English or Japanese about light subjects. As more students entered the class, I would slowly move toward the front, greeting and chatting with other students. Near the beginning of the class period, I would begin the lesson. This soft approach to starting a lesson appealed to enough in class to make a difference. I asked my learners to give pictures of themselves, which I put next to their names in my attendance book. I memorized as many of my students' names as I could and would address them personally in class, in the hallway, or if I met them on the street. Students seemed to like the fact that I was learning their names and using them respectfully. They began to pay more attention in class, and I started to have fewer discipline problems.

Rather than getting through the textbook, I slowed my lessons to allow students to absorb as much of the information in the textbook as possible. This meant spending what sometimes felt like too much time on a chapter, but the students appeared more interested in the lessons and became more confident in trying to use English in the classroom. To supplement the lessons, I moved from controlled pair work and information gap activities to more group tasks. I walked around and spoke to different groups, making a point to tell them things they were doing right. I introduced storytelling to the lessons and was amazed at how even the simplest stories held the students in rapt attention.

After several months, the learners were more active, expressive, on task, and willing to take chances. We feel this change took place partly because the students began to see a change in my teaching and interpreted my attempts to pay attention to their needs as warmhearted, cheerful, and understanding. In response, many began to participate in class, although I encouraged them to study English for themselves.

We finished the year upbeat and energized. Not only did I feel better about myself as a teacher, I also observed a positive turnaround in my classes. Students sometimes sought me out to talk with them about various subjects. Some still visit me 3 years after that initial action research project.

◈ REFLECTIONS

I recently met a student who had participated in this action research project. It had been more than 2 years since I had seen him, and I was surprised how tall he had grown in that time. I was even more surprised when he began to speak to me in fluent English. I asked how it was that he had improved in such a short period of time. He replied, "It was because of your class. When I saw how hard you worked for us, I was deeply impressed. I decided I wanted to become an English teacher like you. So I began to study hard from then. I will go to America in 3 months. When I come back to Japan, I will become an English teacher." He also told me about another student from the class who was now working in the United States and had also become fluent in English.

I thanked him for his kind words and encouraged him to study hard in the United States. We exchanged addresses and had our picture taken with his pocket camera. Then we went our separate ways. Returning home, I felt satisfied that this action research project had also been a benefit to some of the students. A few had even become independent learners.

We call on language teachers to continue in the search for the educational values and affective needs of their learners. Regardless of what may or may not be implemented by education ministries and teacher certification boards, we feel that educating our learners may have a better chance for success when we as teachers understand and appreciate the humanistic concerns of our learners. Often it can make all the difference in the quality and lasting impact of our lessons.

◈ ACKNOWLEDGMENTS

Special thanks to Hiromi Yoshioka Hadley, Niigata University, for her invaluable help in the translation of this research; Confucian scholar A. Charles Muller of Toyo Gakuen University in Chiba, Japan, for graciously allowing the use of his recent translation of Confucius (Muller, in press, *Five Chinese Classics*); Professors Yukio Yamazaki and Kazuo Fukuda of Niigata University, whose spirited discussions of Japanese Confucianism over coffee paved the way for a deeper understanding of this research; and the Fourth Year Teacher Training class at Niigata University, who taught the teacher what it means to be a student. May they all become good teachers.

◈ CONTRIBUTORS

Gregory Hadley is coordinator of the Communicative English Program (CEP) at the Niigata University of International and Information Studies, in Japan. His articles have appeared in *ELT Journal, RELC Journal,* and *Journal of Psycholinguistic Research.*

Chris Evans is a consultant psychotherapist at Rampton Hospital and the associate director of research and development at Tavistock & Portman NHS Trust, in London, England. He taught for many years as a senior lecturer of psychiatry at the University of London.

CHAPTER 13

In Search of Individual, Group, and Institutional Coherence: Does This Compute?

Gavin Melles

⬧ INTRODUCTION

ESOL teaching in the 1990s was marked by the increasing presence of computers in the classroom and in the literature—this being just one instance of a more general movement toward the greater use of educational technology and computers in education. In language teaching, the whole range of available software and environments is flagged as a potential source of independent and collaborative learning activities (e.g., Boswood, 1997; Flowerdew, 1996; Schcolnik & Kol, 1999; Warschauer, 1995). Teachers are enjoined to take advantage of the power of these tools to encourage learner autonomy and to develop more flexible activities and syllabi (Pennington, 1996). There is, therefore, a strong claim that computer-assisted language learning (CALL) can help construct a learner-centered curriculum and develop learner independence.

Of course, learner centeredness as a language teaching philosophy demands a redefinition of teacher and student roles (Tudor, 1996), and the effect of the computer as tool (Levy, 1997) on the teaching environment will, it is claimed, entail further challenges to teacher and student roles and identities. Teacher authority (ego) will be challenged as independent learners forge their own way to learning through interaction with computer-based activities. Consequently, teachers "will have to find new roles, as advisers, as managers, even as fellow learners discovering new insights into language by using the same facilities as their students" (Higgins, 1995, p. 7). In this sense, the computer becomes something of a democratic leveler or instrument of change, in that it forces teacher and student to interact under the constraints of a new relationship.

At the same time, research has begun to investigate, among other issues, teacher resistance to the use of computers (Moore, Morales, & Carel, 1998), the development of autonomy through computer use (Blin, 1998), student perceptions of CALL (Brown, 1998), and the limitations of software applications (Kluge, 1997). What these findings highlight is that we are still very much finding our way in a search for research approaches to CALL in order to measure the actual educational benefits and limitations of computers in language teaching (Chapelle, 1997; Chapelle, Jamieson, & Park, 1996; Motteram, 1998).

An ideal solution for this state of affairs would be to find a research approach that engaged both teachers and students and that aimed at working toward educational improvement broadly conceived to include cognitive and behavioral modifications or adjustments as goals. Action research promises to resolve some of the issues by engaging teachers and learners in a systematic collaborative investigation of their practices and beliefs with a view to transformation and change in the classroom (Cohen & Manion, 1994, Henry & McTaggart, 1998).

Within second language teaching, action research has recently received much attention (Burns, 1999; Chen, 1992; Crookes & Chandler, 1999; Edge & Richards, 1993), although not all of this work has been consistent in its recognition of the critical foundations of action research in education (e.g., Crookes & Chandler, 1999). This lack of attention to educational definitions, history, and discussion of action research has led to an individualistic, descriptive focus that eschews the necessity for change and collaboration (Nunan, 1992b) and supports the idea that action research can be fitted neatly into existing normative research traditions (Carr, 1995).

The issue of concern in this project is the integration of computer-based activities into the ESOL syllabus. It is not about an individual teacher's solution to an immediate classroom problem but about a more open investigation of problematic theme with a broader focus than the classroom to include curriculum policy and the generation and validation of teacher knowledge and reflection. It is about a group of practitioners trying to investigate and transform teaching practice through individual action within a broader group concern. Finally, this report touches on the issue of definitions in teacher research to the extent that participatory action research in practice cannot and should not be bound by method guidelines that exclude flexible responses to local circumstances. Disseminating our experience as collaborative researchers through this report aims not only to represent our voices from the classroom (Bailey & Nunan, 1996) but also to take a stance on what constitutes professional development as a critical endeavor.

◈ SITUATION

ESOL teaching at the Waikato Polytechnic includes a broad range of specific (ESP) and general (EGP) English programs aimed at recent immigrants and international students. Typically, students enroll for a 10-week (term) or 20-week block (semester) and are timetabled for 15–20 hours of classroom teaching. Depending on the nature of the course and the teacher, students will have varying amounts of homework and assignments to complete as part of their program. The teaching timetables of most programs includes a computer hour and some of the assessment tasks, especially in the ESP courses (e.g., English for Tertiary Study, English for Living and Working), which include tasks that mandate or strongly recommend the use of word processing.

Team teaching is the preferred teaching dynamic in the department, and this means that all courses are managed by two or three teachers who will take responsibility for particular areas of the program, for example, reading and grammar. This typically leads to one teacher becoming responsible for the computer hour. All the full-time staff have at least 2 years experience of teaching in the ESOL section, and some have more than 10. Of a total staff (full-time and part-time) of more than 30 people, 2 are male. The typical educational background for teachers is an undergraduate arts degree, a postgraduate diploma in ESL, and roughly 10 years experience in general and ESL education combined. Three staff have MA degrees in language (French), linguistics, or ESOL; other staff are pursuing MAs and other postgraduate courses. Research experience and training is not a major feature of teacher profiles, and academic research (as reported in journals) is not much referred to when teachers talk about their practice.

Despite the difficulties associated with pursuing academic research topics, as well as the doubtful practical relevance with which normative research findings are perceived, a teacher research culture has begun to develop over the past couple of years. The preferred approach has been in the action research paradigm, although other forms of research have also been employed. Naturally, the way the action research paradigm has been explored has differed in each case. This particular project, regarding the integration of CALL into the ESOL syllabus, fits in, then, with an emerging tradition of teacher research in a department where a teaching, rather than an academic, identity is an important factor.

Within the past couple of years, a computer lab has been set up in the department at considerable cost. This includes 10 IBM-compatible and 10 Macintosh computers. Due to poor network connections and other circumstances, students do not have access to the Internet from the lab location; networking problems also lead to substantial and unpredictable down-time for staff and students. Computer lab activities in ESOL have been limited by this constraint, and it continues to be a source of some embarrassment and difficulty for teaching staff who would like to explore the Web with students.

Despite these practical difficulties, the Polytechnic has developed a technology plan that encourages extensive and innovative use of educational technology (Waikato Polytechnic, 1998) and reinforces this discourse in its promotional materials. Thus staff are caught on the horns of a dilemma: They are faced with institutional imperatives to develop and use technology, while in practice they are aware of the limitations of student and teacher access to computer hardware and software.

◈ FOCUS

Within the constraints mentioned above, I had experienced my own difficulties in managing computer-based learning activities within the timetabling of ESOL courses I had taught in the department. In discussing these frustrations in corridor conversations and more formal meeting settings, one of the key terms to emerge for me personally was the notion of *coherence*.

My use of the term *coherence* hinges on a number of senses that were relevant to the question at hand. First, there was my own feeling of the lack of relationship between the computer lab activities students did and the topics they were otherwise studying. My feeling was that there should be a greater integration of computer activities and the ESOL syllabus as it was planned and implemented by teachers. The issue here was whether others shared this perception.

The second sense of coherence that was important related to the team-teaching dynamic. It seemed to me that computer teaching was an isolated optional activity that was not coherently and consistently pursued by coteachers in a course. So, for example, there was no reinforcement of the computer-based activities in the language and activities of team-teaching members not concerned with this issue; incoherence related here to the human dynamic of teaching. Was this simply a personal disjunction? Had others experienced this?

Finally, my feeling was that there was a lack of coherence in the departmental approach to computer-based activities and policies, which seemed ad hoc in their definitions and application. This lack of coherence included the mismatch between the institutional directives embodied in the technology plan and the technological realities of using computers with students. The formula was complicated further by the acknowledged difference of opinion, knowledge, and attitude of staff with regard to the role of computers in ESOL teaching. Was greater cohesion possible at the level of the ESL unit as a whole? Was this a feasible and worthwhile objective? I return to these negotiable notions of coherence and some of the answers we received (or not) in the outcomes and reflections below.

I began expressing my concerns about these issues in e-mails to colleagues, which I sent over a 6-month period (January–June 1999). Colleagues in the department responded encouragingly and critically to my suggestions to pursue a more coherent application of computers to the syllabus. Some felt it was simply a matter of individual choice and decision. Others felt ill-equipped to give answers to these questions. A discussion group formed that debated some of these issues during those first 6 months, and this included some of the teachers who eventually joined in on the project.

At the end of this 6-month period, I proposed that we pursue the issue of CALL and ESOL syllabus integration through a teacher research project, employing an action research framework. I believed that addressing the issue through a research approach that already had an established credibility in the department was an essential factor. Eventually, three other teachers agreed to work together with me, with some participation also from a technical allied staff member.

An essential milestone in this process was the convergence of views on the nature of the issue at hand. This notion of issue is important to stress. Too often, action research is framed in terms of a problem-solution approach for an individual teacher. So, for example, a teacher feels (or is told) that her use of questions in the classroom is not adequate. She, consequently, engages in an action-observation-reflection spiral to discover what is wrong so that she can remedy the situation, that is, so that she now asks more open questions. The difficulty with this kind of framing of the action research topic is that it closes the door on a more open exploration of the educational issues. Where a collaborative group shares a general concern, as in the case of this study, there is no obvious solution nor any specific problem to resolve. There is rather a perception of incoherence and an attempt to clarify what is at stake with a view to improving the correspondence between what we say and what we do in an educational context.

To help focus the thematic concern, I used an instrument called *the Aristotelian table of invention* (Kemmis & McTaggart, 1988). Each prospective member of the action research group received a copy of the table and was asked to explore the table as a way of focusing our concerns. The table and some model answers I supplied as provocateur follow. I need to stress that the answer I suggested for each intersection of the table is only one possibility.

When we had worked through this chart and identified all the intersections we

TABLE 1. SAMPLE ARISTOTELIAN TABLE OF INVENTION

CALL/ ESOL	Teachers	Students	Subject matter	Milieux
Teachers	Teachers do not communicate with others about their experiences and knowledge of CALL.	Some teachers believe students derive little benefit from CALL activities.	Some staff have had training in CALL at University.	Teachers are not fully aware of the computer resources available.
Students	Some students have better computer literacy and knowledge than teachers.	Some students like the independence of working alone at a computer, not with others.	We have students who have poor attitudes to computer-use.	Students are not fully aware of the computer resources on campus.
Subject Matter	Much of the CALL literature is pitched in terms of language that alienates teachers.	There is still not enough computer-based, good quality language learning material.	Critical evaluation of CALL is thin on the ground.	There is quite a lot of discussion about CALL in this milieu.
Milieux	The polytechnic has a strong technology discourse that teachers cannot ignore.	There are a number of access points to computers for students in the institution.	The library has a growing number of texts on computer topics.	Departments do not share information about this.

could, it became clear that we all had some conceptions about why computer-based activities and the syllabus did not work well together. These included, for example, poor attitudes on the part of colleagues, poor knowledge on our part, and difficult jargon in the literature in relation to the topic. This analysis helped give substance and focus to our future work. We discussed each factor that emerged in our team meeting as we worked toward articulating our group concern and our individual action plans for the first cycle.

◈ RESPONSE

Our action research proposal comprised a collaborative investigation broken into three cycles of action-observation-reflection-planning over a 20-week-semester teaching period. At the end of each cycle, there would be a focus group meeting to draw individual and group conclusions and prepare for the cycle ahead. Individual members of the action research group were left to explore the issue of computer and ESOL integration within the limits of their own timetabling. Thus, there was an essential individual element of the research within the framework of the group concern.

Participants

Four teaching staff, including myself, formed the action group. All participants had different roles with regard to the course syllabus, and this introduced an element of diversity and coverage into the project. In my own case, I was a computer tutor not responsible for the course syllabus per se in the ESP course on which I taught. Two of the other tutors involved in the project were responsible for the language syllabus on their course as classroom coteachers. As I discovered, trying to integrate computer activities into the language syllabus where one was not also a classroom teacher, as in my case, strongly emphasized the need for constant communication with classroom teachers. A fourth member of the action team was teaching on-line through an external arrangement that was not linked to teaching students in the department. In essence, she was working on creating and teaching an on-line syllabus in listening outside of the departmental teaching program. We were keen to include her because she was doing on-line teaching, and this was an area that the department wanted to introduce although we were thwarted for some of the administrative reasons noted above. Finally, one of the members of the action research group was a technical support person, whose overall input was limited but, in a collaborative educational context, it is a bonus to have representation from across departmental or institutional boundaries.

Overview

Table 2 illustrates the groups, resources and student feedback mechanisms used by each teacher. Teachers are referred to by pseudonymous three-letter abbreviations.

Action Plans

Individual action plans were formulated to address the following questions:

1. What class am I going to work with?
2. What am I going to do, that is, what software approach am I using?
3. What difficulties do I perceive?
4. How does this work help explore and improve the CALL and ESOL syllabi?
5. How will I gather evidence on student participation and attitudes?

TABLE 2. GROUPS, RESOURCES, AND STUDENT FEEDBACK MECHANISMS USED BY EACH TEACHER

	GBM	JLC	JMS	HKV
Group	Vocational English students	Preparatory EAP group	Beginning ESL students	Two different groups of on-line students
Main resources	PowerPoint 97 Word 97 CD-ROM	Powerpoint 97 CD-ROM	Word processing CD-ROM	Web-based listening course Web-based EAP writing course
Feedback	Student survey forms Record sheets	Student survey and discussion Record sheets	Video recording Student surveys	E-mail and face-to-face surveys

Another member of the action group (the "buddy"), who would comment on the substance of the plan and make any suggestions, then annotated the formulated action plan. Here is an example of annotation, based on HKV's plan to use Sonicmail (1999) in a Web-based listening course for which she was responsible for developing the syllabus in negotiation with students. I responded to her first action plan with the following:

> I will be interested to know how the Sonicmail works, technically I mean. As you know I will be developing an on-line course during this semester, so your experiences are crucial. It is per se interesting to explore listening via web-based teaching because it does require a minimum set of technology standards. It also interests me that you have to deal with the question of individual versus group contact because of time and number commitments; I think this is a reminder that on-line teaching, while it may be more flexible in a sense is not necessarily quicker. The evaluation sheet 3-weekly is a bit of a bind I suppose since you don't know what is happening; can they also send you personal e-mail about individual gripes. I see you have already thought ahead to the questions you need to address in terms of the relationship between what you are doing and syllabus/curriculum integration. Good luck I will try to think of anything that might be useful to read or visit if you want to know. (GBM)

No limitations were set on what constituted valid evidence-gathering instruments. Teachers chose to use video, anecdotal observations, survey forms, and narrative to get responses from students and integrate this into their data collection.

Reflective Journals

All the participants kept reflective journals. Immediately following the teaching session, teachers would record their observations about the class: a basic description of the lesson, an evaluation of success, and a reference to evidence gathered. At a later stage in the week, the teacher would then add a later, slightly distanced reflection. Sometimes these would be motivated by conversations with other teachers or by having read literature. The buddy from the group would then read the reflective note and add her annotation to this comment. By ensuring an ongoing dialogue among participants about the realization of the action plan, we helped promote a critically reflective dimension to the project. Below is an example of a journal entry and annotation.

HKV - July 1999 - Journal Entry 1

Class Description

> My class is a Listening class on-line. In May, I originally had a class of 188. Only 60 of those wrote an introductory letter to me when asked. Only about 20 of them responded to the first lesson sent. After having been away on holiday for 4 weeks, none of them responded to the lesson I sent them. They came from all over the world and from many backgrounds. Quite a few of them were in jobs connected with computers and obviously needed English for their job. I have now asked to be sent a new class and am waiting for it to start.

Evaluation

Obviously, I haven't been a great success at my first attempt to teach on-line.

Evidence about students gathered

I intend to send students an evaluation questionnaire every 3 weeks or so.

Later Reflection on CALL and Syllabus

I have done several things to try and learn what I did wrong. Firstly, I wrote to a mentor on-line. They said that most teachers have a large drop out rate because the lessons are free and most students are already into full time work. The second thing that worried me was that I felt that I couldn't give individual feedback, only group feedback, because of time restraints. I know this would have affected some of the students. The mentor said that group feedback was all right in the circumstances and many teachers do choose to do things that way. I then went and talked to BL. He pointed out perhaps a major aspect of on-line teaching, that of the need for social interaction amongst the class members. He encouraged me to have a Bulletin Board for my next class and to use it every few weeks as part of the lesson. He also showed me some other ways of producing Listening lessons so that I wasn't always just using Sonicmail. I did have quite a few technical problems at first getting used to Sonicmail. Many of the students couldn't hear me. That would have been frustrating for them. All of the above issues are relevant to CALL and the syllabus in that we're on a learning curve and by making mistakes we are learning better ways of doing things for the future. There are major issues involved of time, social aspects, technical knowledge that have to be ironed out early on if we are to be successful in developing future courses.

Annotation

Your frustration with losing a class is something similar to the frustration one feels when technology fails in the lab. It certainly is interesting to see the issue of the social dynamic surfacing everywhere because this is a major research issue also. It certainly is salutary to see the kind of low uptake rate you get with on-line courses and to think about the factors involved. The notion of group and individual feedback is something I am thinking about for my own WebCT course and I am about to give individual feedback to my 12 students in ELW; now those numbers are manageable. I hope you get back on line soon and we can talk about what you and I are learning about that kind of teaching. One question I would ask you is how constrained are you in terms of course design for this listening course because drop out can, of course also relate to poor design and/or teaching. What do you think? (GBM)

Group Focus Meetings

Group focus meetings were planned for the end of each cycle, for all participants to discuss the results of the previous cycle in terms of their action plan and the group theme. The focus group meeting allowed everyone a chance to hear and comment on progress, both their own and that of others. Intended actions and observations measured up more or less with previously stated intentions, and rationalizing (individually) modifications to plans formed part of the interim discourse of the project. The results of these meetings were to lead to the design of modified action plans for the next cycle and the pursuit of revised goals.

I volunteered to record these meetings and then turn them into a summary (not a transcript) for participants to check. A critical incident from the first group focus meeting is represented in the summary extract that follows. One of the participating teachers, with some experience and knowledge of action research, raised the question about whether what we were doing, in fact, measured up to the paradigm.

> JLC questions whether there was any real sense of change in Cycle 2 in particular reference to the work of GBM. GBM responded by saying that there were difficulties in conceiving of the project in the way it had been done before (JNT action research project) because
>
> 1. The area (CALL) was still very uncharted.
>
> 2. There were many constraints, for example, technology, which were part of the environment.
>
> 3. There was a lack of software.
>
> 4. Teacher knowledge was still developing.
>
> 5. Pupil attitudes to computers were not clear.
>
> JNT added that even so, the process had raised broader questions about policy regarding software purchase and what money was available in the account to do this. JNT added that this particular question could become a research focus, that is, purchase policy and analysis of student needs.

As illustrated in the quotation above, group focus meetings are occasions where the history of the project is negotiated, and the outcomes to date inform the next research focus. It is essential at these meetings that participants have an opportunity to describe how their individual action plan is being realized, what some of their conclusions have been on the research process, and what the results are vis-à-vis the students. It is also an occasion where the future begins to be mapped out as the next cycle of planning is decided or debated as a way forward. Finally, it is an opportunity in which existing frameworks (e.g., methodologies and policies) can be challenged and discussed within the confines of a group committed to change.

◈ OUTCOMES

Outcomes in terms of a collaborative research project like this can be conceptualized in at least three ways: milestones, individual/group products, and student benefits.

Milestones

Each group focus meeting has both a retrospective and prospective function. It is a simultaneous opportunity for interim outcomes and critical moments of decision to be noticed and recorded in their own right, and at their own time, as milestones in the project. Action plans are in principle tentative and affected by all the contingencies of teaching during semester, for example, technology breakdowns, teacher illness, and student response. For one teacher (HKV) this meant coping with the fact that an on-line class almost disappeared and trying to understand why, while at the same time reorienting her work to another group so that she could continue her action plan intentions. For myself, it meant describing my difficulties with a group of students who lacked clear personal direction and motivation and therefore frustrated my attempts to be systematic and coherent in ways that seemed valid to me. For all of us, it meant explaining to a greater or lesser extent how classroom and external constraints had thwarted, redirected, and informed what we did. The effect of these milestone experiences extends beyond the project itself.

Individual/Group Products

In terms of measuring up to our goal of improving the integration of CALL into the ESOL syllabus, there were successes and setbacks. Successes came through sometimes as individual development, as teachers talked of their own enlightenment and empowerment through new experiential knowledge. As I listened to recordings of our group focus meetings and revisited the journal entries, there are moments that I identify as critical, moments where, either individually or collectively, we seem to be saying something that shows we have moved on, or that we are distracted enough to want to find out more.

I see some of this at work in the following extract from Action Plan 2, where JNT talks about personal enlightenment and achievement through the experience of the project in her work with beginners:

> I found there is a real interest and motivation for students to actively engage in the learning task with the computer and take control, i.e. not to be passive learners waiting to be directed. This has definite implications for the learning-to-learn aspects of ESOL syllabus, developing autonomy and for a student-led, self-paced syllabus.
>
> From the practical teaching and classroom management side of things, I have learned a lot about how it works in practice with this level: for example, establishing routines of having pen and paper and dictionary handy for taking notes of new vocabulary, printing a hard copy to take away, and gathering the group together at the start of the lesson. I have gained some clarity about CALL and syllabus and the need to be clear about what aspects of the syllabus the lesson is really focusing on, for example, the learning-to-learn syllabus, or vocabulary development, or reading or writing or speaking, and the question presents itself: is word-processing an accepted part of our writing syllabus? One aspect of the writing syllabus which I found the CALL work helpful with at this level was teaching punctuation. (JNT)

A more group-oriented outcome is the coherence that developed in terms of discourse, practice, and social organization within the project constraints. Action research is about improving practice, but improving it in specific ways. One essential element of this improved practice is the development of a more coherent discourse about the issue in question—practitioners began to talk the same language in a way that was not the case before.

This came home to me in an in-house dissemination session held at the conclusion of the project. A slightly skeptical but interested audience asked one of the participating teachers (JLC) whether working with a particular piece of software (Microsoft PowerPoint97, 1996) in a computer environment had in fact been the motivation for an enthusiastic, focused debate about a discussion topic for an English for academic purposes class. The teacher replied that she felt that, yes, it was in fact the environment that had made the difference. Knowing both where JLC had come from in the project (with little knowledge and some skepticism about computer activities) and something about the attitude of the questioner to computer-based activities, this was a significant statement about the power of CALL that had emerged through a knowledge-in-practice experience.

So what about the students?

Whereas the focus of the action research was strongly on ourselves as teachers, the project itself necessarily involved learning and student benefits (and potential hazards). Ongoing reports in journal entries and in group focus meetings highlighted for some how students were enjoying the greater coherence between syllabus/ classroom activities and computer activities. Each of us gathered impressions from students through surveys, questionnaires, and discussions on how they were experiencing our explicit focus on computer-based activities as reinforcing and developing the language syllabus. These reports highlighted a number of key points:

- Teacher enthusiasm and preparation were rewarded by positive evaluations and perceptions of coherence between the computer lab activities and their classroom lessons.

- Positioning students with very different attitudes and experiences of computers was a challenging issue on which we needed to focus.

- The great majority of students wanted more time with the computer. This had not been our impression or experience before, and this issue is being addressed in current scheduling.

Finally, here, an outcome with great future resonance: In the course of our closing group meeting (Cycle 3), JLC reported on her class survey and discussion of what they had done. She found that while students appreciated the focus on computers she had adopted, they did not see the language practice benefits she thought were obvious. For example, when her EAP group used PowerPoint97 (Microsoft, 1996) as a tool for group discussion and consensus building, students were engaged in animated, focused speaking practice, and JLC was amazed at how well the sessions went in comparison to her previous experiences with similar groups in a noncomputer environment. When students reflected on this experience, which they enjoyed, they did not acknowledge the language practice benefits that JLC saw as central to the whole activity—central to her syllabus and plan. Her reporting this incident led to our group's discussing the mismatch of student and teacher perspectives and how we might investigate this gap.

◈ REFLECTIONS

There are five points about the mechanics and nature of the project that I would suggest are worth repeating and considering for those about to engage in teacher research projects.

The Power of the Collaborative Paradigm

Action research in education originated in contexts of collaborative participatory frameworks. The social dynamics of rubbing shoulders with colleagues, students, and administration, with a view to developing a more coherent set of practices, discourse, and organization, is not possible through individualized approaches. In a sense, this project attempted to have one foot in both camps by having teachers as individuals largely steer their action research through their own schedules. Although diary annotations and group meetings kept reminding us what the group issues were and served to keep the encouragement and critique going, the individual responsibility and pathway remained a dominant and somewhat contestable feature of the project. Could we have been more united in our approach? There were different positions on this issue, partly resolved by admitting that we were doing something worthwhile and learning and improving our knowledge and practice.

Open Posing of Problematic Teaching Issues

A problematic theme is much more consistent with collaborative than individual action research in that consensus and negotiation are constantly targeted in the former but not the latter. It was essential in this project because our teaching circumstances, our different computer literacies, and the limits of technology resources made a single focus across all class levels a practical impossibility. There are ways, I think, in which we could have developed a more focused project given other circumstances, and maybe this would have been more satisfying or beneficial. What stands out, however, is that there are clear signals in our texts of what we learned about our limits, and the limits of multimedia, as components of language teaching.

The Need for Data Without Interference

Action research demands a rational approach to data gathering, but data-gathering procedures do not need to mimic normative empiricist research traditions. Laboratory settings typical of normative research are rightly viewed with suspicion by teachers with regard either to the improvement of educational practice or the development of credible educational theory. This means that practitioners should be encouraged within the constraints of their teaching environment and timetable to use those methods that produce evidence sufficient to the individual and the project as a whole.

The Import of Developing a Critical Discourse

It is important to let practitioners question my, your, and our definitions and practices, and to address issues that transcend the classroom and enter the world of policy and institution. The reflective annotated journal used in this project attempts to create this critical dimension and help us probe our own professional beliefs and conceptions. But corridor conversations and the text of more than 200 e-mail messages spanning 12 months of dialogue raised critical issues about ethics, attitudes, ownership, and research methodologies, to mention only some of the more significant themes. As I commented to a colleague at the conclusion of the project, we would like to think this has made a difference not only to ourselves. Has it? How can we know this? These are questions we still need to explore.

◈ CONTRIBUTOR

Gavin Melles is a full-time ESOL lecturer at the Waikato Polytechnic, Hamilton, New Zealand. His research interests are in the area of curriculum and educational research practices in second language teaching. He is an EdD candidate at Deakin University, in Melbourne, Australia.

CHAPTER 14

Going Global:
Communication at (the) Stake

Lesley Pierre

❧ INTRODUCTION

In business circles, globalization has long been recognized as a trend that is gaining ground and momentum. ELT undeniably has a role to play, as English becomes ever more indispensable for conducting business. This, too, has been recognized in business circles. As early as 1994, the magazine *International Management* urged businesses to invest in language training because "the new global aspirations and modern developments in management structures and styles depend even more heavily on good linguistic communication between all members of staff" (Lester, 1994, p. 42). By the same token, practitioners of ELT for professional purposes also need to respond to the "global village" effect (Pauwels, 1993, p. 7) and its possible influences on the very subject matter and target skills that it is the goal of the profession to promote.

With the above in mind, I undertook the present study in order to investigate the influences and complexities involved in communicating in a global business community and to draw conclusions that could shape proposals for improving interactional practices in this environment.

Some initial, informal information gathering hinted at practical and also psychological factors influencing the degree of success in global interaction. Data was therefore collected to get a better picture of the language use and the perceptions of the participants. Subsequent analysis revealed certain discrepancies in the perceptions of different parties, and between these and external observations, as well as a correlation between behavior and experience. Finally, a number of influential factors were identified as meriting pedagogic attention, and a model for dealing with them was formulated.

❧ SITUATION

The French subsidiary of an information technology (IT) company, where I work as in-house English trainer, provides the backdrop for this study. My interest in the effect of globalization on the nature of my work was aroused when I found myself in a position to observe the global village effect taking hold in accelerated form. This evolution is outlined below.

The company, initially headquartered in Italy, was international through its presence in several, mainly European, countries. Although employees in the French subsidiary used their English with various other European nationalities on a limited scale, communication with counterparts in the Italian headquarters accounted for the largest concentration of English. During English training within this context, I had witnessed certain linguistic attitudes of interest. For instance, on having a language item corrected, employees would often remark, "Oh, it doesn't matter, the Italians understand me/say that too/wouldn't understand if I used the correct/polite form."

In 1998, the company was taken over by an American IT company. The aim was to create a global company in keeping with business tendencies. The resulting structural modifications within the new company included the transfer of the world headquarters to the United States, and the setting up of a European headquarters in England. The flow of communication in English was thus greatly modified. The most frequent channels of communication in English for French employees would link France with England and the United States, but far more countries would now be part of the community as well.

This shift meant that a larger proportion of employees would be confronted with the prospect of conversing in English, many not having had much previous experience of this. Moreover, those who already had experience began complaining of greater difficulties, less effective linguistic skills, and a loss of confidence. They also expressed a desire to receive remedial training.

◈ FOCUS

The risks of cross-cultural misunderstanding have already been well documented in the following areas:

- silence, interruption, and overlap (Halmari, 1993; Lehtonen & Sajavaara, 1985; Murata, 1994)

- clarification strategies (Thomas, 1984)

- conversation patterns, subepisodes in phone calls (Godard, 1977; Halmari, 1993)

- politeness on the phone (Sifianou, 1989)

- prosody (Gumperz, 1982)

It seemed likely, therefore, that culturally determined communicative conventions might provide one profitable area of exploration, with a view to implementing suitable troubleshooting action, if necessary.

Another major consideration was that French participants would now communicate far more with speakers whose first language was English. Some recent EFL literature has attempted to draw our attention to the psychological implications inherent in unequal encounters of this nature. Pennycook (1994), for instance, challenges the "bland optimistic view of international communication" that "assumes that this occurs on a co-operative and equitable footing" (p. 9), and Crystal (1997) evokes the possibility that learners may "feel that mother tongue speakers of English have an unfair advantage" (p. 2). Because these factors could influence performance, they also deserved investigation.

Next, the prospect of interacting with speakers whose first language is English would surely introduce new practical difficulties arising from exposure to unfamiliar formulaic expressions, fillers, hesitation devices, and reduced forms. The latter are all typical features of spoken discourse, as has been shown through inspection of various corpora of spoken English (e.g., CANCODE, the Cambridge and Nottingham Corpus of Discourse in English). This corpus prompted Carter (1998) to describe real speech as "messy and untidy" (p. 48) and to claim that "there are many features of real, naturally-occurring spoken standard English grammar which are not recorded in the standard grammars of the English language" (p. 43). It follows that many learners of English might not have been exposed to such features.

Yet another stumbling block might turn out to be parsing the actual stream of speech when participants are unfamiliar with certain models of pronunciation (Brown & Yule, 1983; Ur, 1984). As a consequence, difficulties may arise in recognizing otherwise familiar words, reduced forms, inflectional signals, and message-carrying structures. This can be detrimental to the interpretation of the message because a single phoneme can carry significant weight of meaning (Field, 1998).

Finally, it has been claimed that, in some parts of the world, "English has . . . developed distinct local forms, determined by local norms" (Phillipson, 1992a, p. 25). I therefore wondered if the English used by the French employees who were experienced in conversing with the Italians had become culturally colored.

The above knowledge fed my hypotheses and suspicions. I needed to test and investigate them in the real world. I decided to collect data that would give me insights into underlying perceptions and actual language use. I felt that this two-pronged approach would help to uncover truths concerning practical and psychological realities weighing on the target situation. The data of difficulty and successful outcomes in the new interactional practices might then provide input to language training aimed at both the experienced and the inexperienced groups above.

◈ RESPONSE

Investigating Perceptions

I wanted to find out if participants in my chosen business community had any conscious notions of the issues that could potentially affect communicating on a global scale. I wished to find out, first, the level of awareness of participants whose first language was English (L1Es), concerning the difficulties experienced by those whose first language was other than English (L1Os), and, second, what attitudes they believed themselves to adopt when directly faced with these difficulties.

For the L1Os, I wished to find out, first, what difficulties they perceived themselves to have, as well as differences they believed existed in the English and behavior of L1Es as opposed to other L1Os. Finally, I wanted their impressions as to whether these differences had a psychological or practical influence on their own behavior.

For this purpose I sent questionnaires via e-mail to employees representative of both groups (see Appendix 1).

Questionnaire 1 (Q1) was addressed to 1,850 L1Es randomly spread across hierarchical levels, job profiles, and geographical settings within Britain and

Australia. Other subsidiaries with suitable populations had not yet been connected to the new worldwide network and were therefore excluded for practical reasons. I eventually decided to analyze replies from Australia and Britain separately to see if it would reveal that different native-English-speaking cultures might be a significant variable in accounting for behavior and attitude variation.

Only about 4% of the potential Q1 addressees responded. This could be interpreted as a lack of interest in the issues on the part of L1E speakers. However, the facts must be placed in their global business context. Random distribution meant that targeting those people who indeed had contacts with L1O speakers had been impossible. Answering the survey, moreover, had probably been low on everyone's list of business priorities.

Questionnaire 2 (Q2) was sent to all employees (200) in the French subsidiary. Approximately 22% of Q2 addressees replied. This again is justifiable because the questionnaire seeks information on experience in telephone communication in English. A large percentage of the overall workforce, for whom this was still no more than a prospect, had therefore been excluded. Another factor that probably limited the number of replies was the fact that many employees thought that the survey was to determine candidates for English training. Those who assumed this and who were already involved, or not interested, were also discouraged from answering.

All things considered, the response rates for both questionnaires were sufficient to allow me to continue the investigation. I now had a reasonable number of authenticated perceptions to check against the data of actual interactions.

Investigating Occurrences of Global Interaction

The next step was to test perceptions against recorded data. I decided to collect samples of telephone interaction because this would eventually represent the largest proportion of interaction in English undertaken by the French employees. Conversations in English between L1O/L1O dyads and L1E/L1O dyads were targeted.

Recording material was given to employees who had regular telephone contacts in English, and to those for whom it was exceptional but who were expecting a call or were obliged to make one. Regular correspondents of the French employees were asked for their permission to make recordings at some later, unspecified date. This request was to limit the observer's paradox. For onetime cases, the interlocutor was sometimes asked at the beginning of the call for her consent to record (when participants were at least already acquainted). Failing this, retroactive consent to use the data was sought, and recordings would have been immediately destroyed if it had not been given. (Nobody withheld consent.)

Participant interviews were held wherever possible in order to gain multiple perspectives on the interpretation of the data (see Appendix 2).

Results

I will discuss some of the most salient points arising from the data—those I believe to be influential in swaying communication toward either successful or problematic poles. The data provided a wide variety of random clues, but I will try to draw together the various strands by comparing and contrasting L1E and L1O perceptions and providing illustrations from the recorded data to show matches or mismatches with the more objective record (see Appendix 3 for transcription conventions).

Factor 1: Pitching One's Message Appropriately

Perceptions

A majority of L1E respondents felt that they were able to estimate the English level of their L1O interlocutors, (Q1, Question 1). This was even more prominent in the British results. The Australians justified their answers by referring to their experience of intercultural communication significantly more frequently than the British (21% vs. 2%). This may be a clue as to why a greater percentage of Australians than British, replied negatively because their experience might have taught them that initial perception of performance was often misleading.

Turning to the L1Os' point of view, they declare that their L1E interlocutors "can't imagine that I don't understand" as one of the reasons given for their difficulties in dealing with comprehension problems (Q2, Question 1f). This could arise from L1Es' misjudgment of L1O competence, and if this is so, there seems to be a discrepancy between the perceptions of the two groups.

Recorded Data

First, participant interviews revealed that, in almost all the conversations involving French employees and L1Es, there were stretches of speech that the L1Os had been unable to follow and that the L1Es had been unaware of their difficulties.

The opening to the conversation below, which was one such case, might suggest a source of this common error of judgment. (See Appendix 3 for key to transcription conventions.)

Conversation 1, Extract A

A = L1E (Irish)   B = L1O (French)

1	A	hello, Rose-Marie,
2 =>	B	hello. Jean-Jacques Drué calling from XX France. May I speak to Mrs. Rose-Marie Barnes / / please.
3	A	yur speakin to her
4 =>	B	=uu::hh I'm calling you because I'd like to know if it's possible for you to send us a copy of the contract you have done between you, BHT, and XYZ.

It might be significant that this is a onetime event for both parties, neither having regular contacts with foreigners. B sees this as an opportunity to put into practice some of his rote-learned structures, with a vibrant memory from bygone lessons, that it is of utmost importance to employ polite language when interacting with the British (e.g., Lines 2, 4). This opening to the conversation sets him up as a proficient user of English in A's eyes, and she proceeds to deliver a complex message, in unsimplified terms, at normal speed, with quite a strong regional accent. The length of the exchange prevents me from exemplifying here the extreme difficulties that B runs into in coordinating the rest of the conversation, and A never suspects the extent of the problem because of B's constant display of seemingly proficient language.

It has been noted elsewhere (Gass & Varonis, 1991; Thomas, 1983; Wolfson, 1989) that L1Es are unlikely to imagine that L1Os who appear relatively proficient linguistically may not have mastered sociolinguistic rules to the same level, and that damaging misinterpretation of the intended message can result. It is perhaps necessary to develop a variant of this because in the above, although B does not violate sociolinguistic rules, he might not yet have mastered the interactional skills needed for the situation.

Factor 2: Being Aware of the Nature of L1O Difficulties and Implementing Appropriate Remedial Action

Perceptions

A considerable percentage of L1E respondents (30%) claimed to be ignorant of the nature of L1O difficulties (Q1, Question 2). This is disturbing because having a notion of what constitutes the difficulties must surely be a prerequisite to adapting one's language appropriately when trying to avoid or deal with trouble.

Those with ideas mentioned aspects of vocabulary as the favorite supposed difficulty followed by aspects of delivery of speech. The Australian and the British answers matched closely on these two points. In parallel, rephrasing and slowing down were mentioned as the most popular compensatory reactions in the face of problems for both populations (Q1, Question 3).

On the other hand, a higher proportion of Australians (21% vs. 11%) mentioned potential psychological difficulties (Q1, Question 2) and showed concern for keeping a positive psychological climate (24% vs. 11%; Q1, Question 3). Similarly striking is the higher percentage of British who believed that they did not know how to deal with problems (26% vs. 7%). These figures again raise the possibility that sensitivity to the issues is more widespread in Australia than in Britain.

The L1Os' most frequently cited difficulty was vocabulary, closely followed by "perceiving items in a stream of speech." These tendencies again match L1E perceptions. The fact that some L1Es may inadequately deal with or imagine the nature of the difficulties experienced by the L1Os appears to have been sensed by the L1Os themselves, too, because they clearly preferred interaction with another L1O. They perceived L1Os as more understanding and more able to react effectively to difficulties because their fields of experience overlapped.

Recorded Data

The next two conversations contain problems arising initially from not recognizing or finding an item of vocabulary respectively. They may support the L1Os' feeling that speaking to another L1O is easier.

Conversation 2

A = L1E (British)   B = L1O (French/Italian)

1	A	...is uh ((cough)) is there a slightly earlier flight than u::hm=
2	B	=/ / yes.
3	A	=uh four o'clock?
4	B	(1) at four o'clock.
5	A	um no-no-no-no-no is there one *earlier.* is there one at three o'clock for example.
6 =>	B	(2) u:::h no excuse. would (3) uh, I can, I didn't catch,

7 =>	A	Milan to London.
8	B	Milan to Lon // don.
9 =>	A	na-na don' worry about that Alice, i-its fine. its okay.=
10	B	= It's okay?
11	A	yes.
12	B	(1) okay. I confirm.
13 =>	A	yes. u:h ha-have you booked the tickets?
14 =>	B	yes. I book the tickets and I give you the:::=
15	A	=the reference. // yes.
16	B	reference number
17	A	=yes=
18	B	mh-mh,
19=>	A	=very good.=
20	B	=okay. and for Frankfurt?=
21	A	=yes.
22	B	u::h the first flight, u::h leave on the uh first of November,
23	A	cu-could you send me an e-mail,=
24	B	=yes, I send you an e-mail.
25	A	yup=
26=>	B	=mmm? okay,
27=>	A	=by- = ((sound of telephone being put down))
28	B	=I u::h hallo? hallo?

A problem originates in the first five lines, partly due to B's not perceiving a known word and partly because the question is unexpected (participant interview). A's remedial action unfortunately fails. First, his response to an initial request for clarification (Line 6) directs attention to locations rather than clarifying the fact that he wants to change the flight times (Line 7). Then, he dismisses the point instead of entering into the necessary negotiation of the difficulty (Line 9). B believes that confirmation of this flight has taken place, but A continues to inquire about the subject.

Next, B misses the information-carrying elements of tense, and mistakes "have . . . booked" for reference to what she will do (Lines 14–16). A seems to endorse the interpretation (Line 19). He has, several times already, violated the cooperative principle, which asks us to "make (our) conversational contribution such as is required, at the stage at which it occurs, by the accepted purpose or direction of the talk exchange in which (we) are engaged" (Grice, 1975, p. 45).

He finally issues an ultimate insult in the conclusion of the conversation, by not engaging in the habitual preclosing ritual, effectively hanging up on B (Lines 26–28).

He has contributed to the L1O perception that L1Es are intolerant of their language difficulties and perhaps aggravated the psychological reluctance that B already felt with regard to asking for clarification (participant interview).

Conversation 3

A = L1O (Italian)   B = L1O (French)

1	A	...oka::y well I'll put that one for the time being then, when he has a ne::w one,=
2	B	=yes.= / / he-he's u::h chercher. uh / / ((laughter))
3	A	you know, yeah okay. ((laughter))
4	B	((Italian))=
5	A	=he's looking for. yeah. / / ((laughter))
6	B	yes. thank you. ((laughter)) an address in Italy...

Conversely, in the above, there is solidarity between the participants and a low level of tension, shown in their amusement at the predicament of not finding a word. Furthermore, the collaborative help provided by A provokes no feelings of inferiority or incompetence on B's part (participant interview).

Of course, caution is needed. The above data only exemplifies tendencies voiced in the questionnaire about respondents' perceptions and is not significant in a quantitative sense. The recordings also revealed that it was important not to limit conclusions to each side of a purely L1E/L1O divide. Conversation 4, below, suggests that L1Es who have had considerable experience of international/cultural communication may have found ways of facilitating areas that their correspondents find difficult.

Conversation 4

A = L1E (British)   B = L1O (French)

1=>	A	... I will go and look in my records, and see what the *sig* voltage was, when I tested it. and we will compare it with the eight vol-eight point *two* volts / / for the new one. it says, *new,* eight point two. // you-you see
2	B	yes,
		yes.
3=>	A	that? I will see the figure that I had. when I tested it.

A speaks to L1Os several times a day. The technical profile of his correspondents typically means difficulties with spoken language (many have learned English through reading and are weak on recognizing spoken forms). A seems to have created his own conversational style for dealing with these people. He repeats frequently, checks that his correspondent is following and makes very few contractions, as can be seen from his pronunciation of *will.* In this discussion, all five occurrences of *will* are pronounced in this way. On being questioned, he reveals that he had found that foreign correspondents often missed the notion of future when contracted, so he deliberately used the uncontracted form.

Another strategy used in the data by L1Es and L1Os who tended to have successful interchanges was breaking up the information into manageable chunks to facilitate its assimilation, leaving slight pauses in between to invite feedback (as in Conversation 5). This anticipates a series of potential difficulties ranging from perceiving the message in a continuous stream of speech, to not understanding an item of vocabulary. Furthermore, it allows the other person to confirm, or not, comprehension chunk by chunk, instead of having the additional worry of signaling where the difficulty arose.

Conversation 5

A = L1E (British)   B = L1O (French)

1=>	A	…what we said is that, (3) we believed, (1) that our target audience for France,
2	B	=mmhm=
3=>	A	=is tw-is twenty-four managers. so what we're looking at is,=
4	B	=mmm,=
5=>	A	=taking these twenty-four most senior and middle manage-ment,=
6	B	=oka::y=
7=>	A	=and delivering a management development programme for that twenty-four….

Factor 3: Negotiating Meaning and Requesting Clarification: How Much Is Acceptable?

Perceptions

L1Es overwhelmingly voiced their positive attitudes toward being interrupted for clarification (Q1, Question 4). This was seen as preferable to fostering misunder-standings that might be serious and time-consuming to solve later, and, hence, essential for conducting business successfully.

Ironically, this is one of the actions in which many L1Os felt more reluctant to engage when conversing with L1Es, in order to limit the amount of interaction and minimize the risk of further difficulties (Q2, Question 3). Grounds put forward for this behavior were greater feelings of embarrassment, apprehension, frustration, and the fear of being judged incompetent (Q2, Question 4). Here, there is an obvious mismatch between how the L1Os feel and what the L1Es would have liked them to do.

Recorded Data

There are relatively few occurrences of difficulties being truly negotiated. The inclination to keep the amount of interaction to a minimum holds true in many cases. In Conversation 1, we noted that B got quickly out of his depth. Later, we find an example of his reluctance to clarify a misunderstanding because he wished to limit the conversation to essentials (participant interview). This leads to multiple resurfac-ing of the misunderstanding later, with almost comic effect.

Conversation 1, Extract B

1	B	...my name?
2	A	yeah?
3=>	B	Drué. Jean-Jacques. D R U A.
4	A	mmhmm,
5=>	B	Jean-Jacques, G A R N G A C Q U E S...

((later in conversation))

6=>	A	... your first name is Drua.
7=>	B	yeah Drué. yeah...

((later in conversation))

8=>	A	...just have a word with my manager, and confirm it with him, but Drua that shouldn't be a problem...

(later in conversation)

9 =>	A	...then Drua, thank you. bye bye.

In Line 3, B gives his surname first, as is often done in France. A mistakes this for his first name and the faulty spelling (Lines 3, 5) did not alert her. Later in the conversation, she nevertheless checks the information (Line 6). B overtly avoids the opportunity of clearing up the misunderstanding (Line7). Unfortunately, A uses the "first" name several times thereafter as a sign of her desire to promote rapport with her interlocutor.

Conversation 6

A = (L1O) French   B = (L1E) British

1	A	...=ok. so, you will send this to me?
2=>	B	=uh dju wome te send it t-you or sh'll I send it to Manuel.
3	A	ok. to Manuel....

Here, Manuel is A's subordinate in the company and has been the French contact with B concerning an international contract. Problems have resulted in an escalation to A. A expects B to send the information to him from now on. Unfortunately, he catches nothing in Line 2, except the end, "send it to Manuel" and processes it as a statement rather than a question including an alternative. He imagines that the noise at the beginning of the utterance has perhaps been justification. B, for his part, simply intended to check the changed arrangement, not make a counterproposal. Instead of querying his interpretation (which was face-threatening to his authority) or asking for clarification of the information he had not caught, A admitted openly in the postevent interview that he had preferred to let it drop, rather than engage in further interaction.

Factor 4: Variance in Interactional Behavior: Turn Taking

Perceptions

When asked if anything disturbed them in the behavior of foreign interlocutors, cultural aspects of turn taking constituted one of the reoccurring features in answers of L1Es (Q1, Question 5). For reasons of space, this issue must also stand here as one element of a wider concern with perceptions of politeness, or the lack of it.

L1Os' views on turn taking rate it as problematic relatively rarely compared with other difficulties. More revealingly, when it was mentioned, L1Os traced the difficulty back to blanks resulting from linguistic gaps. Nobody refers to problems arising, not from the blanks, but out of moments when they did indeed have something to say (Q2, Question 1E).

Recorded Data

Turn-taking styles certainly gave the data the appearance of successful or problematic communication. Interestingly, my own interpretations did not always correspond to those of the participants, suggesting different cultural evaluations. Sometimes mismatched styles caused a sense of unease.

Conversation 7

A = L1E (British)   B = L1O (French)

1	A	... i-it I-I was told, that there is no easy way to do that.=
2=>	B	=A:::hh. Oka:y. U:::hm I-I have not checked this point, but I am quite sure that they *are* using SLAM. / / for for this. because i-in the past,
3=>	A	mmm
4	B	they were using uh, I-I=
5	A	=ye / / ah
6=>	B	knew better in the past, they were using uh the orde::r SJC,=
7=>	A	=yeah=
8	B	=and I think it's now they also...((later))... because u:::h they already use SLAM. / / for orders.=
9=>	A	((inhalation))=well I-I'd be inter- ested to understand,
10		ho::w, how you do it though Jean. / / because you know
11=>	B	mmmm I have to check this=
12=>	A	=yeah. because if you're using SLAM...

In the above data, there is a high degree of latching and very little overlap, suggesting finely tuned turn taking. Each person waits respectfully (my interpretation) to hear what the other has to say. When slight overlap occurs, this is usually a case of backchanneling, showing participatory listenership (Lines 2/3, 5/6) (Tannen, 1983).

The only flagrant example of interruption (Line 11) occurs at a potential transition-relevance place (TRP) (Sacks, Schegloff, & Jefferson, 1974). B gives up the floor without a fight (Line 10) to listen to A's comment, only continuing with his own utterance at the next TRP (Line 12).

The above extract is typical of the whole conversation and seemed, to me, harmonious and cooperative. Participant interviews reflected similar interpretations to my own.

A perceptibly different conversational style was present in French/Italian exchanges. An extract from one such conversation follows.

Conversation 8

A = L1O (Italian)   B = L1O (French)

1	A	...he is involvid in another mee::ting. so I don't want to-
		// to::((inaudible))
2=>	B	no no // ((inaudible))
3=>	A	you will you will receive the answer, directly from
		Massimo, within tonight...

((later in conversation))

4	A	...and uh to-to check to go through // the situation
5=>	B	this is one point I
		wanted to check with you today. because,=
6	A	=yeah=
7	B	=u::h according to the // (inaudible) with Italy ((inau-
		dible)) you
8=>	A	yeh, yeh, yeh, yeah,
9	B	told me...

The above illustrates the characteristic features of Italian/French exchanges in the data. Typically there was:

- frequent overlap and interruption at non-TRPs (Line 2)
- competitive bidding for the floor with corresponding upgrading (Levinson, 1983), rendering many sequences totally inaudible (Lines 1–3)
- early bids for the next turn, in anticipation of TRPs, and inattention to the end of the message (Line 5)
- intrusive overlap due to backchannelling, which, while characteristically being brief and quiet (Fasold, 1990), here is extremely animated and can drown the other person's message (Line 8)

For me, the style was frustrating, but participants claimed in interviews that they had felt comfortable and had not noticed any intrusive behavior during the conversation. Further study of the L1O/L1O data seemed to suggest that the above style may be culture-specific to French/Italian interaction. In dyads of other combinations, it was far less present.

It may be significant that the French employee in the next conversation had previously had more experience in speaking to Italians (several communications a week for 10 years) than Anglo-Saxons (a recent development). We could speculate that B had developed a personal style based on experience and had not yet adapted it to her new interlocutors.

Conversation 9

A = L1E (British)   B = L1O (French)

1	A	...is *that* an issue, to do with that or is it / / is it
2=>	B	no! it's a technical problem because u::h even to implant the system, all the instructions are in English,=
3	A	=a / / ha uh ((laughter))
4	B	not even no-not only for me, but for the people who / / ::are
5	A	yes
6	B	uh i-if they want to... ((later))... the menu is in English=
7=>	A	=yes that's right every / / thing i-
8=>	B	so, it's quite difficult for someone who doesn't/ / speak any English, / / to:: begin this kind / / of course so, and
9	A	yes. yes. Okay, le-me let me ask you a question
10	B	yea:::h,,
11	A	(1) Do you ha:::ve (1) an *Intranet*
12	B	(1) ye:::s,...

B's contribution here, and in the preceding section, is delivered at breakneck speed. A is having difficulties taking the floor. His first attempt (Line 1) is met with an interruption at a non-TRP (Line 2). His second attempt (Line 7) is treated similarly (Line 8). There is little overlap compared to Italian/French conversation, but this is because A obligingly gives up the floor to listen to B.

Interestingly, A eventually resorts to tactics resembling B's. He perhaps realizes that to hold the floor, he cannot proceed as usual. He interrupts at a non-TRP (Line 9) and, additionally, employs a preannouncement, which, once acknowledged, gives him the right to the floor (Levinson, 1983). He can then slow down and hope not to be interrupted.

◈ OUTCOMES

Before the investigation, I suspected that the following points might be significant in determining the success of communication in the global business world:

1. culturally determined communicative conventions
2. the psychological, superiority/inferiority implications of being an L1E or L1O
3. practical difficulties involved in the recognizing and processing of spoken forms
4. past experience having colored present performance

Postinvestigation Observations

1. The study of turn taking and politeness in the data seems to reveal that confrontation with cultural conventions different from one's own can lead to errors of judgment and even trouble in interaction.
2. Psychological factors, such as feeling inferior or fear of trouble, influence behavior and conversational outcomes. This can be noted particularly with regard to asking for clarification and negotiating meaning.
3. Processing L1E speech can be a major problem for L1Os.
4. A display of correct and competent-sounding language may not necessarily be in line with a corresponding competence to deal with interaction.
5. Different L1E cultures may have different levels of awareness of and sensitivity to the difficulties.
6. Past experience may indeed color current language use. This can be seen in several aspects of the data:
   - Lack of experience may multiply the difficulty for L1Es of pitching their message appropriately.
   - L1Os (e.g., the Italians) tend to graft their own conversational style onto the foreign language.
   - Some L1Os (e.g., the French who have Italian headquarters histories) have aligned their style to that of their most frequent correspondents.
   - Some participants have simplified their speaking styles to help L1Os.

Pedagogic Implications

Two major considerations stand out. First, it would appear that cross-cultural awareness raising based on the specific conventions of the opposite party may not be enough in today's business world, because the profiles of potential interlocutors change too frequently. Second, experience seems to play a major role. As a result, inexperienced participants in global interaction, whether L1Es or L1Os, may benefit from awareness raising based on potential difficulties and how to deal with them.

Troubleshooting Action Plan

Based on the above observations, I advocate an approach to helping participants that consists of "awareness training" (Erickson, 1979, in Chick, 1996, p. 345), using Erickson's (1985) idea of "retrospective scanning" (in Chick, 1996, p. 345). As Chick points out, this can be doubly beneficial because the insight that interactional "trouble" develops interactionally, rather than unilaterally is itself liberating and allows learners to avoid unhelpful repair strategies based on blaming the other participant or oneself. (Chick, 1996, p. 345)

This approach would, therefore, counter some of the negative psychological influences underlying intercultural interaction. In addition, the actual experiences could become the pedagogic input material.

The following action plan shows one way of translating the above observations and interpretations into interventions:

1. Ask employees to record instances of their intercultural communications in English as was done for this study. When it is explained that the purpose of the recordings is to find ways of facilitating the communicative task at hand, and especially when the people concerned perceive the activity as being potentially beneficial to them in some way, it is not too hard to recruit willing participants.

2. Analyze the data to identify features of communication that contribute to success or to trouble. It is to this stage of the work that I hope this chapter might make some specific contribution.

3. Ask participants for permission to use the extracts for pedagogical purposes. On agreement, organize them into a materials bank and devise corresponding consciousness-raising tasks.

4. Use the materials in training sessions to encourage the development of participants' own sensitivity to

   • what sort of trouble can arise

   • how it is signaled and therefore how it can be recognized

   • which remedial action or repair strategies would be appropriate

   • which techniques or strategies would avoid the trouble in the first place

   Encourage the students to apply the thought processes triggered here to future experiences. The resulting mind set constitutes a constant learning tool.

5. Direct the training at L1E and L1O speakers, particularly those who have had little or limited prior intercultural interaction experiences (e.g., with only one nationality). If both parties are aware of the points discussed in Step 4, this can only maximize the success of the training.

◈ REFLECTIONS

This case study has emphasized that there is a great deal more than just language to be considered when training people to participate in a global communication network. Kachru (1985) asked if the English language training profession had adapted to new pressures arising from ways in which English is now being used in the world. Glancing at pedagogical materials targeted at business English markets today, the question, it seems, remains topical. Globalization is often a subject, it is true. However, the communicative awareness and interactive skills desirable for participating in interaction on a global scale receive little coverage.

This investigation has allowed me to identify some key elements contributing to that communicative awareness and those interactive skills and consider ways of integrating the knowledge into teaching procedures. This, in turn, will lead to training that is more appropriately tailored to professional communication in today's constantly changing global community.

However, I have to close this chapter by asking the reader to return to my earlier comment regarding the potential speed of change of interlocutor in a global market. Following my investigation, the company concerned was bought again, this time by a Dutch concern. I would then invite you to refer again to my opening paragraph, on the importance of communication to organizational effectiveness. As I complete the writing of this report, the new managers have decided, for financial reasons, to close down in-house language training provision, and I am out of a job. We may want to call this an extended reflection stage of action research.

◈ CONTRIBUTOR

Lesley Pierre has been teaching English to professionals in Paris for the past 11 years, both for training organisms and also as in-house English training coordinator for two large international companies. She has recently joined the management team of a small Paris-based language school as pedagogic advisor.

◈ APPENDIX 1: TOOLS FOR DATA COLLECTION

Questionnaire 1: Improving the Spoken Communication Process Between Speakers Whose First Language is English (L1Es) and Speakers Whose First Language is Other Than English (L1Os)

Can you help?

1. In spoken communication with L1Es of English, do you think you can accurately and easily judge their level of competence? Justify your answer.

2. Can you imagine what problems your interlocutor may have? Make suggestions.

3. Do you always know what to do when problems arise? Make comments on your typical reactions.

4. What are your feelings when your L1Os correspondent interrupts you to indicate noncomprehension or to ask for clarification?

5. Have you ever noticed any features in the language or the behavior of your foreign correspondents which disturbs you, frustrates you, or maybe even annoys you?

6. What would you like to know more about, that might help you to be more efficient in dealing with the problems?

7. How would you feel about receiving training on how to more effectively identify and deal with problems which arise when you speak to L1Os?

8. How would you feel about adapting your English so that it becomes closer to the English that L1Os use among themselves?

9. In your opinion, whose responsibility is it to make an effort to facilitate the success of communication on an international scale?

10. How many languages do you speak?

Questionnaire 2: Using English on the Phone

Think about the telephone calls you have to make to, or that you receive from speakers whose first language is English (L1Es), in English.

1. What do you find difficult about the following aspects of the conversation, and why? Make comments.

    a. understanding vocabulary

    b. understanding the notions conveyed by grammar

    c. recognizing the words in the flow of sounds that you hear

    d. interpreting and using the right conventions of politeness

    e. taking your turn

    f. dealing with comprehension problems

    g. other

    Think about the comments you made above.

2. Do these things apply, and to what extent, when you speak on the phone in English to another speaker whose first language is not English (L1O). If not, explain what you feel is different.

3. When you speak on the phone *in English*, do you think you **behave** in the same way towards native and other L1Os? If not, explain what you do differently.

4. How do you **feel** when you have to make, or when you receive a phone call *in English*? Are your feelings the same when you speak to native and other L1Os? Explain what might be the cause of your feelings.

◈ APPENDIX 2: PARTICIPANT INTERVIEWS

Where possible, the recordings of the interaction were replayed to the participants, and interviews were held based on the following points:

Listen to the recorded conversation.

Comment on:

• the tone of the conversation

• the success of the conversation

• the source of any problems

• the strategies used to avoid problems

- the strategies used to try to solve any problems which occurred
- anything you think you should have done differently, with hindsight

In a few cases, no interview actually took place, but comments were collected in note form.

◈ APPENDIX 3: CONVENTIONS USED TO TRANSCRIBE RECORDED TELEPHONE DATA

1. Overlapping utterances: // indicates start of overlap

2. Latched utterances: =

3. Pauses, gaps: (2 seconds) time indicated in brackets

4. Characteristics of speech delivery

[.]	falling intonation contour
[,]	maintained (continuing) intonation contour
[!]	animated tone
[?]	rising intonation contour
[:]	lengthening of a preceding syllable
[-]	abrupt cut-off
[*italics*]	emphasis
[underlining]	louder than surrounding talk
[(( ))]	descriptions

5. Other aspects

[=>]	points of interest
[...]	beginning or end of ongoing talk

References

Adelman, C. (1993). Kurt Lewin and the origins of action research. *Educational Action Research, 1,* 7–24.

Akimoto-Sugimori, N. (1996). An ALT-JTE relationship which failed. In M. Wada & A. Cominos (Eds.), *Japanese schools: Reflections and insights* (pp. 161–167). Kyoto, Japan: Shugakusha.

Aline, D. P. (1996). Teaching in a girls' private high school. In M. Wada & A. Cominos (Eds.), *Japanese schools: Reflections and insights* (pp. 20–26). Kyoto, Japan: Shugakusha.

Allwright, D., & Bailey, K. (1991). *Focus on the language classroom: An introduction to classroom research for language teachers.* Cambridge: Cambridge University Press.

Altrichter, H., Posch, P., & Somekh, B. (1993). *Teachers investigate their work: An introduction to the methods of action research.* London: Routledge.

Arends, R. I. (1989). *Learning to teach.* Singapore: McGraw-Hill.

Atkinson, P. (1992). *Understanding ethnographic texts.* Newbury Park, CA: Sage.

Atweh, B., Christensen, C., & Dornan, L. (1998). Students as action researchers: Partnerships for social justice. In B. Atweh, S. Kemmis, & P. Weeks (Eds.), *Action research in practice* (pp. 114–138). London: Routledge.

Auerbach, E. (1994). Participatory action research. *TESOL Quarterly, 28,* 693–697.

Bailey, K., & Nunan, D. (Eds.). (1996). *Voices from the language classroom: Qualitative research in second language education.* Cambridge: Cambridge University Press.

Bereiter, C., & Scardamalia, M. (1987). *The psychology of written composition.* Hillsdale, NJ: Lawrence Erlbaum.

Blin, F. (1998, July). *Investigating the relationship between CALL and the development of learner autonomy.* Paper presented at the 1998 WorldCALL Conference, The University of Melbourne, Australia.

Boswood, T. (Ed.). (1997). *New ways of using computers in language teaching.* Alexandria, VA: TESOL.

Brown, G., & Yule, G. (1983). *Teaching the spoken language.* Cambridge: Cambridge University Press.

Brown, I. J. (1998, July). *Students' perceptions in CALL—myths and reality: A case study.* Paper presented at the 1998 WorldCALL Conference, The University of Melbourne, Australia.

Brown, P., & Levinson, S. (1978). Universals in language usage: Politness phenomena. In E. N. Goody (Ed.), *Questions and politeness: Strategies in social interaction.* Cambridge: Cambridge University Press. [Reprinted in 1987 (and again in 1989), with corrections, new introduction, and new bibliography as *Politeness: Some universals in language usage.*]

Brown, P., & Levinson, S. (1987). *Politeness: Some universals in language usage.* Cambridge: Cambridge University Press.

Brown, P., & Levinson, S. (1989). *Politeness: Some universals in language usage* (2nd ed.). Cambridge: Cambridge University Press.

Burns, A. (1999). *Collaborative action research for English language teachers.* Cambridge: Cambridge University Press.

Byram, M. (1997). *Teaching and assessing intercultural communicative competence.* Clevedon, England: Multilingual Matters.

Canagarajah, A. (1999). *Resisting linguistic imperialism in English teaching.* Oxford: Oxford University Press.

Carr, W. (1995). *For education: Towards critical educational inquiry.* Buckingham, England: Open University Press.

Carr, W., & Kemmis, S. (1986). *Becoming critical: Knowing through action research.* London: The Falmer Press.

Carter, R. (1998). Orders of reality: CANCODE, communication and culture. *ELT Journal, 52,* 43–56.

Chapelle, C. (1997, July). CALL in the year 2000: Still in search of research paradigms. *Language Learning and Technology, 1*(1), 19–43. Retrieved January 3, 2000, from the World Wide Web: http://polyglot.cal.msu.edu/llt/vol1num1/chapelle/default.html.

Chapelle, C., Jamieson, J., & Park, Y. (1996). Second language classroom research traditions: How does CALL fit? In M. C. Pennington (Ed.), *The power of CALL* (pp. 33–54). Houston, TX: Athelstan.

Charles, M. (1990). Responding to problems in written English using a student self-monitoring technique. *ELT Journal, 44,* 286–293.

Chen, L., & Johnson, D. M. (1992). Researchers, teachers, and inquiry. In D. M. Johnson (Ed.), *Approaches to research in second language learning.* White Plains, NY: Longman.

Chick, J. K. (1996). Intercultural communication. In S. McKay & N. Hornberger (Eds.), *Sociolinguistics and language teaching* (pp. 71–102). Cambridge: Cambridge University Press.

Clark, S. (1997). Beyond the hidden culture. In J. Field, A. Graham, E. Griffiths, & K. Head (Eds.), *TDTR2: Teachers develop teachers research* (pp. 225–241). Whitstable, England: IATEFL.

Clarke, M. (1994). The dysfunctions of the theory/practice discourse. *TESOL Quarterly, 28,* 9–26.

Cochran-Smith M., & Lyttle, S. (1990). Research on teaching and teacher research: The issues that divide. *Educational Researcher, 19,* 2–16.

Cohen, A. (1987). Student processing of feedback on their compositions. In A. Wenden & J. Rubin (Eds.), *Learner strategies in language learning* (pp. 57–69). London: Prentice Hall International.

Cohen, A. (1995). Spoken discourse analysis in Japanese university classes. *Niigata Studies in Foreign Languages and Culture, 1,* 27–32.

Cohen, A. D., & Olshtain, E. (1993). The production of speech acts by ESL learners. *TESOL Quarterly, 27,* 33–56.

Cohen, L., & Manion, L. (1985). *Research methods in education.* London: Croom Helm.

Cohen, L., & Manion, L. (1994). *Research methods in education* (4th ed.). London: Routledge.

Cowie, N. (1995). Students of process writing need appropriate and timely feedback on their work, and in addition, training in dealing with that feedback. *Saitama University Journal, 31,* 181–194.

Cowie, N. (1997). Collaborative journalling by e-mail: Using the structure of cooperative development to become a more reflective teacher. *Explorations in Teacher Education, 5,* 4–11.

Covey, S. (1989). *The 7 habits of highly effective people* New York: Simon & Schuster.

Cox, M., & Assis-Peterson, A. (1999). Critical pedagogy in ELT: Images of Brazilian teachers of English. *TESOL Quarterly, 33,* 433–452.

Crookes, G. (1993). Action research for second language teachers: Going beyond teacher-research. *Applied Linguistics, 14,* 130–144.

Crookes, G., & Chandler, P. (1999). *Introducing action research into post-secondary foreign language teacher education.* Retrieved January 3, 2000, from the World Wide Web: http://www.lll.hawaii.edu/nflrc/NetWorks/NW10/.

Crystal, D. (1997). *English as a global language.* Cambridge: Cambridge University Press.

Cummins, J., & Sayers, D. (1995). *Brave new schools: Challenging cultural illiteracy through global learning networks.* New York: St. Martin's Press.

Dadds, M. (1995). *Passionate enquiry and school development.* London: The Falmer Press.

De Decker, B., & Vanderheiden, M. (Eds.). (1999). TDTR4: Teachers develop teachers research [CD-ROM]. Leuven, Belgium: Centre for Language Teaching, University of Leuven. (Available from Marleen.Vanderheiden@clt.kuleuven.ac.be)

Denzin, N., & Lincoln, Y. (Eds.). (1994). *Handbook of qualitative research.* Thousand Oaks, CA: Sage.

Dewey, J. (1916). *Democracy and education: An introduction to the philosophy of education.* New York: The Free Press.

Dewey, J. (1933). *How we think: A restatement of the relation of reflective thinking to the educative process.* Boston: D.C. Heath.

Diamond, C. P. (1983). The use of fixed role treatment in teaching. *Psychology in the Schools. 20,* 74–82.

Diamond, C. P. (1984). The repertory grid in teacher education. *Bulletin of British Psychological Society, 37,* 57–58.

Edge, J. (1988). Applying linguistics in English language teacher training for speakers of other languages. *English Language Teaching Journal, 42,* 9–13.

Edge, J. (1989). Ablocutionary value: On the application of language teaching to linguistics. *Applied Linguistics, 10,* 407–417.

Edge, J. (1992). *Cooperative development: Professional self-development through cooperation with colleagues.* Harlow, England: Longman. Retrieved October 18, 2000, from the World Wide Web: http://www-users.aston.ac.uk/~edgej/cd/titles.htm.

Edge, J. (1996). Cross-cultural paradoxes in a profession of values. *TESOL Quarterly, 30,* 9–30.

Edge, J., & Richards, K. (Eds.). (1993). *Teachers develop teachers research.* Oxford: Heinemann.

Edge, J., & Richards, K. (1998a). May I see your warrant, please? Justifying claims in qualitative research. *Applied Linguistics, 19,* 334–356.

Edge, J., & Richards, K. (1998b). Why best practice isn't good enough. *TESOL Quarterly, 32,* 569–576.

Elbow, P. (1986). *Embracing contraries: Explorations in learning and teaching.* New York: Oxford University Press.

Elliott, J. (1991). *Action research for educational change.* Milton Keynes, England: Open University Press.

Elliott, J. (1993). Academics and action-research: The training workshop as an exercise in ideological deconstruction. In J. Elliott (Ed.), *Reconstructing teacher education* (pp. 176–192). London: The Falmer Press.

Elliott, J., & Adelman, C. (1975). Teacher education for curriculum reform: An interim report on the work of the Ford teaching project. *British Journal of Teacher Education, 1,* 105–114.

Eriksen, S. (1984). *The essence of good teaching.* San Francisco: Jossey-Bass.

Erikson, E. H. (1968). *Youth and crisis.* New York: W. W. Norton.

Erickson, F. (1979). Talking down: Some cultural sources of miscommunication in interracial interviews. In A. Wolfgang (Ed.), *Non-verbal behaviour* (pp. 294–319). New York: Academic Press.

Erickson, F. (1985). Listening and speaking. In D. Tannen & J. Alatis (Eds.), *Georgetown*

University Roundtable on Languages and Linguistics 1995: Languages and linguistics: The interdependence of theory, data, and application (pp. 294–319). Washington, DC: Georgetown University Press.

Ervin-Tripp, S. (1976). Is Sybil there? The structure of some American English directives. *Language in Society, 5,* 25–66.

Evans, C. (1998). Appendix III: Computer analysis of repertory grids. In J. Houston (Ed.), *Making sense with offenders. Personal constructs, therapy and change* (pp. 204–241). Chichester, England: John Wiley & Sons.

Fasold, R. (1990). *The sociolinguistics of language.* Oxford: Basil Blackwell.

Fathman, A., & Whalley, E. (1990). Teacher response to student writing: focus on form versus content. In B. Kroll (Ed.), *Second language writing* (pp. 178–190). Cambridge: Cambridge University Press.

Feixas, G., & Cornejo-Alvarez, J. M. (1996a). GRIDCOR 2.0. [Computer software]. Barcelona, Spain: University of Barcelona.

Feixas, G., & Cornejo-Alvarez, J. M. (1996b). *A manual for the repertory grid: Using the GRIDCOR programme (Version 2.0).* Barcelona, Spain: Paidós.

Ferris, D. (1997). Influence of teacher commentary on student revision. *TESOL Quarterly, 31,* 315–339.

Ferris, D., & Hedgcock, J. (1998). *Teaching ESL composition.* Mahwah, NJ: Lawrence Erlbaum.

Field, J. (1998). Skills and strategies: towards a new methodology for listening. *ELT Journal, 52,* 110–118.

Field, J., Graham, A., Griffiths, E., & Head, K. (Eds.). (1997). *TDTR2: Teachers develop teachers research.* Whitstable, England: IATEFL.

Flick, S. (1990). Overcoming "feedback block": Using audio-cassettes in writing classes. *Inside English, 17,* 3.

Flowerdew, J. (1996). Concordancing in language learning. In M. C. Pennington (Ed.), *The power of CALL* (pp. 97–114). Houston, TX: Athelstan.

Freeman, D. (1996). Refining the relationship between research and what teachers know. In K. Bailey & D. Nunan (Eds.), *Voices from the language classroom* (pp. 88–115). Cambridge: Cambridge University Press.

Freeman, D. (1998). *Doing teacher research: From inquiry to understanding.* Boston: Heinle & Heinle.

Freire, P. (1982). *Educação como prática de liberdade.* Rio de Janeiro, Brazil: Paz e Terra.

Fullan, M. (1993). *Change forces: Probing the depths of educational reform.* London: The Falmer Press.

Fujita, H. (1991). Educational policy dilemmas as historic constructs. In B. Finkelstein, A. Imamura, & J. Tobin (Eds.), *Transcending stereotypes: Discovering Japanese culture and education* (pp. 147–161). Yarmouth, ME: Intercultural Press.

Gass, S. M., & Varonis, E. M. (1991). Miscommunication in nonnative speaker discourse. In N. Coupland, H. Giles, & J. M. Wiemann (Eds.), *Miscommunication and problematic talk.* London: Sage.

Gebhard, J., & Duncan, B. (1991). *EFL teacher education curriculum development enquiry: The Orosz Szakos Tanarok Atkepzesi program.* Paper presented at the International Conference on Second Language Teacher Educaiton, Kowloon, Hong Kong. (ERIC Document Reproduction No. ED 339 204)

Godard, D. (1977). Same setting, different norms: Phone beginnings in France and the United States. *Language in Society, 6,* 209–216.

Gore, J. (1991). Practicing what we preach: Action research and the supervision of student teachers. In R. Tabachnik & K. Zeichner (Eds.), *Issues and practices in inquiry-oriented teacher education* (pp. 253–272). London: The Falmer Press.

Goswami, D., & Stillman, P. (1987). *Reclaiming the classroom.* Portsmouth, NH: Boynton Cook Heinemann.

Grabe, W., & Kaplan, R. (1996). *Theory and practice of writing.* Harlow, England: Longman.

Graves, K. (1996). *Teachers as course developers.* Cambridge: Cambridge University Press.

Greenwood, D. (1999). *Action research: From practice to writing in an international action research development program.* Amsterdam: John Benjamins.

Grice, H. P. (1975). Logic and conversation. In P. Cole & J. L. Morgan (Eds.), *Syntax and Semantics: Vol. 3. Speech acts* (pp. 41–58). New York: Academic Press.

Guba, E., & Lincoln, Y. (1982). Epistemological and methodological bases of naturalistic inquiry. *Educational and Communication Technology Journal, 30,* 233–252.

Gumperz, J. J. (1982). *Discourse strategies.* Cambridge: Cambridge University Press.

Guntermann, G. (1992). *Developing tomorrow's teachers of world languages.* (ERIC Document Reproduction Service No. ED 350 880)

Hales, T. (1996). Trainee talk. In *Proceedings of the CTEFLA Conference* (pp. 19–23). Cambridge: University of Cambridge Local Examination Syndicate.

Hales, T. (1997). Exploring data-driven language awareness. *English Language Teaching Journal, 51,* 217–223.

Hales, T., & O'Donoghue, C. (in press). What was that you said? Trainee-generated language awareness. In H. Trappes-Lomax (Ed.), *Language in language teacher education.* Amsterdam: John Benjamins.

Halmari, H. (1993). Intercultural business telephone conversations: A case of Finns vs. Anglo-Americans. *Applied Linguistics, 14,* 408–430.

Head, K. (Ed.). (1998). *TDTR3: Teachers develop teachers research.* Whitstable, England: IATEFL.

Henry, C., & McTaggart, R. (Eds.). (1998). *The action research reader* (4th ed.). Geelong, Australia: Deakin University Press.

Heron, J. (1996). *Co-operative inquiry: Research into the human condition.* London: Sage.

Higgins, J. (1995). *Computers and English language learning.* Oxford: Intellect.

Higgins, T. (1986). *Wednesday's child.* Stuttgart, Germany: Klett.

Hopkins, D. (1985). *A teacher's guide to classroom research.* Milton Keynes, England: Open University Press.

Jarvis, G. A., & Bernhardt, E. B. (1987). *The status of foreign language teacher education today.* (ERIC Document Reproduction Service No. ED 289 362)

Johnson, D. W. (1986). *Reaching out: Interpersonal effectiveness and self-actualization* (3rd ed.). Englewood Cliffs, NJ: Prentice Hall.

Johnson, K. (1999). *Understanding language teaching: Reason in action.* Boston: Heinle & Heinle.

Johnston, B. (1999). Putting critical pedagogy in its place: A personal account. *TESOL Quarterly, 33,* 557–565.

Kachru, B. B. (1985). Standards, codification and sociolinguistic realism: The English language in the outer circle. In R. Quirk & H. G. Widdowson (Eds.), *English in the world: Teaching and learning the language and literatures* (pp. 11–30). Cambridge: Cambridge University Press.

Kelly, G. A. (1955). *The psychology of personal constructs* (Vol. 1). New York: W. W. Norton.

Kemmis, S., & McTaggart, R. (1988). *The action research planner* (3rd ed.). Geelong, Australia: Deakin University Press.

Kenny, B. (1993). Investigative research: How it changes learner status. *TESOL Quarterly, 27,* 217–232.

Kerr, P. (1993). Language training on pre-service courses for native speakers. *Modern English Teacher, 2*(4), 40–43.

Kerr, P. (1996). Grammar for trainee teachers. In J. Willis & D. Willis (Eds.), *Challenge and change in language teaching* (pp. 93–98). Oxford: Heinemann.

Kluge, D. (1997). The Internet: Promises, problems and possibilities. *The Language Teacher Online, 21*(6). Retrieved January 3, 2000, from the World Wide Web: http://langue .hyper.chubu.ac.jp/jalt/pub/tlt/97/jun/promises.html.

Kobayashi, J. (1991). Cross-cultural difference in classroom management: Coping with student silences and communication failures. *The Language Teacher, 15*, 17–18.

Kramsch, C. (1994). *Context and culture in language teaching.* Oxford: Oxford University Press.

Lake, N. (1997). Survey review: Learner training in EFL coursebooks. *ELT Journal, 51*, 169–180.

Lantolf, J., & Appel, G. (1994). *Vygotskian approaches to second language research.* Norwood, NJ: Ablex.

Leather, S. (1998). Reflections on feedback. *Modern English Teacher, 17*, 62–64.

Leech, G. (1983). *Principles of pragmatics.* London: Longman.

Lehtonen, J., & Sajavaara, K. (1985). The silent Finn. In D. Tannen & M. Saville-Troike (Eds.), *Perspectives on silence.* Norwood, NJ: Ablex.

Lester, T. (1994, July/August). Pulling down the language barrier. *International Management.*

Levinson, S. C. (1983). *Pragmatics.* Cambridge: Cambridge University Press.

Levy, M. (1997). *Computer-assisted language learning: Context and conceptualization.* Oxford: Clarendon Press.

Lewin, K. (1946). Action research and minority problems. *Journal of Social Issues, 2*, 34–46.

Lewis, M. (1997). *Implementing the lexical approach.* Hove, England: Language Teaching Publications.

Littlewood, W. T. (1981). *Communicative language teaching: An introduction.* Cambridge: Cambridge University Press.

MacLure, M. (1996). Telling transitions: Boundary work in narratives of becoming an action researcher. *British Educational Research Journal, 22*, 273–286.

Maneekhao, K. (in press). Using the Internet as a resource for learning English. *rEFLections, 3.*

McMahon, T. (1999). Is reflective action synonymous with action research? *Educational Action Research, 7*, 163–169.

McNiff, J. (1988). *Action research: Principles and practice.* London: Routledge. (Reprinted in 1997)

Merritt F., & Wheldall, K. (1990). *Positive teaching in the primary school.* London: Chapman.

Microsoft PowerPoint97 [Computer software]. (1996). Redmond, WA: Microsoft.

Miklowitz, G. (1985). *The war between the classes.* Stuttgart, Germany: Klett.

Mitchell, J. (1976). Amelia. On *Hejira* [record]. Los Angeles: Elektra/Asylum Records.

Miyoshi, M. (1996). Cultural bumps and icebergs. In M. Wada & A. Cominos (Eds.), *Japanese schools: Reflections and insights* (pp. 195–199). Kyoto, Japan: Shugakusha.

Moore, Z., Morales, B., & Carel, S. (1998). Technology and teaching culture: Results of a state survey of foreign language teachers. *CALICO, 15*, 109–128.

Motteram, G. (1998, July). *Changing the research paradigm: The use of qualitative research methodology in CALL classrooms.* Paper presented at the 1998 WorldCALL Conference, The University of Melbourne, Australia.

Muller, A.C. (in press). *Five Chinese classics: New translations of the basic texts of East Asian indigenous thought.* Taipei, Taiwan: Jin Luen.

Munby, H. (1982). The place of teacher beliefs in research on teacher thinking and decision making, and an alternative methodology. *Instructional Science, 11*, 201–225.

Nattinger, J. R., & DeCarrico, J. S. (1992). *Lexical phrases and language teaching.* Oxford: Oxford University Press.

Murata, K. (1994). Intrusive or co-operative? A cross-cultural study of interruption. *Journal of Pragmatics, 21*, 358–400.

Nicol, C. (1998). *Finally saying no: An examination of second level refusals to polite proposals.* Unpublished manuscript, Aston University.

Nozaki, K. N. (1992). The Japanese student and the foreign teacher. In P. Wadden (Ed.),

A handbook for teaching English at Japanese colleges and universities (pp. 27–33). New York: Oxford University Press.

Nunan, D. (1988). *Syllabus design.* Oxford: Oxford University Press.

Nunan, D. (1989). *Understanding language classrooms: A guide for teacher-initiated action.* London: Prentice Hall International.

Nunan, D. (1991). *Language teaching methodology: A textbook for teachers.* London: Prentice Hall International.

Nunan, D. (1992a). *Collaborative language learning and teaching.* Cambridge: Cambridge University Press.

Nunan, D. (1992b). *Research methods in language learning.* Cambridge: Cambridge University Press.

Nunan, D. (1998, August 31). Interview. *New Routes, 3,* 5–9.

Nunan, D., & Lamb, C. (1996). *The self-directed teacher: Managing the learning process.* Cambridge: Cambridge University Press.

Okuyama, M. (1996). Teacher-student relationships in Japanese high schools. In M. Wada & A. Cominos (Eds.), *Japanese schools: reflections and insights* (pp. 89–93). Kyoto, Japan: Shugakusha.

Olson, J. (1981). Teacher influence in the classroom. *Instructional Science, 10,* 259–275.

Oxford, R. (1990). *Language learning strategies: What every teacher should know.* New York: Newbury House.

Paul, D. (1996). Why are we failing? *The Language Teacher, 20,* 29–30, 39.

Pauwels, A. (1993). Communicating across cultures: An Australian case study of language related research on cross cultural communication in the professions. In T. Boswood, R. Hoffman, & P. Tung (Eds.), *Perspectives on English for professional communication* (pp. 7–36). Hong Kong: City Polytechnic of Hong Kong.

Peck, A. (1988). *Language teachers at work: A description of methods.* London: Prentice Hall International.

Pennington, M. C. (1996). The power of the computer in language education. In M. C. Pennington (Ed.), *The power of CALL* (pp. 1–14). Houston, TX: Athelstan.

Pennycook, A. (1994). *The cultural politics of English as an international language.* London: Longman.

Pennycook, A. (Ed.). (1999). Critical approaches to TESOL [Special issue]. *TESOL Quarterly, 33*(3).

Phillipson, R. (1992a). ELT: The native speaker's burden? In T. Hedge & N. Whitney (Eds.), *Power, pedagogy and practice* (pp. 23–30). Oxford: Oxford University Press.

Phillipson, R. (1992b). *Linguistic imperialism.* Oxford: Oxford University Press.

Pope, M., & Keen, T. R. (1981). *Personal construct theory and education.* Ontario, Canada: Academic Press.

Prawat, R. (1991). Conversations with self and settings: A framework for thinking about teacher empowerment. *American Educational Research Journal, 28,* 737–757.

Prendergast, M. (n.d.). *Seven stages in my first action research project.* Retrieved August 14, 2000, from the World Wide Web: http://educ.queensu.ca/projects/action_research/michael.htm.

Proposed teacher reviews draws fire. (1996, October 30). *The Japan Times,* p. 2.

Revans, R. W. (1980). *Action learning: New techniques for management.* London: Blond & Briggs.

Richards, J. C. (1998a). *Beyond training.* New York: Cambridge University Press.

Richards, J. C. (Ed.). (1998b). *Teaching in action: Case studies from second language classrooms.* Alexandria, VA: TESOL.

Richards, J. C., & Nunan, D. (1990). *Second language teacher education.* New York: Cambridge University Press.

Roche, D. (1999, August 9). Going nowhere fast. *Time Magazine,* p. 23.

Rosenshine, B., & Meister, C. (1993). The use of scaffolds for teaching higher-level cognitive strategies. In A. E. Woolfolk (Ed.), *Readings and cases in educational psychology* (pp. 219–227). Boston: Allyn & Bacon.

Rubin, J., & Thompson, I. (1991). How to be a more successful language learner. In D. Nunan, *Language teaching methodology: A textbook for teachers* (p. 171). London: Prentice Hall International. (Extract originally published in 1983 in *How to be a more successful language learner.* New York: Heinle & Heinle)

Ryan, S. (1998). Student evaluation of teachers. *The Language Teacher, 22,* 9–11, 43.

Sacks, H., Schegloff, E. A., & Jefferson, G. (1974). A simplest systematics for the organisation of turn-taking for conversation. *Language, 50,* 696–735.

Sakamoto, A. (1993). Cognitive complexity and the evolution of sociocognitive systems. Tokyo: Kazama Shōbo. (in Japanese)

Sakamoto, A. (1996, August). *Cognitive complexity and the number of points for rating.* Paper presented at the 103rd American Psychological Association Convention, Toronto, Canada.

Sakamoto, A., & Numazaki, M. (1989). The effect of time for rating on a cognitive complexity scores of the rep test. *The Japanese Journal of Psychology, 60,* 316–319. (in Japanese with English abstract)

Scarcella, R. C., & Oxford, R. L. (1992). *The tapestry of language learning: The individual in the communicative classroom.* Boston: Heinle & Heinle.

Schcolnik, M., & Kol, S. (1999, March). Using presentation software to enhance language learning. *The Internet TESL Journal, 5*(3). Retrieved January 3, 2000, from the World Wide Web: http://www.aitech.ac.jp/~iteslj/Techniques/Schcolnik-PresSoft.html.

Schmidt, R., & Richards, J. (1980). Speech acts and second language learning. *Applied Linguistics, 1,* 129–157.

Schon, D. (1987) *Educating the reflective practitioner.* San Francisco: Jossey-Bass.

Scott, M. (1996). *Wordsmith tools.* Oxford: Oxford University Press.

Searle, J. R. (1969). *Speech acts.* Cambridge: Cambridge University Press.

Sewell, K. W., Adams-Webber, J., Mitterer, J., & Cromwell, R. L. (1992). Computerized repertory grids: Review of the literature. *International Journal of Personal Construct Psychology, 5,* 1–23.

Shimizu, K. (1995). Japanese college student attitudes towards English teachers: A survey. *The Language Teacher, 19,* 5–8.

Sifianou, M. (1989). On the telephone again! Differences in telephone behaviour: England versus Greece. *Language and Society, 18,* 527–544.

Somekh, B. (1993). Quality in educational research: The contribution of classroom teachers. In J. Edge & K. Richards (Eds.), *Teachers develop teachers research* (pp. 26–38). Oxford: Heinemann.

Sonicmail [Computer software]. (1999). (Available from http://www.lycos.com/computers /downloads/lycosware/sonicmail.html)

Sparks-Langer, G. M., & Colton, A. B. (1993). Synthesis of research on teachers' reflective thinking. In A. E. Woolfolk (Ed.), *Readings and cases in educational psychology* (pp. 16–24). Boston: Allyn & Bacon.

Stake, R. E. (1995). *The art of case study research.* Thousand Oaks, CA: Sage.

Stenhouse, L. (1975). An introduction to curriculum research and development. London: Heinemann.

Stewart, V., & Mayes, J. (1997). *The repertory grid interview.* Wellington, New Zealand: Enquire Within Developments.

Stoppard, T. (1993). *Arcadia.* London: Faber & Faber.

Storch, N., & Tapper, J. (1996). Patterns of NNS student annotations when identifying areas of concern in their writing. *System, 24,* 323–336.

Takagi, E., & Sakamoto, A. (1991). Changes in national images due to Seoul Olympics: Panel survey using college students. *Shakai Shinrigaku Kenkyu (Social Psychology Research), 6,* 98–111. (in Japanese with English abstract)

Tannen, D. (1983). When is an overlap not an interruption? In R. DiPietro, W. Frawley, & A. Wedel (Eds.), *The first Delaware symposium on language studies.* Newark: University of Delaware Press.

Taylor, D. H. (1990). *Toronto at Dreamer's Rock.* Berlin: Cornelsen.

Tharp, R., & Gallimore, R. (1988). *Rousing minds to life.* Cambridge: Cambridge University Press.

Thomas, J. (1983). Cross-cultural pragmatic failure. *Applied Linguistics, 4,* 91–112.

Thomas, J. (1984). Cross-cultural discourse as unequal encounter: Towards a pragmatic analysis. *Applied Linguistics, 5,* 226–235.

Thompson, E. (1968). *The making of the English working class.* Harmondsworth, England: Penguin Books.

Tollefson, J. (Ed.). (1995). *Power and inequality in teacher education.* Cambridge: Cambridge University Press.

Tribble, C. (1996). *Writing.* Oxford: Oxford University Press.

Tribble, C., & Jones, G. (1990). *Concordances in the classroom.* London: Longman.

Truscott, J. (1996). The case against grammar correction in L2 writing classes. *Language Learning, 46,* 327–369.

Tudor, I. (1996). *Learner-centredness as language education.* Cambridge: Cambridge University Press.

Ulichny, P., & Schoener, W. (1996). Teacher-researcher collaboration from two perspectives. *Harvard Educational Review, 66,* 496–524.

Ur, P. (1984). *Teaching listening comprehension.* Cambridge: Cambridge University Press.

Ur, P. (1996). *A course in language teaching.* Cambridge: Cambridge University Press.

van Lier, L. (1996). *Interaction in the language curriculum: Awareness, autonomy & authenticity.* Harlow, England: Longman.

The Waikato Polytechnic. (1998). *The Waikato Polytechnic technology plan.* Hamilton, New Zealand: Author.

Wallace, M. (1991). *Training foreign language teachers: A reflective approach.* Cambridge: Cambridge University Press.

Wallace, M. (1993, May). *Action research: How to do it.* Unpublished paper presented at the 2nd International Conference of the Malaysian English Language Teaching Association (MELTA), Kuala Lumpur, Malaysia.

Wallace, M. (1998). *Action research for language teachers.* Cambridge: Cambridge University Press.

Warschauer, M. (Ed.). (1995). *Virtual connections: Online activities and projects for networking language learners* (Technical Report No. 8). Honolulu: University of Hawaii at Manoa: Second Language Teaching & Curriculum Center.

Watson-Gegeo, K. A. (1988). Ethnography in ESL: Defining the essentials. *TESOL Quarterly, 22,* 575–592.

Watson Todd, R. (1999). Integrating task and content in the language classroom. *KMUTT R&D Journal, 22,* 11–25.

Watson Todd, R. (2000). On course for change: Self-reliant curriculum renewal. *rEFLections, 2,* 1–20.

Wenden, A. (1990). Helping language learners think about learning. In R. Rossner & R. Bolitho (Eds.), *Currents of change in English language teaching* (pp. 161–175). Oxford: Oxford University Press.

Williams, M. (1988). Language taught for meetings and language used in meetings: Is there anything in common? *Applied Linguistics, 9,* 45–58.

Willis, D. (1990). *The lexical syllabus: A new approach to language teaching.* London: Collins.

Willis, J. (1996). *A framework for task-based learning.* Harlow, England: Longman.

Willis, J. W., & Mehlinger, H. D. (1996). Information technology and teacher education. In J. Sikula, T. J. Buttery, & E. Guyton (Eds.), *Handbook of research on teacher education* (2nd ed.) (pp. 978–1029). New York: Simon & Schuster Macmillan.

Wilson, E. (1999). *Consilience: The unity of knowledge.* London: Abacus.

Winter, D. A. (1992). *Personal construct psychology in clinical practice. Theory, practice and applications.* London: Routledge.

Wolfson, N. (1989). *Perspectives: Sociolinguistics and TESOL.* New York: Newbury House.

Woods, P. (1996). *Researching the art of teaching: Ethnography for educational use.* London: Routledge.

Yin, R K. (1994). *Case study research: Design and methods* (2nd ed.). Thousand Oaks, CA: Sage.

Yorke, D. M. (1985). Administration, analysis and assumptions: Some aspects of validity. In N. Beail (Ed.), *Repertory grid technique and personal constructs: Applications in clinical and educational settings* (pp. 383–399). London: Croom Helm.

Zamel, V. (1985). Responding to student writing. *TESOL Quarterly, 19,* 79–101.

Zeichner, K. (1993). Connecting genuine teacher development to the struggle for social justice. *Journal of Education for Teaching, 19,* 5–20.

Index

Also available from TESOL

Academic Writing
Ilona Leki, Editor

*American Quilt: A Reference Book
on American Culture*
Irina Zhukova and Maria Lebedko

*CALL Environments:
Research, Practice, and Critical Issues*
Joy Egbert and Elizabeth Hanson-Smith, Editors

*Common Threads of Practice:
Teaching English to Children Around the World*
Katharine Davies Samway and Denise McKeon, Editors

*Implementing the ESL Standards for Pre-K–12 Students
Through Teacher Education*
Marguerite Ann Snow, Editor

Integrating the ESL Standards Into Classroom Practice: Grades Pre-K–2
Betty Ansin Smallwood, Editor

Integrating the ESL Standards Into Classroom Practice: Grades 3–5
Katharine Davies Samway, Editor

Integrating the ESL Standards Into Classroom Practice: Grades 6–8
Suzanne Irujo, Editor

Integrating the ESL Standards Into Classroom Practice: Grades 9–12
Barbara Agor, Editor

For more information, contact
Teachers of English to Speakers of Other Languages, Inc.
700 South Washington Street, Suite 200
Alexandria, Virginia 22314 USA
Tel 703-836-0774 • Fax 703-836-6447 • publications@tesol.org •
http://www.tesol.org/

DATE DUE